# Trading Market Dynamics

# Using Technical Analysis

# Trading Market Dynamics
# Using Technical Analysis

CONSTANCE M. BROWN, CFTE, MFTA

ROCKVILLE, MARYLAND
INTERNATIONAL FEDERATION OF TECHNICAL ANALYSTS
2022

LIBRARY OF CONGRESS CATALOGING-IN-PUBLICATION DATA

International Federation of Technical Analysts
Trading Market Dynamics Using Technical Analysis/Constance M. Brown
Includes bibliographical references and index.
Summary: Trading Market Dynamics Using Technical Analysis is an educational textbook for traders, investors, analysts, and business students. It teaches how technical analysis charting skills can be used to understand, and interpret price movements and trends in global markets. (BEGINNER TO INTERMEDIATE LEVEL)"—provided by the Author.
ISBN—978-0-578-38286-9 (alk. paper)

1.      Investment analysis. 2. Speculation. 3. Technical Analysis. 1. Title

# INTRODUCTION

**M**arket movement is about people. The dynamics of mass crowds exerting their singular will on markets force us to read more than technical signals and indicators to be successful. We teach about the dynamic pressure and influences of crowds after we study techniques. Should not the influence of crowds be an integral part of the discussion from the beginning?

The definition of a professional trader changed during the Covid-19 pandemic. Professionals worked from home as the next generation of market influencers discovered that their large numbers had weight and influence in market direction, trend duration, timing, and swing amplitude.

Both groups face new challenges. A re-thinking of the application of classic technicals is one result. In 1996, my book Technical Analysis for the Trading Professional first introduced the concept of signals in the mid-range of oscillators to show that these are of greater value than divergences at the extremes. As a front-line trader living and dying on the decisions I make daily, it is clear technical analysis for portfolio management and trading for your personal income are very different applications.

This book is dedicated to the many educators who helped me within our global member societies of IFTA. Trading had been their clear priority. Many expressed the need to refresh our thinking on how best to teach our craft for effective market participation post-Covid. I am immensely grateful to Saleh Nasser of the Egyptian Society of Technical Analysts who heads the Education Committee for IFTA. On a single phone call he ignited a passion within me to write about market pressure as an integrated discussion with technical analysis.

Constance Brown, CFTe MFTA
February 20, 2022

# ACKNOWLEDGEMENTS

This project would not be possible without our software vendors. There are four vendors contributing to the charts in this book.

Charts created using Optuma have a blue band over the chart. (C) Market Analysts International Pty Ltd., 2022, All rights reserved. No investment or trading advice, recommendation or opinion is being given or intended. Please visit optuma.com. All of my Gann and longer horizon chart work depends on the Optuma Gann Edition.

The cycles charts on pages 102 to 108 were created with TimingSolution Software. There is no better cycle research product on the market. However, this software requires knowledge before you begin and is therefore better suited for intermediate and higher levels. Please visit timingsolution.com.

TradeStation is my trading platform. Charts created using TradeStation are (C) TradeStation Technologies, Inc., All rights reserved. No investment or trading advice, recommendation or opinion is being given or intended.

A fourth vendor offers easy-to-use technical analysis features as an online subscription product called StockCharts.com. This is a low cost entry level offering with numerous prepared charts in professional logic trees. If you need to know how to approach your mornings, or how to easily find common market or stock groupings such as the stock symbols of sectors or composition symbols within ETFs, this is a great way to access this time-consuming collection of data. It is the only software I use that offers equivolume charting. They also create the best Point-and-Figure charts in the business.

A special thank you to the Foundation for the Study of Cycles. Pages 110 and 111 are from the Edward Dewey library of extensive research on cycles. Please visit https://cycles.org for membership. Members receive an exceptional magazine exploring Dewey's work and world of cycles.

I had promised myself after book nine, never again. But here we are with the tenth book. It is my sincere hope that it helps our newest traders coming into our industry. May this book help you see how one trader combines methods in a real-world example. You will add and subtract methods you feel are beneficial. It is an evolving process. I have been hunting in the world markets for more than thirty years. What joy!

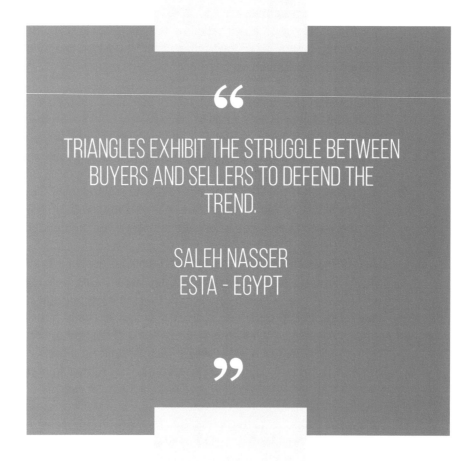

"

TRIANGLES EXHIBIT THE STRUGGLE BETWEEN BUYERS AND SELLERS TO DEFEND THE TREND.

SALEH NASSER
ESTA - EGYPT

"

# CONTENT

Technical analysis is presented in a unique way in this book. This is a discussion by a professional trader. Methods are introduced as they are needed to support the continuous dialogue. Please read chapters in sequence. This book will help you understand why and when certain methods are applied, what questions they answer, and will enhance your skills to trade and manage the risks.

# THE WORLD MARKETS ARE ABOUT PEOPLE AND COMMERCE

# CHAPTER ONE

# The Universe of Markets

## MARKETS ARE CONNECTED. A MAJOR EVENT IN ONE MARKET CAN IMPACT ALL MARKETS.

**M**arkets are about people. People in large numbers make decisions that an individual might not make on their own. Mass psychology is fascinating to study. Price action in markets is the study of people's assumptions, hopes, fears, and yes, greed. While you may think you only have to understand stocks, if that is your primary interest, you may want to look at an event in history that puts market dynamics into context.

In baseball the biggest event is the World Series. Now coming from Canada I always found that an odd name. It only includes American teams and no teams from other countries. However, it goes on every year and is the event that captures all Americans every fall. The die-hards know the statistics for every player - similar to you knowing all you can about a stock and the statistics or technicals one could collect for that company.

Finally the big day arrives on October 17, 1989. Hundreds of thousands of people are watching and the media is creating the buzz in anticipation. Tables of performance stats and forecasts about who will win are being broadcast. Suddenly, the live prime time show from Candlestick Park in Oakland, California is suspended by a Richter Scale 6.9 earthquake. The live opening

# The World Series Earthquake

youtube.com/watch?v=viE_yQNFvhM

broadcast from ABC, by the American Broadcasting Company, can be viewed at YouTube/watch?v+Z8ExMR0c0aM or scan the QR Code at left. The link above shows the event in a broader context.

The announcers Al Michaels and Tim McCarver did not know bridges and large buildings had just collapsed. The stadium itself became unstable and at risk of collapse. Outside the stadium thousands became homeless in those few brief minutes they went off air. How does this event relate to stocks you may wonder? Imagine you have studied your charts and finalized your plan to execute a position in a specific stock. This is no different than the people who held all their lists of baseball stats in hand that October day in 1989. Nothing else is of interest to you as the market is about to open and you are about to buy your selected stock. You have experience to support your belief that only the stock market in your country needs your attention. Suddenly, your charts are showing a wild fluctuation and you struggle to obtain a reason why the market has suddenly made these movements without warning. What are people thinking to cause this?

Like the earthquake that suspended the World Series in California, a sudden shock within the Foreign Exchange Currency markets will override the dynamics of stocks in a heartbeat. There is a hierarchy order within markets and the FOREX, or foreign exchange markets around the world, can be viewed as the largest domino in a series of aligned market dominoes. If a shock occurs in a major currency market; you can be assured, world markets will react.

History provides us several examples of how market shock waves ripple through other markets as people around the world react. But in order to have this conversation with examples, we need to look at the basic ways we read prices. The price action movements on our screens in a single market can

Figure A
Watch the video from the History Channel link above.

Foreign exchange currencies lead the hierarchy order for all global markets.

help us understand what people are thinking and why they are reacting as they do.

You may already know what a bar chart is and how to create this basic chart style to map price movements, but has anyone ever sat down with you to explain how to read a bar chart? It is rich with details to help us understand who has control, where the most important price ranges are located, where people are battling for control of a trend and who could win. We know if the number of buyers is dissipating and holding a weak position. We can read specific triggers created from the open and closing prices for a specified time period relative to the time period behind it. Does the trigger tell us to take action, be more patient, or hold our ground firmly in the market? Can one market lead another to warn us of the approach of a directional change which has already happened elsewhere? All of these questions can be answered if you understand how to read a bar chart and mine the price action for the hidden gems it contains.

As your ability to read and understand chart price action grows within a single market, we can then look at how different markets interact with one another and what markets have the greatest influence on the one you are focused upon. It is the best chess game in the world and the playing field is without question a three-dimensional board. When you make a smart move today, you can come back tomorrow and see who is doing what to whom and how you might then define your own strategy. All this from a price chart? You can bet on it!

Figure 1.1 is a weekly bar chart of December 2021 Crude Oil Futures. One vertical bar records the price high, range, and low traded in a single week. Most people look at the direction of the bars and conclude the Oil market had a sharp decline that was followed by a rally retracement, or price swing back to a price near 48.

HAS ANYONE EVER SAT DOWN WITH YOU TO EXPLAIN HOW TO
READ A BAR CHART? IT IS RICH WITH DETAILS.

CLZ21 - Weekly PC=82.66 O=**82.25** Hi=82.37 Lo=82.10 **-0.54** 07:34:48 PM 10/27/21

Figure 1.1
December 2021 Crude Oil
Futures - weekly

Chart by TradeStation

Each vertical bar has a small marker to the left of the bar showing the opening price for that time period, in this case where the week begins, and to the right showing the closing price for that week. When bar charts are taught, few really explain what all these open and closing markers on each bar can tell us about what people are thinking.

- Green arrow '1' points to the middle of two bars. The closing price of the left bar and the opening price for the next weekly session are the same price. What does that tell us? The bar on the right of '1' declines, but the warning was in the range knowing buyers failed to move prices higher than the price high of the range in the prior week. That is a failure and the sellers take control. The weekly bar '1' closes just off the price lows for the week. That is weakness. The buyers could not restore the uptrend with a stronger close.
- Bar '2' opens the week lower than the close of the prior week. A feeble bounce up within '2' fails to equal the closing price of the prior week. This failure is a sell trigger signal that experienced traders recognize and the sharp decline follows in price bar '2'. The close for bar '2' is just off the price lows for the week.
- Bar '3' opens on the low for the week and lower than the price range low of the prior week. Never a good sign. The buyers try to pressure the market up during the week, but they fail to print a price higher than the range low made three weeks ago. (Two bars left of '2'.) That bar relationship warns that the sellers will retake control and we see the close for the session is barely above the price low from the session's open. The week's gains were lost by the close and the close is below the close of the prior week. That is trouble ahead.
- Bar '4' opens well below the close of week '3'. The buyers try to fill the gap and fail. We know several things about what buyers and sellers are thinking. Bar '4' is where we know everyone is on the same side of the market. The buyers are forced to sell. The sellers are aggressively adding to short positions. Experienced traders who missed the selling opportunity above the gap know they must sell as soon as possible into the attempt to fill the gap. Everyone is on the same side. How do we know this? Under the price bars are blue vertical bars showing us the total number of trades or volume recorded as a histogram plot. Price bar '4' shows volume increased.

In short horizon periods like intraday bars, we can use tick volume which is a record of trades by minimum price fluctuation.

- The close in bar '4' is below the open. We know something about this type of high volume activity in a wash-out declining price bar. It is called capitulation when the bulls panic and run from their opinion that the market is in an uptrend. The traders holding long positions  without deep pockets

continued ...

# HOW TO READ BAR CHARTS

to hold through a deep decline are forced out. But the high volume that occurs in this bar is rarely the final move down. *Trends rarely terminate on high volume.* People cannot be run over by a truck and feel like they want to try it again immediately. The sellers take the market down again but people selling are declining in numbers. We know this because the volume at 'a' under the price bar '6' is lower than the volume that occurred in the

A narrowing price range with marginal new highs and higher shallow lows on declining volume is a major red flag.

 ALWAYS WAIT FOR THE TEST ON LOWER VOLUME BEFORE YOU TAKE A POSITION IN A REVERSING TREND.

decline for bar '4'. Bar '5' also has less volume than bar '4' .

- The volume or selling pressure is weakening because there are fewer orders coming into the market when we make a comparison between bars '5' and '6'. But the rebound that follows is a weak 'hand' rally because the closing bars all fail to make a close that is higher than the relative close of the prior week.
- The bears try to crush the buyers one last time and the volume histogram bar marked 'b' shows the volume is lower than the high volume in bar '4'. This is a confirmation that the sellers are exhausted. Now is the time for the buyers to make their move. The lower volume tells buyers that it is safer to step in because the selling pressure has diminished. Always wait for the test on lower volume before you take a position in a potential reversing trend.
- Bar '7' in Figure 1.1 is the early buyers' trigger signal that the market direction is reversing. Why? Bar '7' has a closing price that is above the

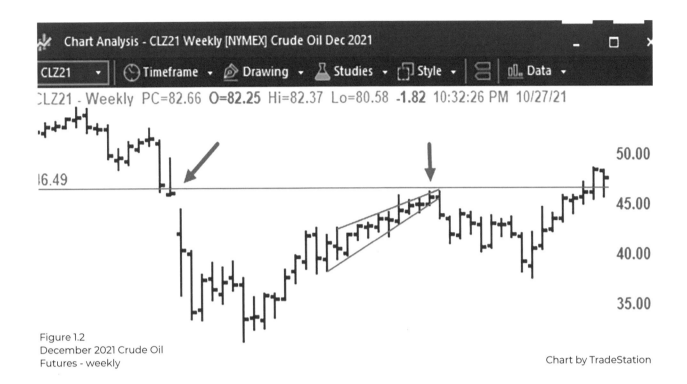

Figure 1.2
December 2021 Crude Oil
Futures - weekly

Chart by TradeStation

price high of the bar to the immediate left of '7'.

- The blue line below bars '8' and '9' is the classic definition of a confirmed trend line because the price lows touch the line three times. However, we need to clarify the definition for a trend line later as our industry uses lines haphazardly and calls all lines trend lines. That is incorrect. What is of greater value is to see that the rally now develops higher price highs and higher price lows.

- Point '9' is a pattern. While the open is slightly lower than the close of the prior week, the price low in the second bar in the circle is higher than the low of the prior. While subtle, this is important. Which direction is the pressure building? Correct. Upwards. From bar '10' to '11' the market prices work higher.

There is a problem developing in the rally. Figure 1.2 draws two red converging lines. While the price direction is upwards, the range for each bar is narrowing as minor new highs and rising lows form the wedge. *The volume under each bar is declining.* Where did the buyers' conviction go? The throw-over bars do not change the growing concern because the open and close for these bars are within the narrowing range.

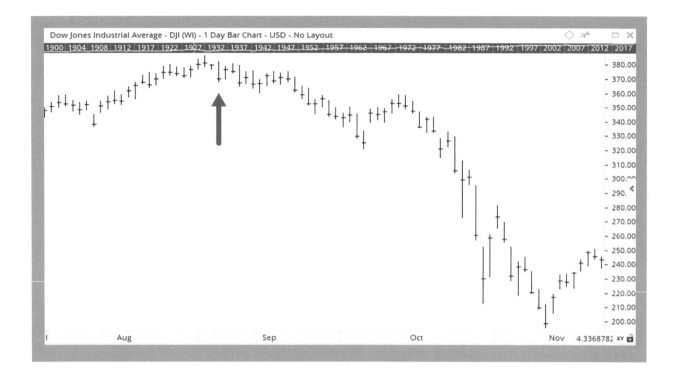

Dow Jones Industrial Average - DJI (WI) - 1 Day Bar Chart - USD - No Layout

While buyers were able to fill the gap, there are no other buyers coming into the market once the price gap was filled. Figure 1.1 at '11' shows declining volume in the last 3 bars into the swing high. The sellers see this weakness and step in to sell. The market begins to decline. The bar at '12' opens below the close of the bar at the top of the wedge. The volume picks up in the next bar. Now this is important:, the decline that follows then retraces the rally that started the wedge pattern in Figure 1.2. Figures 1.1 and 1.2 look a little different because the y-axis scale is more compressed. But it is the same data. This narrowing range of higher highs and shallow higher lows is called a termination wedge. You can see why and it is nearly always retraced back to the base where the pattern began. Bar '13' in Figure 1.1 allows you to see that buyers are stepping into Crude Oil with conviction as volume is increasing and exceeding the volume highs that developed during the decline. That is where the buyers take control and keep it for the balance of the chart.

One final point regarding Figure 1.1 and for all charts you create.

- Always know which price bar is the longest one in the chart. That is significant. Know the length of the longest bar in an uptrend and in a decline for later comparisons. When the longest bar is exceeded in the opposite direction within a swing, a new trend is trying to develop.

A famous single reversal price bar in history is described in the book, *The Day the Bubble Burst: A Social History of the Wall Street Crash of 1929* by Gordon Thomas and Max Morgan-Witts (1979) New York, Doubleday Publishers. One smart

Figure 1.3

DJIA 1929 - daily

A woman's cable to her broker from a ship traveling across the Atlantic to "SELL EVERYTHING" triggers the first selling panic by First Class passengers in 1929.

woman read the sentiment of travelers crossing the Atlantic. Everyone was talking about the bull market. She walked to the wire room and sent one sentence to her broker. "SELL EVERYTHING." I'll let you read who it was who sold. The message was spread via rumor throughout First Class and the oil and railroad tycoons duplicated her message to their brokers in New York as they knew she had an uncanny sense of timing. I guess I like this story because it tells how a woman triggered the first early warning of the Great Crash. Another who was known to sell right at the market top for similar reasons was Charlie Chaplin. A shoe-shine man told him to buy a stock. Chaplin sold everything.

Do you know another famous person who sold based on consumer sentiment in September of 1929 before the Great Crash? The grandfather of Jacqueline Kennedy, John Vernou Bouvier Jr., a stockbroker and lawyer who sold his entire extensive portfolio. He saved the family's fortune and likely Jacqueline's future.

Markets are about people, regardless of what time horizon you may trade, invest, or analyze. We read bar charts to understand what people are thinking and may do next. Now we have the basics to connect people across different markets and countries. Our next step is to look at the universe of global markets.

> **"**
> IT IS NOT ABOUT EXECUTING A TRADE; IT IS ABOUT MANAGING THE TRADE AND KNOWING THE COMPLETE PROCESS.
> COSTA PERDIKIS, TSAA - SOUTH AFRICA

**LEARNING OBJECTIVES**

Understand Buyer/Seller market pressures. Learn directional signals using price open and close comparisons. Detect weakening conviction or activity of the market's trend followers. Know when to enter a trend reversal.

# MONEY FLOWS BETWEEN MARKETS TO CHASE BASIS POINTS (BPS)

I recall reading in *The Day the Bubble Burst* that on September 4, 1929 Jesse Livermore's desk received three messages. The first was from a high official in the Bank of England. London was five hours ahead of New York and it read, "The American bubble has burst." The second message stated that the Bank of England was planning to raise interest rates a full percentage point. Such a move would be very significant to stocks.

The backdrop to these first two messages was the knowledge that the outflow of gold from Great Britain in July and August of 1929 had greatly reduced the bullion reserves of gold in the Bank of England to a mere £137 million.

The third message to Jesse Livermore concerned a high net worth investor in London that was about to fail and would cause an exchange margin call problem. Jesse Livermore sold stocks short all afternoon as the tape confirmed numerous stocks had begun to rollover.

We need to unpack several aspects of this story and these critical messages to really comprehend the magnitude of this information given to Livermore.

Figure 1.4
Lamborghini Aventador -
Carbonado

Before we can move forward, people new to the stock market often find the concept of short selling stock a way to short-circuit their brains. The blank stares and confused looks are a common occurrence. Here is how I seem to help them over that hurdle. You have been asked by a neighbor to watch over their Lamborghini Aventodor S car. They will be away for a full year.

Now here is the part we have to overlook the moral, legal, and ethical issues of my example. You know Lamborghini cars have been in an over-heated buyer's market. It will not last. So you sell your neighbor's car for $825,914, being the top price in 2020. Several months later knowing the market prices have fallen, and aware you must have the EXACT same car in the garage when your neighbors return, you buy the EXACT replacement car for $750, 914. You keep the price difference of $75,000 from selling high and buying the car back at a lower price. The car has been returned and all is well.

When you decided to sell your neighbor's car, which you did not own, it is similar in a way to what happens when you sell stocks short. You do not own them either. You have to reserve them from your broker as they must confirm they have stock you can sell. The owner of the stocks forgot long ago that their agreement with their brokerage firm has a little clause in the contract that states that they agree their stocks can be sold short. So you have permission to sell stocks you do not own. The owner is not told their stocks have been put on reserve for short selling.

If everyone just sold stocks short in a crash without any checks or balances, you could be selling stock that does not exist by selling stocks in numbers that exceed the number of outstanding shares a company has issued. That means you could not buy the stock back to return it to the account of the original owner whose shares were put on reserve for you. So short selling always has to have a buy order later to offset a short position. To prevent this huge problem of not finding stock to buy back, you need your brokerage firm to confirm that the stock exists before you sell. The brokerage firm sets the method for how you can reserve stocks to short. Moreover, they may not let you sell some issues short at all because they either do not have them to reserve or the market is so thin you might not be able to buy the shares back that you want to borrow.

Jesse Livermore was famous for selling stocks short at the top of the Dow Jones Industrial Average, September 4th of 1929. The sentiment of the public toward short sellers of the stock market is one of anger and outrage. That is still true today. Short-sellers find market bottoms because short-sellers must buy to cover their short positions when there are no other buyers to be found in a market. All you have to do is look at the Saudi stock market called the Saudi Tadawul All Share Index (TASI). This exchange does not permit short selling. As a result the crash in 2008 was even more extreme than other indexes that allow short selling. Livermore was much hated by the public. But short sellers are not the enemy hidden within the crowd. Without short sellers there could be no hedge funds. They can both buy and sell and give positive returns for their investors regardless of the direction the market moves. Mutual funds can only buy. Well, that's not exactly true. That's why exchanges introduced some Exchange Traded Funds (ETF's) structured to create gains when the market declines. They will have the term 'short' in the name of the ETF. If you see the term 'ultra-short' in the ETF's name, it will have a *beta* greater than one.

Beta is another term that may need explaining. If you have a basket of stocks that move up or down the same percentage gain or loss as the index the stocks are members, the beta is equal to the value of one. If our little basket of stocks moves up or down 20% whenever the index moves up or down 10%, the portfolio of stocks will have a beta of 2. The stock portfolio moves twice as much as the index. It is more volatile than the index by a factor of 2. The term 'ultra' in an ETF name warns you that the fund will have greater leverage,

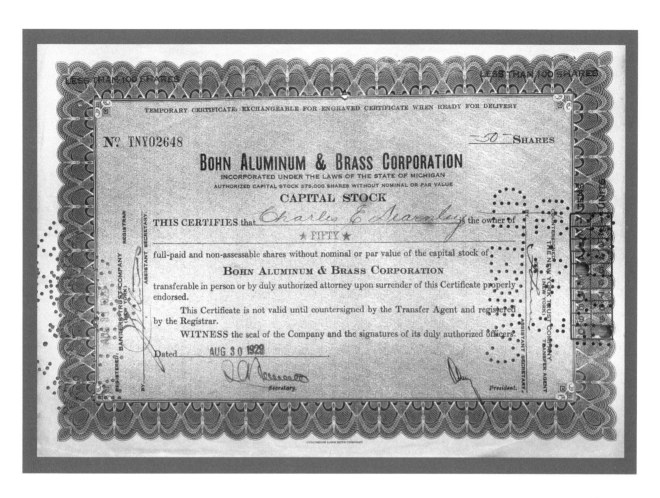

Figure 1.5
50 Shares Bohn Aluminum & Brass Corporation
Purchased August 30, 1929 - (Connie Brown Library)

Google the company name. Wikipedia shows their futuristic vision of an
ocean liner that looks like a torpedo. The company survived the crash
and Great Depression. It then merged into Universal American in 1963.

a higher beta, than the index of comparison. The price swings for ETF's with
names ultra-short and ultra-long will move significantly more than the index.
The ETF name may state 2X or 3X giving you the expected beta.

Consider the messages Livermore received before the Great Crash. The first
message stated that the "American bubble has burst". A rather odd message
to come from a banking community without additional facts. It is not until later
that we understand why such a statement could have been made. Livermore is
told in the second message that the Bank of England is going to raise interest
rates a full percentage point. To fully understand this statement, we need to
talk about basis points.

It does not matter if you are investing in stocks, bonds, gold, real estate, bitcoin, commodities, or an asset class yet to be created, every asset class has a common denominator. What is the return on my money? What percentage gain will my investment yield? Then you will expect a higher return on your money if the risk to your underlying principle increases. It is this common denominator of percentage gain for risk taken that is pulsing through different asset classes that creates the flow of cash from one market to another. You can never just look at stocks alone because they are the last domino in the series of dominoes that connect all financial markets. No question stocks will be impacted negatively from a full 1-percent rate hike proposed by the Bank of England.

One percent is equal to one hundred basis points. Another way to say the same thing is that one Basis Point (BPS) is equal to 1/100th of one percent. If a stock increases 5.5 percent in a single day on news, people have pushed the stock up 550 BPS. This is a unit of measurement and is easy to convert. Divide Basis Points by 100 to obtain percent and multiply the percent by 100 to obtain basis points. Basis Point is an absolute unit and solves the problem when relative percentage change is discussed. An increase from 11% to 12% is an absolute change of 100 BPS. But the relative change is 9.90%. Referencing BPS is a much better way to look at change and compare different returns in different investments.

For a Central Bank to raise interest rates one hundred BPS is a huge and troubling move that will ripple and shake through the entire financial chain of market dominoes and their subsidiary asset classes. The Bank of England wants money to stay in England and they are willing to pay for it. They also want to make it more expensive to borrow money and hence tighten credit by having all British banks charge people more on their loans and credit instruments in the commercial and private sectors. Here is how such a change would flow through the markets.

The first and immediate impact will be felt in the yield curve and through interest rates. To ensure you understand what the yield curve is we should pause here to discuss it. Regardless of the market of greatest interest to you, we need to understand what the yield curve is and what it can tell us. The data above was obtained from the St. Louis Federal Reserve. The address is https://www.treasury.gov/resource-center/data-chart-center/interest-rates/Pages/TextView.aspx?data=yield, or you can use the QR-code.

Treasury Yield Curve Rates are commonly referred to as 'Constant Maturity Treasury' rates. They are based on the closing market bid yields on actively traded Treasury securities in the over-the-counter market. The curve is created from the daily yield from a series of government securities based on their time to maturity. In the United States the debt maturities sold by the federal

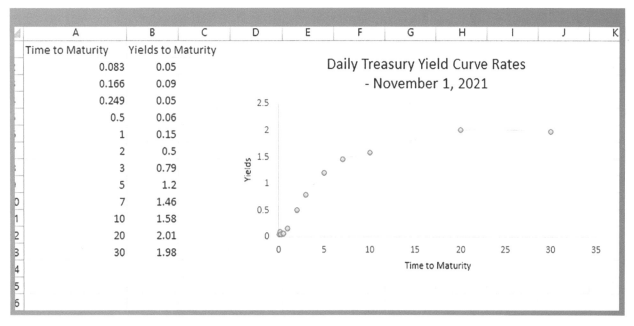

| | A | B | C | D | E | F | G | H | I | J | K |
|---|---|---|---|---|---|---|---|---|---|---|---|
| | Time to Maturity | Yields to Maturity | | | | | | | | | |
| | 0.083 | 0.05 | | | | | | | | | |
| | 0.166 | 0.09 | | | | | | | | | |
| | 0.249 | 0.05 | | | | | | | | | |
| | 0.5 | 0.06 | | | | | | | | | |
| | 1 | 0.15 | | | | | | | | | |
| | 2 | 0.5 | | | | | | | | | |
| | 3 | 0.79 | | | | | | | | | |
| | 5 | 1.2 | | | | | | | | | |
| | 7 | 1.46 | | | | | | | | | |
| | 10 | 1.58 | | | | | | | | | |
| | 20 | 2.01 | | | | | | | | | |
| | 30 | 1.98 | | | | | | | | | |

Figure 1.6
St. Louis FRED Economic Data.
Daily U.S. Treasury Yield Curve Rates

government are the 1, 2, 3 and 6-month Treasury Bills, and then the Treasury Notes with maturities of 1, 2, 3, 5, 7, 10, and Bonds with maturities of 20, and 30-years. Each country has their own series of government securities, and not every country has a 30-year bond. When we compare treasury markets between countries the 20-year bond is the best maturity to compare. We say that the securities plotted with maturities in months are the short end of the curve. The 30-year bond is the long-bond on the far end of the yield curve.

The yield curve in Figure 1.6 will be a historic chart someday. It is a normal shaped curve, but the yield spread between the T-Bills and long-bond is only 2-percent. Would you want your cash locked up for 30 years if it were only going to pay you 2 percent? Not me, or anyone else with options. So who would buy the long end of the yield curve? The government is the buyer. Sell the long-bond and you only pay 2-percent to borrow money for 30-years. Good deal if you can create bonds to sell to borrow cash from the public.

When the short end of the yield curve is in essence zero, the government cannot lower rates further which is done in the Federal Funds Rate off the yield curve plot further to the left. It controls everything in the curve as the starting reference for all other securities. If you want to stimulate a sick economy and cannot lower the Fed Funds Rate, because rates are on the bottom already, what other options does a government have?

# HOW TO CHART A YIELD CURVE IN MICROSOFT EXCEL

If you do not have a Bloomberg terminal, you are going to find it is difficult to see a Yield Curve graph from a product for technical analysis. I hope this changes! However, we can manage by creating one in MS Excel. Figure 1.6 shows you the raw data from the St. Louis Federal Reserve.

Here are the steps I used to create the scatter plot chart with connected lines in Figure 1.6.

1. In cell A1 is a label 'Time to Maturity'. Cell B1 has the label 'Yields to Maturity'.

2. I cannot use in the spreadsheet 1-month, 2-month, 3-month, and 6-months because I also want to plot years with them on the x-axis. So I used a decimal equivalent for maturities less than a year and filled the balance of the securities in cells A2 to A13.

3. Cells B2 through B13 will be the yields to maturity as reported by the Federal Reserve.

4. Now create the chart. Select cells A2 to A13, and B2 through B13 as you hold down the shift key. In the top menu tap 'INSERT' in the top menu. In the fourth box are the Chart options. Select 'SCATTER' and then click on 'SCATTER WITH SMOOTH LINES and MARKERS'.

5. Last step is to tap the chart itself. Select 'Chart Elements'. Then select 'Axis Titles'. You will find one for horizontal and one for vertical. Just click the text place holder in the chart to add the labels. Do not forget to add a title as well.

One option is to buy the long end of the curve. What effect would this have on a troubled economy? There is an inverse relationship between bond prices and yield. Some in the retail market just don't get this one. You are promised a fixed yield on the maturity date of your treasury security. If the price goes up, *the yield has to go down as the promised return is fixed*. If you make more in the face value because price rises, you will make less on the interest rate paid so it still comes out to equal the fixed promised maturity rate. When treasury futures rise in price, the yield chart for that same maturity duration must decline. If treasury future prices decline, then rates must rise to keep the maturity rate of return the same.

If one has a hard time with the inverse relationship between price and yield, this could be even harder. The formula for the return rate assumes the cash paid out on a coupon will be *fully reinvested for the remaining duration of the underlying security at a similar or better rate of return*. Therefore, you cannot spend it. If a 5% bond pays a coupon today, where are you going to find a 5% investment when the 30-year U.S. Treasury bond pays only 2-percent? Not going to happen. People who think they are making 5% on a government security and do not know the catch about reinvesting the coupon payments, or worse, spend the coupon payment, are making far less on their money than they know.

Quantitative Easing is when the central banks print money as a first step. Then when the government's hands are tied and they cannot lower interest rates on the short end of the curve, they can buy treasuries on the long-end of the curve. Price goes up and yield on longer maturities declines. If you lower interest rates on the long-end of the curve you are lowering mortgage rates. Lower mortgage rates lead to people buying houses and all the goodies that go with it. In essence the government found another way to stimulate the economy when they could not lower interest rates on the short end of the curve. Eventually the government will taper their purchase and stop buying treasuries all together. What happens then? Prices begin to fall on bonds and rates rise. If they are too late, normally the

LEARNING OBJECTIVES

Learn how to create a Treasury market yield curve using Microsoft Excel. Understand why yield curves change shape and the emotions behind slope changes. Learn how to detect an approaching recession.

case, they have an overheated economy and inflation takes off. We say the Fed is chasing the curve because now they have to chase a problem. Through all these changes the most stable part of the yield curve is in the middle. The 5-Year Treasury Note  can be seen as the fulcrum point of the curve.

Is this technical analysis? This is understanding why things go bump in the night. It impacts why markets move as they do. The fundamentals behind treasuries are complex and I suspect this discussion will make those experts cringe, but it gives a basic picture for those of us who are not treasury experts. When examining other markets, we cannot compartmentalize what is technical and what is the study of people.

The yield curve in Figure 1.6 is an arching, upward slope because bond investors should be compensated for the risk of loaning their money to the government for a longer period of time as defined by the maturity. When the long bond pays considerably more than the short maturities we say the yield curve is steep. When the spread is narrow between the short and long end of the curve, it can take on a flat line appearance.

While rare, it is possible for a yield curve to invert. That is when the shorter-dated securities are paying higher rates of return than longer-dated maturities. This is always trouble. Yield curve inversions typically precede recessions.

In February of 2020, the yield curve inverted between the 3-month U.S. Treasury Bill (T-Bill) that was paying more than the yield of the 10-Year Treasury Note (T-Note). The last time this occurred was July/August of 2007. The failure of Lehman Brothers in mid-September of 2008 was not the start of the Great Financial Crisis.

# FEBRUARY 2020  U.S. INVERTED YIELD CURVE

| Date | 1 Mo | 2 Mo | 3 Mo | 6 Mo | 1 Yr | 2 Yr | 3 Yr | 5 Yr | 7 Yr | 10 Yr | 20 Yr | 30 Yr |
|---|---|---|---|---|---|---|---|---|---|---|---|---|
| 02/12/20 | 1.57 | 1.59 | 1.58 | 1.56 | 1.49 | 1.44 | 1.42 | 1.45 | 1.55 | 1.62 | 1.93 | 2.09 |
| 02/13/20 | 1.59 | 1.59 | 1.59 | 1.56 | 1.48 | 1.44 | 1.42 | 1.43 | 1.53 | 1.61 | 1.91 | 2.07 |
| 02/14/20 | 1.60 | 1.60 | 1.58 | 1.56 | 1.49 | 1.42 | 1.40 | 1.42 | 1.51 | 1.59 | 1.89 | 2.04 |
| 02/18/20 | 1.61 | 1.60 | 1.58 | 1.56 | 1.47 | 1.41 | 1.37 | 1.39 | 1.48 | 1.55 | 1.85 | 2.00 |
| 02/19/20 | 1.61 | 1.61 | 1.58 | 1.56 | 1.47 | 1.42 | 1.39 | 1.41 | 1.50 | 1.56 | 1.86 | 2.01 |
| 02/20/20 | 1.61 | 1.60 | 1.58 | 1.55 | 1.46 | 1.39 | 1.35 | 1.37 | 1.45 | 1.52 | 1.81 | 1.97 |
| 02/21/20 | 1.60 | 1.60 | 1.56 | 1.53 | 1.43 | 1.34 | 1.30 | 1.30 | 1.39 | 1.46 | 1.75 | 1.90 |
| 02/24/20 | 1.60 | 1.59 | 1.53 | 1.49 | 1.35 | 1.26 | 1.21 | 1.21 | 1.30 | 1.38 | 1.68 | 1.84 |
| 02/25/20 | 1.59 | 1.58 | 1.53 | 1.47 | 1.30 | 1.20 | 1.16 | 1.16 | 1.25 | 1.33 | 1.63 | 1.80 |
| 02/26/20 | 1.59 | 1.56 | 1.53 | 1.42 | 1.26 | 1.16 | 1.14 | 1.14 | 1.25 | 1.33 | 1.64 | 1.81 |
| 02/27/20 | 1.56 | 1.53 | 1.45 | 1.33 | 1.18 | 1.11 | 1.08 | 1.11 | 1.22 | 1.30 | 1.61 | 1.79 |
| 02/28/20 | 1.45 | 1.37 | 1.27 | 1.11 | 0.97 | 0.86 | 0.85 | 0.89 | 1.03 | 1.13 | 1.46 | 1.65 |
| 03/02/20 | 1.41 | 1.27 | 1.13 | 0.95 | 0.89 | 0.84 | 0.85 | 0.88 | 1.01 | 1.10 | 1.46 | 1.66 |

Figure 1.7

(February 2020 above) (July 2007 below), February 2020 the U.S. 3-month Treasury Bill paid more than the 10-year Treasury Note causing a rare inverted yield curve.

https://www.treasury.gov/resource-center/data-chart-center/interest-rates/Pages/TextView.aspx?data=yieldYear&year=2020

# JULY/AUGUST 2007  U.S. INVERTED YIELD CURVE

| Date | 1 Mo | 2 Mo | 3 Mo | 6 Mo | 1 Yr | 2 Yr | 3 Yr | 5 Yr | 7 Yr | 10 Yr | 20 Yr | 30 Yr |
|---|---|---|---|---|---|---|---|---|---|---|---|---|
| 07/24/07 | 5.05 | N/A | 5.02 | 5.08 | 4.97 | 4.77 | 4.76 | 4.82 | 4.87 | 4.94 | 5.13 | 5.05 |
| 07/25/07 | 5.04 | N/A | 4.99 | 5.05 | 4.95 | 4.74 | 4.74 | 4.80 | 4.85 | 4.92 | 5.12 | 5.04 |
| 07/26/07 | 4.98 | N/A | 4.92 | 4.96 | 4.83 | 4.56 | 4.54 | 4.61 | 4.68 | 4.79 | 5.02 | 4.95 |
| 07/27/07 | 4.89 | N/A | 4.85 | 4.94 | 4.82 | 4.56 | 4.53 | 4.60 | 4.68 | 4.80 | 5.03 | 4.95 |
| 07/30/07 | 4.95 | N/A | 4.96 | 5.00 | 4.87 | 4.59 | 4.57 | 4.64 | 4.71 | 4.82 | 5.05 | 4.97 |
| 07/31/07 | 5.13 | N/A | 4.96 | 4.99 | 4.85 | 4.56 | 4.55 | 4.60 | 4.67 | 4.78 | 5.00 | 4.92 |
| 08/01/07 | 5.05 | N/A | 4.89 | 4.96 | 4.82 | 4.56 | 4.53 | 4.60 | 4.66 | 4.76 | 4.99 | 4.90 |
| 08/02/07 | 5.02 | N/A | 4.89 | 4.95 | 4.83 | 4.59 | 4.57 | 4.62 | 4.68 | 4.77 | 5.00 | 4.91 |
| 08/03/07 | 4.94 | N/A | 4.85 | 4.91 | 4.76 | 4.46 | 4.45 | 4.52 | 4.59 | 4.71 | 4.96 | 4.87 |
| 08/06/07 | 4.92 | N/A | 4.88 | 4.92 | 4.76 | 4.46 | 4.45 | 4.52 | 4.60 | 4.72 | 4.98 | 4.89 |

# U.S. 10-YEAR TREASURY CONSTANT MATURITY MINUS 2-YEAR TREASURY CONSTANT MATURITY

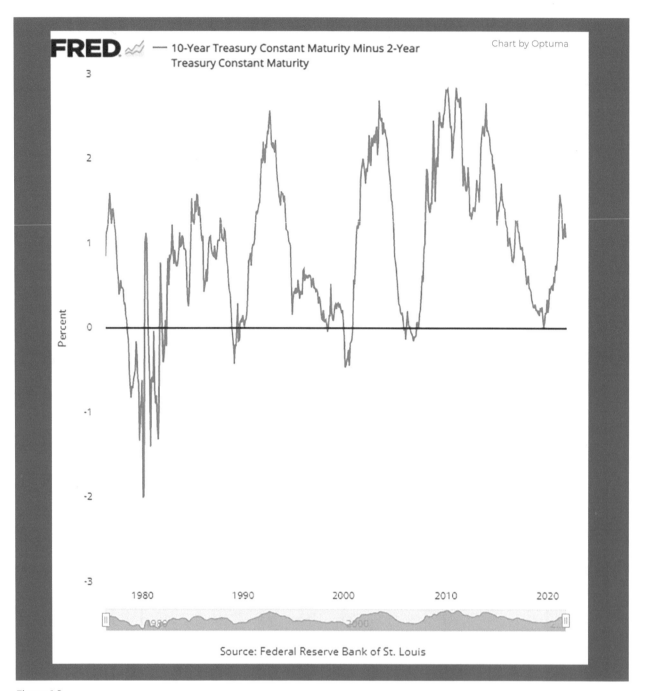

Figure 1.8
June 1976 to September 2021
U.S. 10-Year Treasury Constant Maturity Minus 2-Year Treasury
Constant Maturity Recessions marked by gray vertical bars.
fred.stlouisfed.org/series/T10Y2Y#0

It is very rare for the one-month T-Bill and the 10-Year T-Note to invert. The convention is to graph the yield differential between the U.S. 10-Year T-Note minus the yield of the 2-Year T-Note. Figure 1.8 allows us to visualize this spread from June 1976 to September 2021. Each time the spread falls below the zero line, the yield curve had inverted.

The gray vertical bars in Figure 1.8 mark when a recession occurred. It makes it easier to understand why we say that an inverted yield curve means there is trouble ahead. Each time the data breaks the zero line, a recession soon followed. This chart is so widely monitored it is a standard setup prepared by the St. Louis Fed. Just go to fred.stlouisfed.org/series/T10Y2Y#0

While most leave the discussion here, we need to consider why the yield curve can invert periodically. What is the sentiment of investors to cause this rare negative spread? There is a panic unfolding. People are scared. When people are scared, they do not want their money sitting exposed in a long-term investment. To feel safer about where their money is parked, they move their money down the yield curve into short-term maturities. That way they can move out of it easily when conditions seem more stable, and fear begins to dissipate.

When the inversion developed between the 1-month T-Bill and 10-Year T-Note, this was particularly troubling. Why? The T-Bill has an insurance policy backing it so to speak. The T-Bills should not ever default because they are backed by the government's ability to tax its citizens. Therefore, the government website treasurydirect.gov can make the statement, "T-Bills are backed by the Government's full faith and credit". That is true up to 1-year T-Bills, but do not believe that to be true for U.S. T-Notes and T-Bonds. South America has a history of government bond failures. Government Bonds can fail. Therefore, when people are fearful and unsure, they scramble down the yield curve into T-Bills for safety. If a private individual wanted to buy U.S. T-Bills, they would open an account from treasurydirect.gov.  All my clients have accounts. It is like having a bank account and you just transfer funds by tapping a few buttons. Safer than cash in a bank. Why? Banks loan your cash out to other people who may fail to payback their loan to the bank. Only purchase 4-week T-Bills. You can roll them over several times automatically if you want to avoid the hassle of doing it yourself every four weeks.

We have learned how to create a yield curve graph; we also know where to obtain the data and your country's government will have similar data available. We know the normal relationship between maturities from short-term to long-term should be a graph with an upward sloping arch. We know that all these government securities are calculated off the Fed Funds rate or the benchmark rate defined by your government or Central Bank. But the yield curve we have discussed only contains government securities.

One could also create a Corporate Bond Yield Curve in a similar manner. The arching upward curve from different maturities for corporate paper, notes, and bonds would be offset slightly higher as compared to the government yield curve. Corporate securities are viewed as riskier than government securities, so they demand a slight interest rate premium across their yield curve for the higher risk. The greater the risk, the higher the yield will be paid. But when the Fed Funds Rate is increased by the Federal Reserve, it has an immediate impact throughout the entire chain of interest rate securities from government securities to quality Aaa Corporate Bonds, to High Yield securities; (nicknamed; Junk Bonds), mortgage rates and mortgage-backed securities, credit card rates, you name it. Everything is impacted because the basis points charged by the Federal Reserve for banks to borrow directly from their discount window will be passed on with immediate consequences. The greater the BPS change, the greater the impact across all financial markets.

You will recall Jesse Livermore was told that the Bank of England would raise rates a full 100 basis points. Central Banks normally make changes of +/-25 basis points at a time. To change the anchor rate by 100 BPS is extraordinary. This would have triggered a major ripple effect beyond the British borders. In comparison this would be the earthquake that suddenly suspended the World Series that began our discussion.

September 4, 1929 Jesse Livermore was told the Bank of England would raise rates by 100 BPS. He knew a major chain reaction would follow.

## WHAT REACTION WOULD THE PUBLIC HAVE TO THESE SUDDEN MARKET CHANGES?

Sell stocks to take profits and run to safety simply because they do not understand the sudden volatility in multiple markets. wiser investors would know a sudden increase in rates means the credit system was in trouble in some way. sellers lead to more selling and then a spiral event develops fueled by growing fear.

# RIPPLE EFFECTS THROUGH MARKETS:

THE TRIGGER: The Bank of England unexpectedly raises rates by 100 BPS.

- Yields on treasury securities increase
- Yield on corporate debt instruments increase including mortgage rates
- Yields increase and treasury market prices decline sharply.
- British Pound strengthens or appreciates sharply because of the higher interest rate.
- Cross-rate currencies against the British Pound weaken. Now other Central Banks and countries are forced to consider increasing rates to support their own currency.
- Currency instability usually triggers a flight-to-safety in Gold. Will that be Bitcoin today?
- Bond prices are in a free-fall, bonds lead stock indexes.
- Stocks selloff because higher interest rates slow the economy impacting earnings.

CHAOS. The markets are in turmoil because of the action of a single Central Bank. Consider today's markets.

- Specific stock sectors will be impacted in different ways in today's markets.
- Bank stocks may rally because their principle revenue stream comes from the credit card divisions of a bank. But a weaker economy may increase defaults. Tough one here.
- A sudden stronger British Pound and weaker U.S. Dollar impacts trade balances within Europe and the United States
- Several countries have currencies pegged to the U.S. Dollar in Asia. Therefore their currencies would decline rapidly.
- Sudden higher rates charged for business loans is a liquidity tightening event making loans harder to obtain.
- Tight credit for businesses has a negative effect on the Economy.
- Because of the lessons of 1929, Central Banks take a different response today. They LOWER interest rates to increase lending.
- The EURUSD is the critical currency for Oil. A 100 BPS change by a Central Bank would impact the Oil market.

Table 1.1.
Domino effect and repercussions through financial markets

# INTEREST RATES & STOCK MARKETS

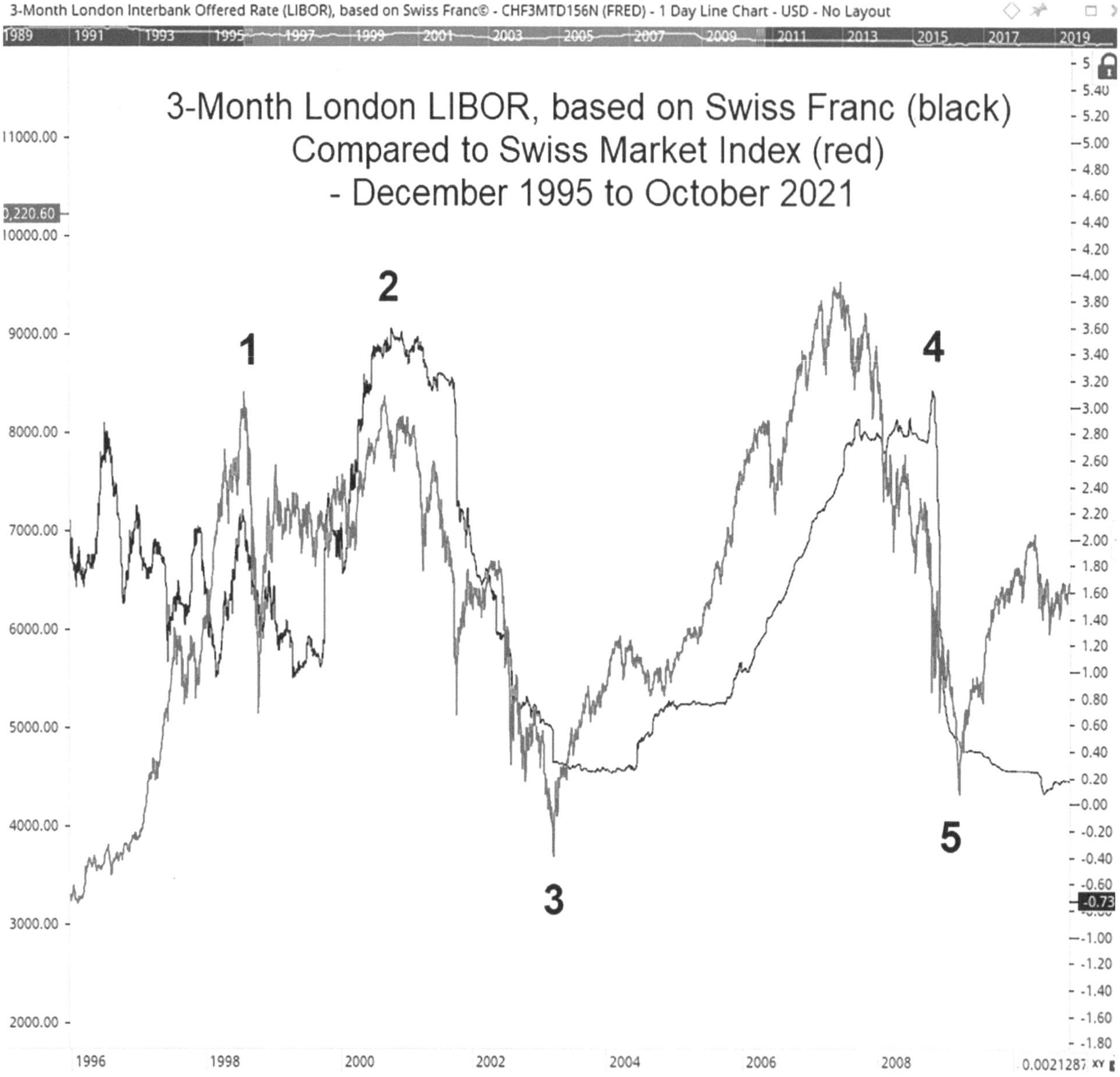

Figure 1.9
LIBOR (SF) and Swiss
Market Index

Many books about intermarket relationships state that interest rates lead the stock market indexes. I am not so sure about this claim. When I read a book, or hear such a statement, I always create a visual chart using an overlay of the two market references. Figure 1.9 shows a correlation, but stocks lead, and it is the Central Bank's benchmark interest rate that lags. Therefore, governments are chasing the people in control of the stock index trend that reflects the sentiment of the buyers and sellers. Opinion within the public about economic stability is important.

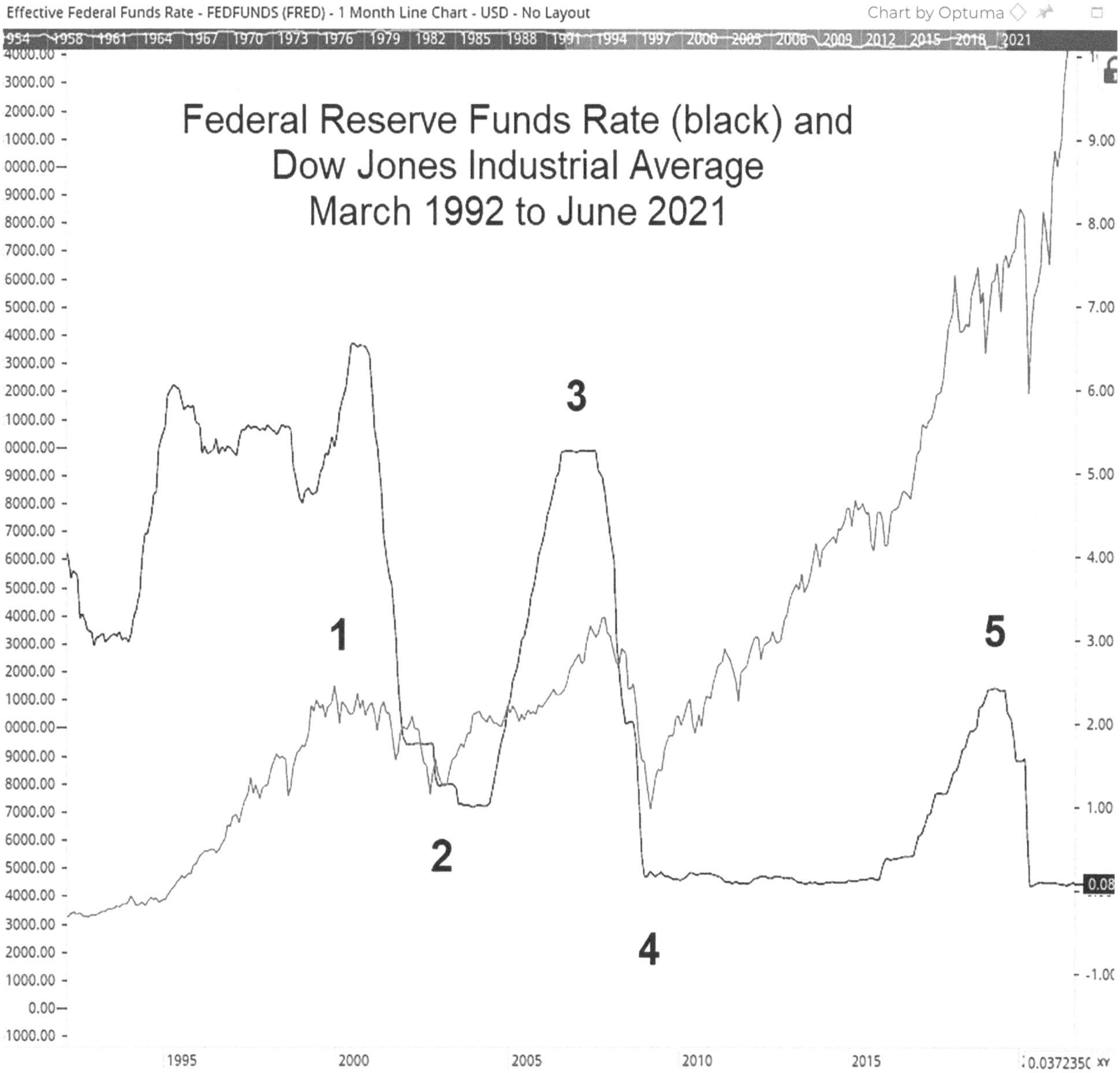

Figure 1.10
Fed Funds Rates (USD)
and Dow Jones Industrial
Average

Figure 1.9 compares the 3-month LIBOR or London Inter-bank Offered Rate in Swiss Franc currency. That way both datasets are in Swiss Francs.Outside of the United States the LIBOR rate is the primary benchmark. LIBOR rates are calculated for five currencies and seven different periods from overnight to one year. LIBOR will soon be replaced. I will explain in a moment.

Figure 1.10 compares the U.S. Fed Funds Rate to the Dow Jones Industrial Average. The comparison in Figure 1.10 does show that changes in the

# BENCHMARK INTEREST RATES

benchmark interest rate lead the stock market index at points 3, 4, and 5. Therefore, what I have read is true, but only some of the time. This raises an interesting question. What relationship do we have between two different government benchmark interest rates? This is like asking, "Which came first, the chicken or the egg?"

While the patterns are different, it is clear the U.S. Federal Funds Rates lead the LIBOR rates most of the time. The world markets are connected, and we cannot ignore these relationships. The reaction could be delayed, but you know a countermove is coming that will impact the entire chain of financial markets.

The process we just followed should never end. Take the step of asking, I wonder what that would look like?. Make a chart to help visualize the relationships. Don't take anyone's word for it, prove it to yourself that a correlation is present and

Figure 1.11
Fed Funds Rates (USD) and
LIBOR Rates

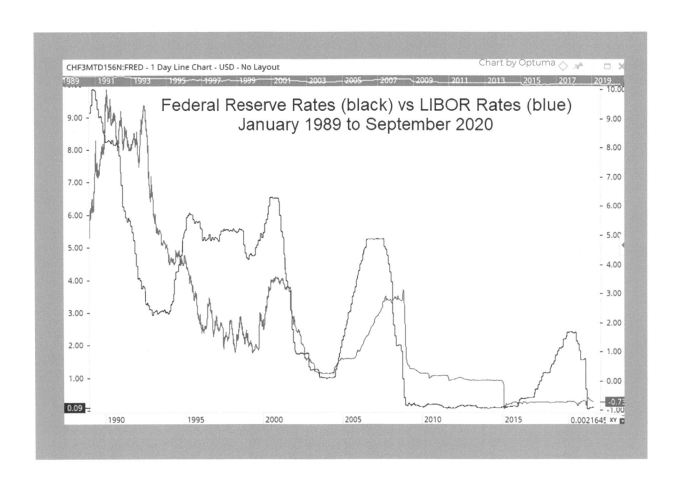

what it looks like in a chart.

In Chapter Three, we will go step-by-step to learn how to use *Microsoft* Excel to evaluate correlations objectively. You just need the raw data, and you can then answer any market relationship question you may have in mind. However, you need to think about how you compare the two markets. If you only look at their relationship when other indicators tell you a major turn is near, do not expect the correlation to track 100% of the time when it is tested. The best question to ask to learn more about market relationships is, 'What if...?' Then start down the path to find the answer by looking at the chart.

Now we need to continue our discussion concerning LIBOR rates because a big change is coming. Knowing the history behind the approaching change will help.

The London Inter-Bank Offered Rate and primary benchmark will be discontinued. The LIBOR is prepared for all sterling, euro, Swiss franc, and Japanese Yen. Why? LIBOR is an average from interest-rate information submitted by primary banks in London on what they charge to borrow from other banks. Sounds simple enough. Why change? The problem began in 2012 when Barclays Bank uncovered significant fraud in the information coming in to create the average. The British Banker's Association transferred the oversight of LIBOR to regulators. Because of this history LIBOR is being discontinued.

LIBOR is being replaced with the Secured Overnight Financing Rate (SOFR) and Sterling Overnight Index Average (SONIA). Regulators pushed the industry to strengthen existing benchmarks for interbank offered rates (IBORs). SOFR is for U.S. Dollars and SONIA for GBP, British Pound Sterling currency. A change is coming and it is called the 'Benchmark Transition Event'.

In March 2021 the United Kingdom stopped entering new contracts using LIBOR as the reference rate. Therefore, Figure 1.11 captures data up to September 2020 when both rates basically run across the chart at zero.

The one rule I have over my long carrier is this; once I figure something out regarding a market, you can be assured someone will change the rules that used to be in place! Change is the only constant.

# FACTORS THAT INFLUENCE A CURRENCY

The exchange rates between countries have several factors that will affect their currency valuation. Interest rate is one factor. When the benchmark interest rate increases it will cause the country's currency to appreciate as banks have to pay more interest. This will then attract more foreign capital because investors can earn more, or more basis points, by holding cash in this higher paying currency. Banks pay a higher rate when the benchmark rate

Figure 1.12
Euro / British Pound
Sterling - EURGBP -
monthly

British Pound Sterling / US Dollar - GBPUSD (FX) - 1 Month Bar Chart - USD - No Layout

Chart by Optuma

Figure 1.13
British Pound Sterling
/ US Dollar - EURUSD -
monthly

increases.

Another factor that impacts the currency exchange rate between countries is inflation. A country with higher inflation depreciates their currency against a country with lower inflation. A country with excessive government debt does not buy another country's bonds. Excessive debt is risky, as foreign governments will sell the government bonds they hold due to risk or for

# CREATING A SYNTHETIC FOREX CROSS-RATE

political clout. This devalues the debtor country's currency.

A country's currency can be devalued when it buys more product overseas than it sells. That is why the Trade Balance Reports move currency rates. The ratio of export prices to import prices is also a factor. Political stability, recessions, and market speculation all impact a country's exchange rate. The good news is we technical analysts have all we need in our chart price data. We can read a great deal about what people are thinking from our charts directly. We have ways to build charts that will help us construct an opinion when the principal exchange rate itself is very cloudy to determine.

Figures 1.12 and 1.13 show the exchange rate between Euro / British Pound Sterling (EURGBP) and British Pound Sterling / U.S. Dollar (GBPUSD). They are both monthly bar charts. British Pound Sterling is also called Cable because telephone cable had to be dropped across the floor of the Atlantic Ocean in 1956 to facilitate trade. Hence the nickname. The first telegraph cable was laid across the Atlantic in 1858.

Consider Figure 1.12. Which currency is strengthening when price is rising, and which one is weakening? The currency that leads is in the name. EURUSD is rising or falling when the data is trending up or down. The second currency is weakening or strengthening against the first.

Now it gets a little squirrelly. Hang in there with me. Figures 1.12 and Figure 1.13 are rather interesting. If you bought EURGBP by purchasing Euro currency by selling British Pound Sterling, and then bought GBPUSD, or bought the same amount of British Pound Sterling by selling U.S. Dollars, do you have two positions or one?

## THE CHART FOR EURCHF MAKES US WONDER IF EURO CAN SURVIVE.
### PATRICK PFISTER - SAMT-SWITZERLAND

You cannot be long Euro and short GBP in one position; then, long GBP and short U.S. Dollar. You have created what we call a synthetic cross-rate. Within these two currency crosses you would be short GBP and long GBP at the same time. An equal weighting will cancel GBP out of the equation. That would leave you with a position that is long Euro currency and short the U.S. Dollar. You have created a position in EURUSD. Why would anyone do that? Traders do it all the time,. (I'll explain in a moment), but as an analyst the two charts may give a clearer trend direction for EURUSD that is not visible in the EURUSD chart alone.

Figure 1.14
Foreign Exchange (FOREX)
Cross-Rates

| | Symbol | Description | Rate | Change | % Change | |
|---|---|---|---|---|---|---|
| 1 | Secondary | | | | | |
| 2 | AUDUSD | Aust Dollar / US Dollar | 0.73879 | -0.00121 | -0.16% | 877 |
| 3 | SGDJPY | Singapore Dollar/Japanese Yen | 84.049 | -0.153 | -0.18% | 045 |
| 4 | US Dollar - USD is Primary Symbol | | | | | |
| 5 | USDCHF | US Dollar / Swiss Franc | 0.91656 | 0.00409 | 0.45% | 654 |
| 6 | USDCAD | US Dollar / Canadian Dollar | 1.24486 | -0.00118 | -0.10% | 481 |
| 7 | USDDKK | US Dollar / Danish Krone | 6.45581 | 0.01883 | 0.29% | 570 |
| 8 | USDSEK | US Dollar / Swedish Krona | 8.59565 | 0.00870 | 0.10% | 510 |
| 9 | USDNOK | US Dollar / Norwegian Krone | 8.58253 | 0.02730 | 0.32% | 176 |
| 10 | USDJPY | US Dollar / Japanese Yen | 113.690 | -0.065 | -0.06% | 688 |
| 11 | Euro - Euro is Primary Symbol | | | | | |
| 12 | EURUSD | Euro / US Dollar | 1.15207 | -0.00339 | -0.29% | 207 |
| 13 | EURGBP | Euro / British Pound | 0.85543 | -0.00049 | -0.06% | 540 |
| 14 | EURCHF | Euro / Swiss Franc | 1.05597 | 0.00167 | 0.16% | 594 |
| 15 | EURAUD | Euro / Australian Dollar | 1.55941 | -0.00200 | -0.13% | 937 |
| 16 | EURNZD | Euro / New Zealand Dollar | 1.62414 | -0.00269 | -0.17% | 410 |
| 17 | EURSEK | Euro / Swedish Krona | 9.90285 | -0.01860 | -0.19% | 230 |
| 18 | EURNOK | Euro / Norwegian Krone | 9.88761 | 0.00226 | 0.02% | 662 |
| 19 | EURJPY | Euro / Japanese Yen | 130.980 | -0.455 | -0.35% | 978 |
| 20 | British Pound | | | | | |
| 21 | EURGBP | Euro / British Pound | 0.85543 | -0.00049 | -0.06% | 540 |
| 22 | GBPUSD | British Pound / US Dollar | 1.34682 | -0.00311 | -0.23% | 678 |
| 23 | GBPCHF | British Pound / Swiss Franc | 1.23442 | 0.00266 | 0.22% | 436 |
| 24 | GBPNZD | British Pound / New Zealand $ | 1.89865 | -0.00196 | -0.10% | 850 |
| 25 | GBPJPY | British Pound / Japanese Yen | 153.118 | -0.441 | -0.29% | 111 |
| 26 | Japanese Yen | | | | | |
| 27 | USDJPY | US Dollar / Japanese Yen | 113.690 | -0.065 | -0.06% | 688 |
| 28 | AUDJPY | Aust Dollar / Japanese Yen | 83.993 | -0.185 | -0.22% | 990 |
| 29 | EURJPY | Euro / Japanese Yen | 130.980 | -0.455 | -0.35% | 978 |
| 30 | CHFJPY | Swiss Franc / Japanese Yen | 124.040 | -0.624 | -0.50% | 035 |

## THE BASICS
# FOREX MARKETS FROM THE BEGINNING

FOREX synthetic cross-rates. Yikes! That was over the top was it not? Feel a bit like a fog developed around you? Well, that is by design. While synthetic cross-rates are real, the fuzzy understanding you may have felt is how many people trade or analyze FOREX cross-rates. They do not really understand what they are looking at. I see LinkedIn charts with price target spreads that are irrational for the time horizon of their chart, and this reveals lack of understanding of what the quote values mean. We don't want you to fall in with this group.

Money flow in FOREX is all about sentiment as the mass herd oscillates between fear and greed over the chase for more basis points. We know basis points and interest rates are glued relatives. So why do most FOREX traders fail to look at rates, especially bonds? We will look at this.

The king pin today is still the U.S. Dollar viewed as the currency of first reserve. What does that really mean? It is the bedrock under every capital market. This may change some day, but the U.S. Dollar is the one currency we really need to understand. Money flow drives every market and for this reason, everyone should learn the basics of the FOREX market.

Let's say your last name is Soros and you want to sell Euros to buy U.S. Dollars. The problem is that your last name is Soros. You do not want the world to know what you are really doing. Therefore, you cannot just sell Euros for U.S. Dollars without the world knowing it. (Short EURUSD). Ah, but if you want to be sneaky about it, you could construct a synthetic position that achieves the exact same thing. That is one reason why synthetic cross-rates are constructed: to be in stealth mode.

From the beginning we know an exchange rate is the price at which a currency can be bought or sold in terms of another. A cross-rate is really a catch-all term we toss around, but actually a cross-rate is only one type of exchange rate. There are four types of exchange rates.

**Direct Quotations:**
There is an internal exchange rate expressed in units of the national currency. As example when you, an American, are in Germany, one U.S. Dollar would be worth 'x' Euros.

The most important financial markets are often the least understood.

### Indirect Quotations:

A trader in New York would deal on an indirect basis with traders outside the United States.

Why is the British Pound quoted in reverse to how most currencies are quoted by showing the U.S. Dollar first? The United Kingdom is one of the countries that quote the exchange rate based on their national currency first. The foreign currency is always second. New York uses the national currency, the U.S. Dollar first, and the foreign currency second. If you are in London with U.S. Dollars in hand, the U.S. Dollar will be quoted as 'x' units of dollars worth one Pound Sterling. A London visitor in New York would receive a quote in their national currency first, GBP, and U.S. Dollars second. That's the indirect quotation system.

### Cross-Rates:

A currency exchange rate is called a cross-rate *only when the national currency is not part of the transaction*. If you are a Swiss Bank and want to sell Japanese Yen for U.S. Dollars, you would use a cross-rate quote because Swiss Francs are not part of the transaction.

The U.S. Dollar and Euro have an interesting role. Let's say your Malaysian company needs to buy French Francs by selling Malaysian Ringgits. If you have a very large transaction, it might be difficult for you to obtain a competitive and fair quotation. You can accomplish the exact same thing by buying U.S. Dollar with Malaysian Ringgits, then buying the French Francs by selling your U.S. Dollars. More steps, but the net result is you just bought French Francs by selling Malaysian Ringgits. You do not have to go through the U.S. Dollar, but it might be the only way to complete a large transaction when you are selling a secondary market currency.

### Forward Rates:

The fourth type of exchange rate is a forward rate that we will pass over at this time.

**LEARNING OBJECTIVES**

The FOREX markets are about money flow and participant sentiment. Develop a solid foundation of how these markets work. Learn the types of exchange rates.

## THE BASICS
# FOREX MARKETS CONTINUED...

The spot rate for a currency is the price quoted for the nearest standard settlement date for the transaction. Spot rates can be free-floating or fixed. Fixed spot rates are caused by authorities demanding an exact buy/sell rate for goods and services. China comes to mind.

In countries with free floating rates the rates are determined by market-makers. They reside in the large commercial banks and institutions. Now read this next part VERY CAREFULLY.

How are spot rate quotes communicated? Two companies, Bloomberg and Reuters, have a monopoly on the accuracy of the currency spot rate quotes. They were very clever. They developed trading platforms to facilitate the foreign exchange market. Then they placed their terminals in the largest trading firms with a contract requirement; only they can collect the exchange rate of the transactions passing through their terminals. So the companies with the greatest number of transactions collected will have the most accurate indication of where the market exchange rate  and value is currently for a FOREX market. **None of these transactions will be shared with the other quote vendors.**

A software vendor may state that they have foreign exchange rates available on their platform, but if they have access to only a few trading rooms, you are flat out of luck as far as knowing the true and accurate exchange rate as you only see the valuation for trades outside the larger concentration of transactions taking place. The market could be trading at levels your display cannot record. This is a big problem when you trade futures and place what is called an 'exchange for physical' stop order. It means if the FOREX market trades your spot market price, you are stopped out of your futures position. How did I learn this charming fact? Yes, the hard way. I rolled up to my screen one morning and my futures position had been stopped out. My exchange for physical stop had been hit in the overnight session. But when I looked at my screen, the FOREX market never traded the price that would trigger the washout. That's when I was told, "it must have traded somewhere to have stopped you out". Tilt! What do you mean? Then I learned about how the prices are collected by each vendor and how vendors do not have access to the same trades to produce their quotes. The giants are Bloomberg and Reuters. Most FOREX trades pass-through these two vendors and will not be shared with other software systems. Beware.

# How Dealers create a FOREX quote.

Most people learning about markets avoid currencies because they do not understand what they are looking at in the table of flashing quotes. We need to change this with a few examples.

AMAZON, based in the USA, wants to buy foreign currency GBP. The bank they contact in New York City gives a quote of 1.3510-15. The quote is competitive to other banks. They decide to buy £1,000,000 at 1.3515. The bank is selling high and the company is buying high. On the spot date the New York bank will pay Amazon £ 1,000,000 and receive US$ 1,351,500.

Overseas Business XYZ Inc., needs to buy product from the USA to sell in their chain of stores in their country. They need to settle the purchase in U.S. Dollars. They want to buy US $ 1,000,000 at an exchange rate of 2.0020. To know what they owe on the spot date, they must divide one million by 2.0020. They will be paying 499,500.50 in theircurrency to the bank.

How do you calculate the rate when the transaction will pass-through a third currency? In this example the transaction desired is GBP/AUD. I like the number 2 as the big number within the example, though it is not a real price.

One pound sterling  US$2.0010-15
One US dollar        AU$1.5000-15
          The first rate will be the value of one GBP in dollar terms.
          The second rate is the value of one dollar in Australian dollar
          terms.

The rate at which the customer can obtain Australian dollars against sterling is by multiplying 2.0010  by 1.5000 = 3.0015 and conversely, she sells AUD at 2.0015 x 1.5005 = 3.00325075. This degree of accuracy would never be used. 3.0015-35 would be more realistic. The real spread is wider because a break-even calculation in the third currency causes a margin in percent. But these three examples demonstrate what the exchange rates mean and how they are utilized.

It can be said that FOREX is the fulcrum point for all other markets. It is certainly the biggest and most liquid. A county's currency is a battle ground for central banks and governments. The battle is about people wanting economic or political gain. Then people follow the path where they can make a few more basis points than they are making currently. The 'smart' money reads people, and not just price, to detect change.

The financial implosion of 2008 was a game changer. Currencies do not trade only based on interest rate differentials anymore. Now we face governments that must intervene more often. It does not discredit our chart work, but it does force us to be far more aware when intervention measures may enter the market. The setup is often seen beforehand in the technical methods we apply to our price charts. The shock wave then ripples through all the other markets.

We now have sufficient background to really start a more meaningful discussion about intermarket relationships and examine who is pushing or pulling whom. This is the fun part. There are several currency charts, and I am confident the price data will now be more informative.

Before we dive into charts, just a few pointers I have found helpful that I would like to pass on to you.

PLOTTING MARKET OVERLAY CHARTS:

- Always display a y-axis price scale. You will need a right and left-hand y-axis for two markets. It is rare I add a third in the same frame. Usually adding a left scale is an option you select before you add the second dataset.
- Never use semi-log scale. Use arithmetic spacing for the y-axis or price display range.
- Be prepared to adjust the y-axis scale of your price datasets. It is never just a simple drop the data in the frame and you are done.
- Look for proportions that give you the easiest display to compare market directional changes within each market and to each other.
- This last recommendation might be harder for some: Often the best correlation between markets is seen when they are based on the same underlying currency. You will see like currencies in some of the market overlay examples that follow.

# INTERMARKET RELATIONSHIPS AND GLOBAL CASH FLOWS

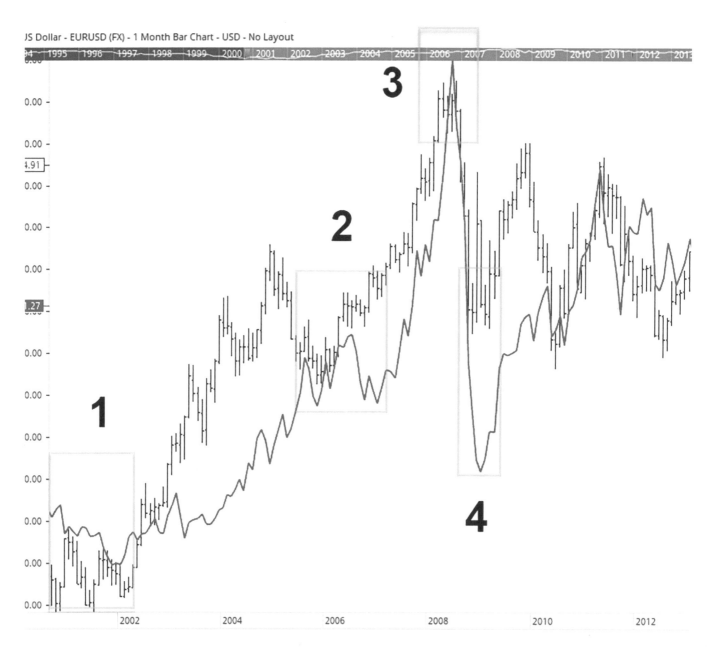

JS Dollar - EURUSD (FX) - 1 Month Bar Chart - USD - No Layout

Because most transactions for Crude Oil are made in EURUSD currency, it is common to overlay these two markets together for comparison as displayed in Figure 1.15. The bar chart is the EURUSD currency, and the blue line is Crude Oil futures charting only the closing price for each month. The time intervals in each market must be the same.

Figure 1.15
Euro / US dollar - EURUSD - bar chart - month
Light, Sweet Crude Oil Futures (NYMEX) (USD) - Line-on-close - month

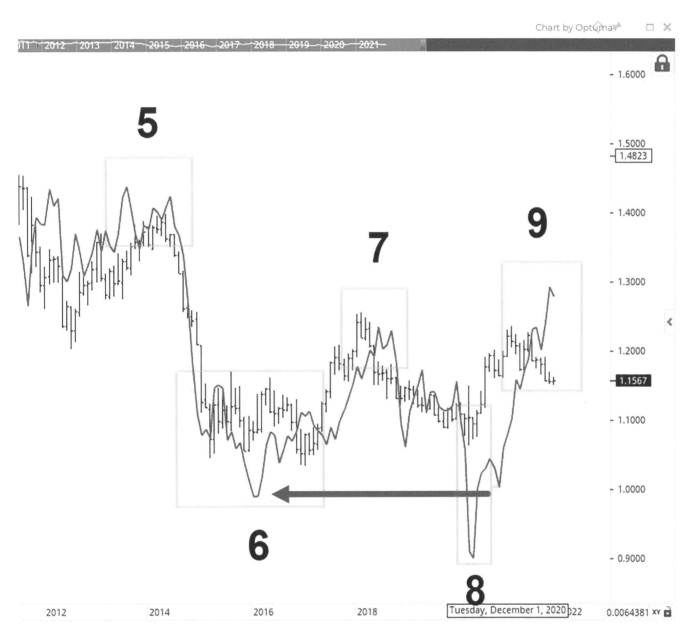

Several boxes are numbered to aid our evaluation. Box '1' shows the EURUSD making a double bottom where price challenges the same lows. The sellers cannot push the Euro currency lower.

Then above the 2002 date, sellers of Euro currency make a third attempt, but fail to push price to the bottom of the box. This is a higher low than the prior two price lows. The Euro currency sellers are losing the battle, or it could be said that the buyers of U.S. Dollars are weakening their conviction.

The Oil market also reverses direction. But a close comparison shows Crude Oil lags the EURUSD in Box 1. It is the EURUSD battle into the bottom of the box that warns us there may be a trend reversal developing in Crude Oil.

Both market prices trend upwards. The Euro currency is strengthening against the U.S. Dollar. Crude Oil is appreciating.

The EURUSD has a setback before Box 2. Once again it leads the Crude Oil market, this time by several months. We take notice of this, but the comparison in Box 2 is extremely interesting. Crude Oil pulls back as the EURUSD makes the last swing down within its decline. Then EURUSD starts to advance. Crude Oil makes a double bottom near the bottom of the box, yet the entire time Oil is forming a correction, EURUSD is on the rise. This is the warning of what is to come. Both markets explode out of Box 2 and rally toward the 2008 highs.

Box 3 is the high into 2008. Which market tops first? Again, it is the EURUSD. The high in the Euro currency is in April 2008. The same market retests the high in July 2008 making a double top. The price high in Crude Oil Futures was June 2008. The double top or failure of Euro currency buyers to make a new high in July was a confirmation that the sentiment in the mass crowd was changing.

When mortgages begin to fail and mortgage-backed securities begin to selloff and unwind causing a deep financial crisis, the crowd sells the Euro currency and most others, to buy U.S. Dollars. The U.S. Dollar is viewed a safer currency. Now if that is true or not is a debate that cannot be answered here. But the psychology of the masses is clear from what we see in the chart price direction. The declining prices indicate Euro

currency is being aggressively sold in favor of U.S. Dollars.

Box 4 shows Crude Oil makes a 'V' reversal in the middle of the box as EURUSD develops a double bottom. Euro currency buyers reverse the trend though it is a struggle after the high made November 2009. The struggle forms a sideways market as the larger trend is directionless until March of 2014. Do notice as the EURUSD swings within a range, Crude Oil also has a narrowing range develop from September 2011 into June 2014 when the markets then breakdown.

Which market leads the breakdown in Box 5? Crude Oil leads at peaks in Box 5. Then a lower high in the second peak develops compared to the first. We call this a divergence when we compare it to the same time interval in the EURUSD which is still advancing.

You may have a different opinion. The entire price action in the EURUSD bar chart shows five narrowing swings following box 4. The top of the third swing is near the right-hand side of page-left. Then the fourth swing, is the first price swing low, on the far left-side of page-right. The fifth swing in this contracting price over several years ends in box 5. That pattern of contracting price swings is a battle of mass crowd confusion. It ends when the fifth swing tops in EURUSD which leads the Crude Oil peak made the second time.

In addition, EURUSD makes a double top if you look very closely under the second peak in Oil within Box 5. The two charts have been split from a single chart and shifted so the page margin does not hide the data. I use a narrow repeat in the price action to help your eye connect the page split.

There is another warning that was developing in EURUSD. From the price low to the left of Box 5 on the right-hand page, into the high that marked the start of the next wash-out, the pattern from low to high is a known corrective pattern. We will learn about patterns and directional signals in Chapter 4. Then we could have a very interesting debate concerning which market was leading the other; currency or oil traders.

Box 6 in Figure 1.15 is not as simple as it may first appear. It would be easy to get stung into this bottom. Box 6 in the EURUSD bar chart data shows people are totally confused. Both sides of the crowd have losses as the price action is just sideways.

But Box 6 shows the Crude Oil crowd has a stronger conviction and the middle of the box is a 'V' bottom. Prices continue to advance forming divergence between the two markets. The shallow pullback near the end of Box 6 in Oil is where the EURUSD crowd regains their conviction and clarity. EURUSD makes a strong move up beyond the outer frame of Box 6.

When long price bars form, it is the place of recognition for the market participants in EURUSD. Everyone finds themselves on the same side of the market. The people who thought the Euro currency would weaken against the US dollar are scrambling to reverse their holdings as the stronger the move against them the deeper loss they are experiencing. All the people who wanted to buy the Euro currency are being pushed to jump in and sell their U.S. Dollars. Everyone who was right before the move wants more. So everyone is on the same side buying Euros against the U.S. Dollar. It creates a strong price bar and it continues for several months. Oil is clearly the lagging party crowd when you examine the end of Box 6 into the start of Box 7.

In Box 7 it is easy to read that the EURUSD price

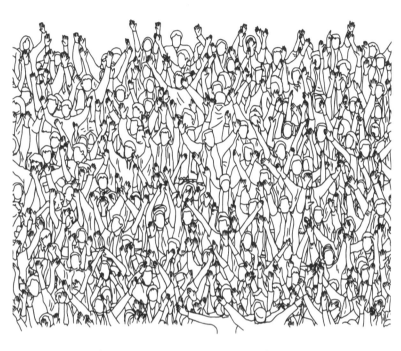

Figure 1.16
The outcry system of trading in Future pits at physical exchanges became a global public outcry system when the world moved to digital.

direction reverses well before Crude Oil. The decline for both continues into Box 8.

Box 8 reflects the unforgettable public panic wash-out due to the unknowns of Covid-19. Oil tankers were sitting at ports with nowhere to unload. All the storage areas in the United States were full. The panic was so great that I remember watching my computer screens do the impossible; Oil was free-falling deep into the negative scale. "Well, there's another first!" I thought. One of my rules is 'do not ever trade the unknown. Box 9 shows a clear divergence.

# FOREX CADJPY AND CRUDE OIL FUTURES (USD)

Canadian Dollar / Japanese Yen - CADJPY (FX) - 1 Month Bar Chart - USD - No Layout

While most people will watch the EURUSD against Crude Oil, there is another pairing of interest. Figure 1.17 has replaced the EURUSD with the Canadian / Japanese Yen (CADJPY) in comparison to Crude Oil. Why? Canada is an Oil producer and exporter. Japan must import all their Oil. Therefore, when Oil prices rise it is a positive for Canada's economy and a negative for Japan's. The CADJPY in Figure 1.17 is the bar chart dataset. The market topped in November 2007 and Crude Oil Futures topped in June 2008. That was a tremendous lead time. Does this relationship continue? No. We can see

Figure 1.17
Canadian Dollar / Japanese Yen - CADJPY bar chart - month
Light, Sweet Crude Oil Futures (NYMEX) (USD) - Line-on-close - month

Notice the recent data far-right shows no divergence
between the two markets that is present in Figure 1.15.

Crude Oil defines a top in June 2014, well ahead of the CADJPY reversal. In 2018 the CADJPY leads the decline once again. The CADJPY defines a double top with price highs that sharply reverse in September 2017 and January 2018. If we can chart the impact of Crude Oil prices on these two economies, what other markets might be of interest? An equity stock market: The Saudi Tadawul All Shares Index (TASI) against Oil.

# CRUDE OIL FUTURES (USD)
# AND SAUDI TASI INDEX (USD)

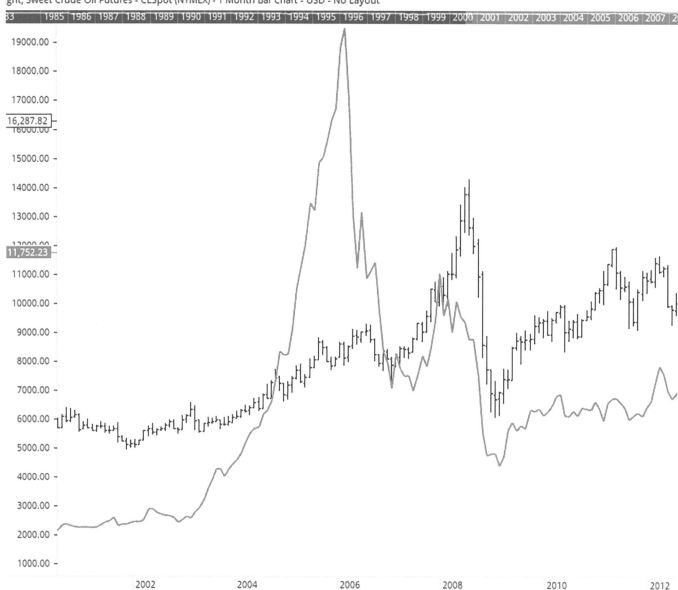

In Figure 1.18 the bar chart is the monthly spot Crude Oil Futures and the green line-on-close is the monthly Saudi Tadawul All Shares Index (TASI). This chart shows a dramatic top in TASI in February 2006. A sharp decline follows into a double bottom in TASI June 2007.

Oil tops in July 2008, but TASI's market high developed seven months earlier. The Great Recession was in large part caused by a deep loss in confidence by people in banks. Banks and financial institutions would not loan money causing a panic for credit. The credit crunch caused stock

Figure 1.18
Light, Sweet Crude Oil Futures - bar chart - month
Saudi Tadawul All Shares Index - TASI- Line-on-close - month

markets around the world to crash, the U.S. Dollar to strengthen, and caused governments to lower their prime interest rates rapidly to save their banks and financial systems.

Ben Bernanke in 2008, then chairman of the U.S. Federal Reserve, (search Brooking-Ben Bernanke-2018/09/13/financial-panic-and-credit-disruptions) stated how their models in spring of 2008 did not see the problem approaching. Charts gave the warning. It was just a question of "when?"

# TORONTO TSX COMPOSITE (CAD) AND SAUDI TASI (USD)

If the Saudi TASI stock market can lead Oil, and the CADJPY can lead Oil, remove Oil from the chart. Just graph the two stock markets for the Oil producing countries. Figure 1.19 is a bar chart of Canada's Toronto S&P TSX Composite Index (TSX) against a line-on-close monthly graph for the Saudi TASI. The Saudi TASI topped before the Toronto TSX in 2008. TASI was already in a steep decline starting April 2008 when Bernanke claimed there were no warnings present.

The Toronto TSX bottoms before the Saudi TASI in

Figure 1.19
Toronto TSX Composite Index - bar chart - month
Saudi Tadawul All Shares Index - TASI- Line-on-close - month

January 2016. The Saudi TASI bottoms much later in September 2016.

As the comparisons are made throughout the chart, it is clear this divergence between markets is valuable, but does not give a time signal when the two markets will begin to track together again. This is important to know. We are going to look at 'time' in Chapter 2.

We compared two stock market indexes as they had similar economies being energy producers. We can compare other stock indexes if we know the sector weightings.

# THE TOP THREE SECTOR WEIGHTINGS IN TWENTY-TWO GLOBAL EQUITY INDEXES

As curious as we likely are now to compare stock market indexes for various exchanges, we need to first look at the composition differences to learn how each index is constructed. As example, The Japanese Nikkei 225 and NASDAQ 100 stock indexes are both heavily weighted to technology stocks. More than 43 percent of the NIKKEI 225 is weighted to technology and the NASDAQ 100 is more than 50 percent weighted to technology. It makes sense to compare these two indexes together. However, one index trades in Japanese Yen and the other in U.S. Dollars. We will convert our graph shortly, so both are displayed in the same currency. This will further tighten their correlation.

What are weightings? Each stock can be weighted by the proportion of their market capitalization (cap) to the total market cap of all the stocks in the index. When a stock price rises, or the market cap rises (total number of outstanding shares * share price), the stock will have a larger weighting within the index. The weightings of stocks for companies in like sectors can be tallied together. The three sectors with the highest weightings in 22 global indexes are listed in Table 1.2.

Not every exchange calculates their stock index in the same way. Some indexes limit the weighting of an individual stock. Therefore, creating a table like Table 1.2 is considerable work. Generally, the weighting percentages change from year-to-year, but the top three sectors rarely change. Major changes primarily occur after a market crash cycle. Exchanges then toss out the worse performing companies and replace them with companies that will make their index look stronger. Stock indexes are marketing products for their exchange. Do the changes invalidate the historical record of the index? No. Why? Mainly because the index is a measure of sentiment within a mass crowd and that never changes. The transition from fear to greed within a mass crowd will create repeatable patterns, regardless of the decade.

The take-away from this table is for you to see how important the Bank and Financial Sectors are to world equity indexes. What impacts the revenue of banks? Interest rates. We can never ignore treasury markets and yield curves. The markets are all connected and stock traders just learning will experience many hard lessons that teach not to hyper-focus on just a group of favorite stocks.

Table 1.2 (page right)
Sector Weightings in Global
Equity Indexes

| | 1ST | 2ND | 3RD |
|---|---|---|---|
| AUSTRALIA S&P/ASX 200 | FINANCIALS 29.9 % | MATERIALS 19.3 % | HEALTH CARE  10.6 % |
| FTSE NEW ZEALAND (AUG 31, 2021) | HEALTH CARE 31.65% | UTILITIES 21.72 % | INDUSTRIALS 18.46 % |
| CHINA SHANGHAI COMPOSITE (DEC 31, 2020) | FINANCIALS AND REAL ESTATE 33.2 % | INDUSTRIALS 18.7% | CONSUMER DISCRETIONARY  10.2 % |
| FTSE CHINA 50 (AUG 31, 2021) | BANKS 21.05 % | TECHNOLOGY 16.8 % | RETAILERS 13.35 % |
| SINGAPORE STRAIT TIMES (AUG 31, 2021) | BANKS 43.51 % | REAL ESTATE 22.34 % | INDUSTRIAL GOODS & SERVICES 10.02 % |
| SINGAPORE SHARIAH INDEX (AUG 31, 2021) | BANKS 35.7 % | REAL ESTATE 27.39 % | INDUSTRIAL GOODS & SERVICES 10.07 % |
| FTSE BURSA MALAYSIA KLCI (AUG 31, 2021) | BANKS 29.05 % | FOOD , BEVERAGE, TOBACCO 11.95 % | INDUSTRIAL GOODS & SERVICES 9.34 % |
| FTSE BURSA MALAYSIA EMAS SHARIAH COMPLIANT (AUG 31, 2021) | FOOD , BEVERAGE, TOBACCO 16.32 % | HEALTH CARE 13.44 % | TELECOMMUNICATIONS 13.39 % |
| HANG SENG INDEX (AUGUST 2021) | FINANCIALS 35.43 % | INFORMATION TECHNO-LOGY 26.12 % | CONSUMER DISCRETIONARY 10.38% |
| NIKKEI 225 (DECEMBER 30, 2019)* | TECHNOLOGY 45.73 % | CONSUMER GOODS 24.50 % | MATERIALS 14.11 % |
| FTSE VIETNAM 30 (AUG 31, 2021) | REAL ESTATE  40.04 % | FOOD , BEVERAGE, TOBACCO 21.13 % | INDUSTRIAL GOODS & SERVICES 16.17 % |
| EGYPT EGX70 * (SEPTEMBER 21, 2021) | REAL ESTATE 37.74% | BASIC RESOURCES 13.68 % | FOOD , BEVERAGE, TOBACCO 11.98 % |
| FTSE SAUDI ARABIA INDEX (AUG 31, 2021) | FINANCIALS 43.81 % | BASIC MATERIALS 22.79% | TELECOMMUICATIONS 9.64 % |
| INDIA NIFTY 50 | FINANCIAL SERVICES 37.58 % | INFORMATION TECHNO-LOGY 18.51 % | OIL & GAS 11.39 % |
| DAX INDEX (SEPT 20, 2021)  (AUTOS ARE 10.19 %) | CHEMICALS 15.81 % | INDUSTRIALS 15.14% | PHARMA & HEALTH CARE 10.25 % |
| SWISS MARKET INDEX (SPIDER WEB CHART IS A TOUGH READ) | HEALTH CARE 43 % | CONSUMER GOODS 25 % | FINANCIALS 18 % |
| FRENCH CAC 40 ** (SEPTEMBER 24, 2021) | LVMH LOUIS VUITTON 11.41 % | TOTALENERGIES SE 7.17 % | SANOFI (PHARMA) 7.12 % |
| FTSE ITALY 30 (AUG 31, 2021) | BANKS 18.67 % | UTILITIES 18.56 % | AUTOMOBILES & PARTS 13.65 % |
| FTSE 100 (AUG 31, 2021) | ASTRAZENECA 6.81% GLAXOSMITHKLINE 3.73 % (PHARMACEU-TICALS) | UNILEVER 5.46 % | HSBC HLDGS 4.08% (BANK) |
| S&P 500 (DEC 22, 2020) | INFORMATION TECHNOLOGY 27.6% | HEALTH CARE  13.44% | CONSUMER DISCRETIONARY  12.7 % |
| NASDAQ 100 (JUNE 4, 2021) | TECHNOLOGY 55.0 % | CONSUMER SERVICES 22.0 % | CONSUMER GOODS  10.0 % |
| DOW JONES INDUSTRIAL AVG (AUG 21, 2021) | INFORMATION TECHNOLOGY 22.4% | FINANCIALS 16.7% | HEALTH CARE  16.6% |

**SECTOR WEIGHTINGS in GLOBAL EQUITY INDEXES**

# NIKKEI STOCK AVERAGE 225 (USD) AND NASDAQ 100 (USD)

Nikkei Stock Average 225 - NI (WI) - 1 Month Bar Chart - USD - No Layout

By converting the Nikkei 225 to U.S. Dollars rather than Japanese Yen, we can make it easier to compare the technology index with the NASDAQ 100 that also trades in U.S. Dollars. When we do this the currency basis spread is removed.

We do not make price projections from this modified data; we just make a comparison of the datasets as we did for Figure 1.15. Does one market lead the other in tops with the other leading near price bottoms? Has there been a change in leadership? Does a rising trend in one help to clarify a consolidation developing in the other?

Figure 1.20
Nikkei Stock Average 225
(USD) - bar chart - month
NASDAQ 100 Index (USD)-
Line-on-close - month

This is demonstrated in the data through 2012. The triple top in the Nikkei 225 in 2007 warned well in advance of the top in the NASDAQ 100. What is important is to know that big trend reversals do not happen in just one equity index. By tracking several around the world you can see when trouble is ahead or selling exhaustion is developing. Other methods will help us time a major trend reversal, but the early warning will come from multiple markets giving the same warning.

# HANG SENG INDEX (HKD), HOCHIMINH VIETNAM INDEX (USD), AND JAKARTA STOCK EXCHANGE COMPOSITE (IDR)

Figure 1.21
Hang Seng Index (HKD)- bar chart (black) - weekly
Jakarta stock exchange composite Index- (IDR) Line-on-close (blue) - weekly
HoChiMinh Vietnam Index- (USD) Line-on-close (purple)- weekly

When three markets are mapped together it is still best to use one bar chart with two line-on-close graphs. The Hong Kong Hang Seng used to be the

primary market in Asia until China's takeover. The Indonesian Jakarta Composite Index made several notable leading trend reversals shown in blue. Vietnam's HoChiMinh Index (purple) lagged the Jakarta Composite for years until 2019. Vietnam has made great strides in the world of finance and

their stock market reflects their changing position in the world. With the Hang Seng rapidly losing world preference, how do we identify the new market that will take its place?

# HANG SENG (HKD)
# AND GERMAN DAX (USD)

The monthly chart above of the Hang Seng and German Dax shows divergence in 2020 between these two markets. Convert the German Dax from Euro currency to U.S. Dollars which will produce a tighter correlation between the two datasets.

Next, compare the Singapore Straits with the

Figure 1.22
Hang Seng Index (HKD) - bar chart - month
German DAX (USD)- Line-on-close - month

# SINGAPORE STRAITS TIMES INDUSTRIAL INDEX (SGD) AND GERMAN DAX (USD)

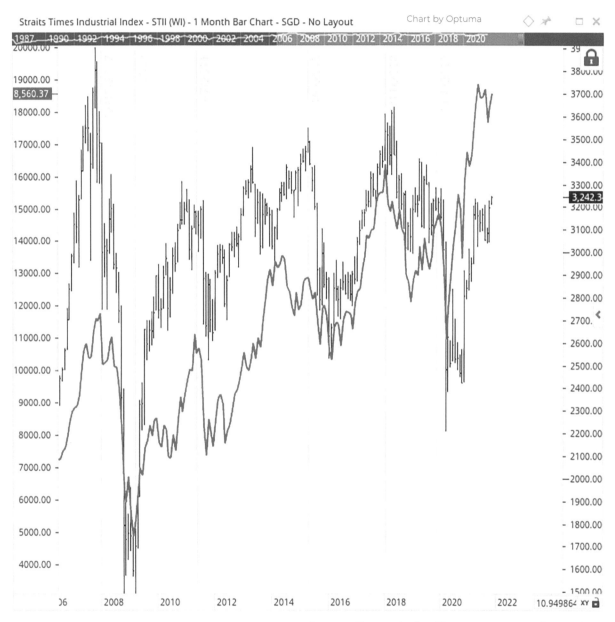

Figure 1.23
Singapore Straits Times Industrial Index (SGD) - bar chart - month
German DAX (USD)- Line-on-close - month

German Dax. It is the Singapore Straits that is the new 'Hang Seng' for Asia. Cash is flowing into Singapore and out of Hong Kong based on regional corporate relocations. Another metric to monitor is real estate prices with total number of sales or purchases by region per quarter.

# S&P500 INDEX (USD)
# AND GERMAN DAX INDEX (USD)

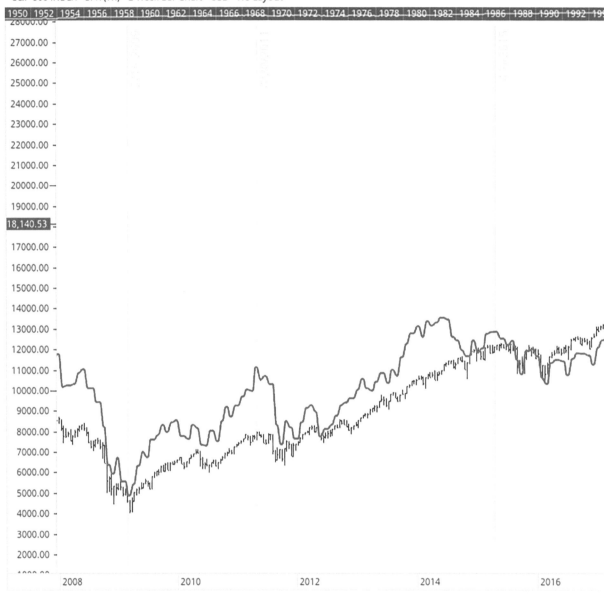

The German Dax is a stock market index with a unique property, it is not weighted to the bank and financial sector as are most world stock markets. By comparing markets, like the S&P 500 Index to the German Dax, it allows a comparison of indexes weighted to different sectors. Therefore, we will not be blindsided when the banking sector offers no warning.

Figure 1.24 compares the 2-week bar chart of the S&P 500 with the German Dax. Dropping down to a lower time interval shows more detail between

Figure 1.24
S&P 500 (USD)
2-week bar chart
German Dax Index- (USD)
2-week Line-on-close

the two markets so that may be easier to read regarding the market that is leading or lagging. The most important message in this chart is the lag in the European rally compared to the benchmark index in the United States. Do you trade the lead or lagging market? We should return to this question and market divergence when we have the tools needed for further evaluation such as oscillators, pattern recognition, and price calculations for support and resistance.

# FTSE JSE AFRICA ALL SHARES (ZAR CURRENCY) AND GERMAN DAX (USD)

The Johannesburg Stock Exchange (JSE) has posted descriptive information on 114 different stock exchanges from around the world with many difficult to obtain. (See sseinitiative.org/exchanges-filter-search/) The FTSE JSE Africa All Share Index (ALSH) can be compared to the German Dax in Euro currency

Figure 1.25
FTSE JSE Africa All Share (ZAR) - bar chart - month
German Dax (USD)- Line-on-close - month

# FTSE JSE AFRICA ALL SHARES (ZAR) AND NIKKEI AVG 500 (JPY)

Figure 1.26
FTSE JSE Africa All Share (ZAR) - bar chart - month
Nikkei Stock Average 500 (JPY) - Line-on-close - month

or U.S. Dollars. ALSH does not show the same divergence with the Dax as seen with the S&P500 in Figure 1.24.

Then make the same comparison to the Nikkei 500. What market is out of sync with the rest of the world? The S&P 500 is far more exuberant.

# AUSTRALIA ALL ORDINARIES (AUD) AND SHANGHAI COMPOSITE (CNY)

There are three important comparisons between the Australia (XAO) and China's Shanghai Composite. The first rectangle shows how China lags as cash is flowing into Australia. We assume this is cash from China as the reaction was greater than any other English-based government we could compare. In the

Figure 1.27
Australia All Ordinaries Index (AUD)
- bar chart - month
Shanghai Composite Index (CNY)
- Line-on-close - month

# AUSTRALIA ALL ORDINARIES (AUD) AND GERMAN DAX (EUR)

Australia All Ordinaries Index - XAO (WI) - 1 Month Bar Chart - AUD - No Layout    Chart by Optuma

Figure 1.28
Australia All Ordinaries Index (AUD)
- bar chart - month
German Dax Index (EUR) - Line-on-close -
month

second rectangle XAO still leads China. In the third rectangle, China leads the decline ahead of Australia. Then they uncouple. China lags and the media reports Australian companies are disengaging from China. The chart above shows that the All Ordinaries and German Dax are better comparisons since 2018.

Forum

Join ATAA

Login

Membership ⌄

Events ⌄

Resources ⌄

Education ⌄

About ATAA ⌄

Home

Australian
Technical Analysts
Association

https://ataa.asn.au

**IFTA**

Where Market Technicians from Around the World
**Speak the Same Language**

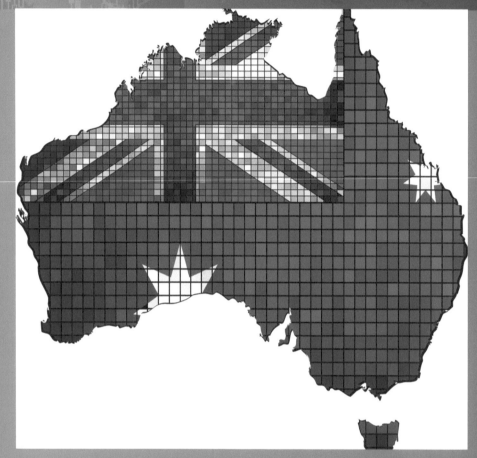

ATAA: A MOSAIC OF CONNECTED CHAPTERS

**In-person/Online Events**

**International Educators**

**A Welcoming & Diverse
Community for All Levels**

**Established in 1990**

Figure 1.29
Australia S&P/ASX 200 (XJO)- Candlestick chart - weekly
S&P500 (SPX) - Bar Chart- weekly (blue)

Figure 1.29 compares the American S&P500 (SPX) to the Australian S&P/ASX 200 (XJO). The XJO is plotted in a method called candlestick charting. The open and closing price for the period is drawn as a narrow rectangle called the real body. The price action outside this area is the wick. S&P500 in blue is a traditional bar chart. Divergences in corrections between the two markets are meaningful. Which market is lagging or leading? Oscillators in Chapter Five will help to answer this question.

**2**

LEARN THE LANGUAGE OF CYCLES
AND HOW CYCLES ARE MEASURED

# CHAPTER TWO

# CYCLE PRINCIPLES

## IT IS EASY TO FIND A RHYTHM IN A CHART OF PRICES, BUT THE MISSION IS TO FIND THE RHYTHM OR PERIODICITY OF SIGNIFICANCE IN A TIME SERIES.

**W**hat is a cycle? A cycle describes a series of events or phenomena that repeat with regular occurrence over time.

Edward R. Dewey (1895-1978) was Chief Economic Analyst for the U.S. Department of Commerce in 1930 to 1931. He was given the task by President Herbert Hoover of finding the cause of The Great Depression. The task launched Mr. Dewey towards a lifelong search and he concluded, "Everything that has been studied has been found to have cycles present." Mr. Dewey's Foundation for the Study of Cycles (FSC) compiled an extensive body of historic cycle research in the fields of business, economics, natural and social sciences.

Dewey stated in his FSC August 1964 Research Bulletin, "The 17.7-Year Cycle in War 600 B.C. to A.D. 1957," that the term 'cycle' has several meanings. He concluded by stating that cycles are a series of oscillations, whether rhythmic or periodic, that come around to the place of beginning.

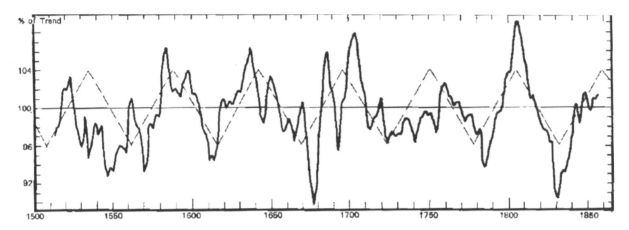

Figure 2.1
Wheat Prices from 1500 to 1869. Solid line = actual prices (smoothed, detrended),
dashed line is the idealized cycle.
(Detrending will be described in Cycles: Part Two)
Source:   Foundation for the Study  of Cycles, Edward R. Dewey

Cycle analysis is truly fascinating. But Dewey believed a cycle that is recurrent but not rhythmic, that is, where the crests and bottoms do not necessarily occur at regular intervals, is not a true cycle. The catch word here is regular. If a cycle beat repeats in a rhythmic increasing frequency pattern and then resets to begin the series exactly as a repeating unit of beats, is it a cycle? The repeating secondary and tertiary beats could be a mathematical ratio of an underlying fundamental cycle with a fixed period. The fixed period itself would not change. So our discussion will just focus on fundamental cycle periods in Part One to avoid moving ahead too quickly causing confusion. Cycles are not difficult, but if your definitions are a little fuzzy it can become difficult very easily.

Classic cycle theory is demonstrated in Figure 2.1 for Wheat prices. There is an idealized fixed interval, and we examine how theory compares to the actual occurrences. A fixed period cycle does not mean we should expect an exact alignment to the theoretical forecast because the cycle can be pulled by shorter or longer forces. There will be multiple cycle rhythms oscillating through a data set. Our mission is to identify the ones of greatest influence and importance.

Though we will only study symmetrical fixed period cycles, we know that markets exhibit cycles both symmetrical and asymmetric in character. To study either we need to know the language of cycle researchers  and we need to understand the mathematics used to detect cycles. We must then determine what cycles are significant statistically so we can be confident that what we see is not a random event. The last step is to determine if the cycle is still relevant in nearby price action.

# CLASSIC CYCLES
# GLOSSARY OF DEFINITIONS

The language of cycle analysis:

- CYCLE ANALYSIS - The study of rhythmic or periodic occurrences in a time series.
- PERIOD - The length of time required to complete a cycle. The ideal (or average) wavelength (in time) between successive crests, troughs, or any other epochs.
- EPOCHS -Critical points in time on the curve such as the times of crest or trough but can also be the time of upward or downward crossings.
- PERIODICITY - A succession of waves which repeat at precise and unvarying intervals of time.
- RHYTHM - refers to movement with fairly regular recurrence of alternating ups and downs.
- WAVELENGTH - The distance over which the wave's shape repeats.
- CREST or PEAK - The highest point of a wave.
- TROUGH or BOTTOM - The lowest point of a wave.
- SHAPE - The cycle's *shape* is symmetrical when the right-side of the wave form is a mirror reflection about the vertical axis compared to the left-side. Not all cycles are symmetrical.
- AMPLITUDE - The size of the cycle swing expressed as half the difference between the peak value and trough, or minimum value of the cycle.
- FREQUENCY - The rate at which cycles occur. Frequency is the reciprocal to a cycle's wavelength.
- PHASE - The position in time of a wave.
- HARMONIC - A unit fraction of some base wavelength known as the fundamental.
- HARMONIC ANALYSIS - A specific branch of mathematics concerned with the functions of a basic wave. This is the study of Fourier analysis.
- OVERTONE - Any frequency greater than the fundamental, but harmonic overtones are reserved for frequencies that are integral multiples of the fundamental cycle.
- STATISTICAL SIGNIFICANCE - The probability that a given behavior is not the result of chance.

**LEARNING OBJECTIVES**

Understand the language and definitions of cycle analysis. Learn the math skills we use to identify the presence of cycles. Evaluate the significance of a cycle within the data set.

## CLASSIC CYCLES
# PART ONE: CYCLES MOVE HISTORY INTO THE FUTURE

In horror, we all watched the red dots expand and spread on global maps as Covid-19 shut the world down. Cycles show us we have been down the same road before, and the latest pandemic struck humanity right on the beat of past occurrences. Consider prior pandemics as we struggle to exit the Covid-19 Pandemic of 2019 to 2022 (?).

A one-hundred-year cycle brought seven devastating pandemics upon the world. How many years would we need to know the occurrence is not a random event of coincidence? The data must have a range that is at least three times the length of the cycle's period. In this example our data sample would require a minimum of three hundred years.

- The earliest recorded smallpox pandemic was 568 CE in Africa.
- 1520 a Smallpox Pandemic kills millions of native inhabitants of Mexico
- 1617-1618 Smallpox killed 90% of Massachusetts Bay Indians in the USA.
- 1717 Smallpox and Measles Pandemic of Britain
- 1721 Smallpox Pandemic in Boston
- 1817-1824 Cholera Pandemic in India spreading to all Asian Countries
- 1918-1920 Influenza Pandemic
- 2020-2022(?) Covid-19 Pandemic

Does the one-hundred-year cycle repeat with a regular interval between events? Yes, it does.  This is the period. A cycle that skips 20 years, as for example the Great Crash of 1929 shifted some cycles,  and then restarts the fixed-period anew, is a cycle with a new base-year. We start the count again one-period after the new base-year, but to be confident the old period is still valid we would like to see the occurrences fall on the beat at least two more times from the new base-year. Was the pandemic cycle active in the most recent calendar timing? Unfortunately, Covid-19 struck right on the beat and in rhythm to pandemics in our past. The heartbeat for this 100-year cycle remains active in current times. Now we have an opportunity to help you become more familiar with the

Figure 2.2
2020: The Year World Travel was Parked. Endless rows of dormant planes filled every field and airport runway around the world.

language we use to describe cycles. We will learn how to read cycle analysis developed by others. What do we compare and how do we explain why cycles seem to shift their timing when compared to idealized cycles? Why do people seem to forget past cycles every twenty years and we have to go through similar experiences all over again? Why does the media seem so fixated on the same economic indicators? Do we have any information that is a leading indication of what is coming and how timely is it? There are answers to these questions through the study of cycles.

Why do markets and economies of nations run through "boom-to-bust" expansion and contraction phases? Human nature never changes though the circumstances appear to be different. The great debate among economists is always what factors are causative, and whether the fluctuation is the result of exogenous (external) factors, or endogenous (internal) causes. They will never agree on a final cause/effect conclusion. Why? Because the real driver is in the knowledge that people and human nature do not change.

Every twenty years due to our human life expectancy, we skip one generation in units of 10-years, and then the next generation believes they can and will do better than their parents. They are the next generation that can right all the wrongs they perceive their parent's generation has created. The new generation will be so much wiser. But it never happens that way. It looks to be different on the surface, but once we dig past the surface, it is the same thing over and over within a different picture frame. Why? The basic fears, hopes and dreams that humans they have for themselves and their children never change.
The real question is how do we measure where we are within this repeating pattern of human hopes and fears?

Figure 2.3
The Fibonacci Spiral

Figure 2.3 is the Fibonacci Spiral that contains an expansion and contraction ratio found in nature and present in all living things. The question for you to ponder is, Is this a cycle? Maybe several cycles?

It is not because cycles must have a *linear time scale*. Figure 2.3 does not have a linear time series because it is a repeating pattern that always returns to the same axis within a 360-degree pattern. The next circle is altered by a factor that circles without end towards infinity.

Now this will be much harder. Figure 2.4 is what we call a seasonal chart study. Does Figure 2.4 demonstrate four cycles? No, it does not. It is a study where we have cut a single cycle at exact points in a calendar that begin on a specific day and end 12-months later. Seasonal charts are always annualized as the scale must have a range that covers twelve months, but they do not have to start from January 1st. For example, Figure 2.4 begins on March 21st for all four lines plotted.

Seasonal charts do not have to compare *sequential* time intervals. Figure 2.4 graphs four annualized seasonal periods in non-sequential years. Each 12-month block of time has met a pre-defined condition so we can see the effect on the market when the condition is present. What Figure 2.4 tells us is price trends in this direction when condition 'y' is active.

The seasonal study shows that the Dow Jones Industrial Average declined in all four annualized comparisons near 100 degrees past March 21. When is that? One hundred degrees from March 21st in a 12-month circle calendar falls on July 4th and 5th. The dataset is daily, so we find something many people already know; people in the United States tend to sell into major national holidays to bank some of their profits. It happens again near the 320-degree interval. When does that occur within a 12-month calendar period starting on March 21st? The graph tells us price corrections that develop in January tend to find bottoms and reverse near February 10th. But this conclusion is only true when the original condition is present. It does not mean this seasonal trend will happen every year because the underlying condition does not repeat every year. Seasonal studies utilize cycles, but they themselves are not cycles.

Why did I use degrees and not label months on the x-axis? That is a good question. Figure 2.4 shows a ribbon of changing shades of white to gray to black on the x-axis. The computer cannot use text for computation. Here the computer is detecting when the hot zones of high occurrence develop. The range from 100 to 120 degrees is black meaning this is the hottest zone of interest being flagged for us in the study.

What if I want to know how a market trends within a 24-hour period for intraday trading? The 360-degree x-axis scale would be a range of 24 hours. How could I use such information? I can determine if Gold futures often move a certain direction 40-minutes after the futures market opens the new trading session.

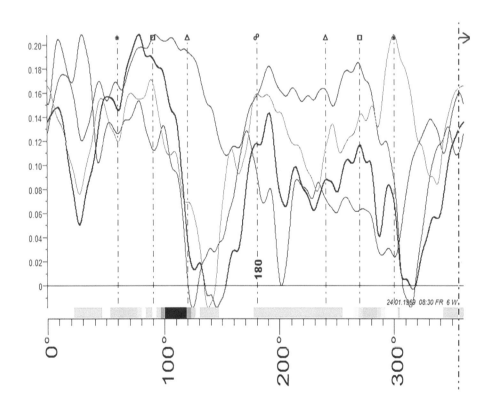

Figure 2.4
Annualized Seasonal Study of the Dow Jones Industrial Average when a specific event occurs.

Chart by TimingSolution

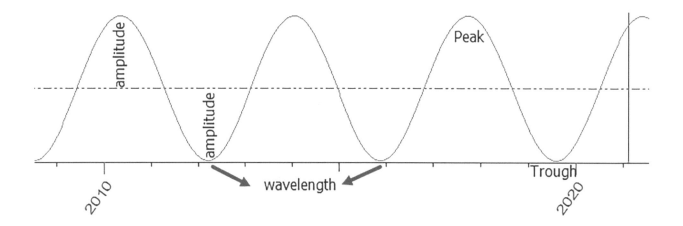

Figure 2.5
Sine Wave - Repeating Cycle
Chart by TimingSolution

A simple cycle is displayed in Figure 2.5. The cycle repeats when one wavelength is completed. In Figure 2.5 the epoch can also be when the cycle crosses up through the mid-line each time.

The peak, also called the crest by some, and trough of the oscillation are at the maximum +/- displacements from the center line. The amplitude is a displacement measurement from physics. Many in finance do not have training in the sciences and incorrectly label the amplitude as the sum of both the +/- amplitudes. Financial cycle research is beginning to advance towards the sciences, and we all need to stay true to physics principles to avoid later confusion. It is the field of harmonic cycles that is forcing us all to clean-up some of our incorrect definitions.

We know stock market indexes graph prices in an upwards trending slope as business grows with periods of corrective interruptions of varying severity. Then the larger trend resumes upwards. How we flatten these undulations along a rising slope to look like those represented in Figure 2.6 will be explained later in this chapter. But first we need to learn what data we may want to use and what the oscillations mean.

Figure 2.6
Economic Business Cycle - Expansion with strong economic growth, Peak with stagnant economic growth, the Contraction with economic decline. The trough with stagnant exonomic growth. The recovery follows with Expansion and strong economic growth. The cycle repeats.

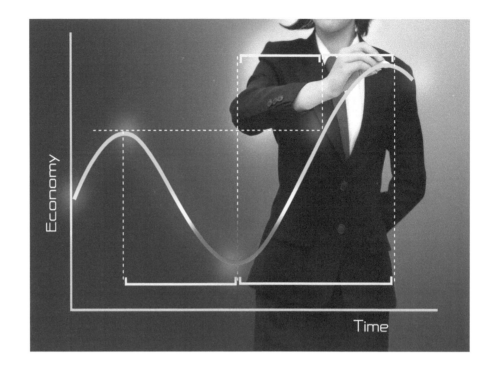

The rhythm in Figure 2.6 is a line we know when moving upwards represents an expansion phase of the cycle. When it rolls over and moves back down, we say the dataset is contracting. If we are looking at a business cycle that is expanding and contracting, what is expanding? What is contracting? Do all businesses in different sectors expand and contract together? Figure 2.6 raises many more questions than it can answer when we begin to think about it. Adding a few labels or areas of color is hardly a complete self-defining story of what people are experiencing.

When the cycle falls or rises representing a business contraction or expansion, often this is a short-hand reference to the Gross Domestic Product (GDP) for a nation. It is the economic output, or the inflation-adjusted value of all new goods and services produced by labor and property. Governments have various ways they collect, bundle, and conduct their data analysis. But the bottom line is simply the need to know when the businesses of a nation are growing or not.

I've been around long enough to know that economic indicators often boil down to just plain common sense. The politicians change the rules so everyone qualifies for a mortgage so they can attract more votes; loans by banks for real estate explode upwards; eventually, that idea goes bust because we know not everyone should be given credit to carry a mortgage. When they

"

BUSINESS CYCLE INDICATORS ANALYZE
ALTERNATING SEQUENCES OF ECONOMIC
EXPANSIONS AND CONTRACTIONS KNOWN
AS BUSINESS CYCLES.

*St. Louis Federal Reserve*

"

do they bring a whole lot of people down with them in the process. The 2008 crisis was felt around the world because we are all so interconnected. But there were data indicators warning that the house-of-cards would collapse.

In the early dot.com era banks had no idea what to do with all the cash rolling in. What do banks do? Exactly what they did before when the railroads were being built across Europe and America and were viewed as a new technology. Invest in South America which has a two-hundred-year history of bond defaults bringing the whole ball of wax down with them. Yes, it happened again that a default caused a global shakedown in the nineties. Did banks want any part of the dot.com industry in the beginning? No. Deemed too risky. Banks are always late to the party of a new developing technology or industry. Private enterprise and entrepreneurs funded the start of the dot.com era. Some will debate the ethical role of some people like Michael Milken of Drexel Burnham Lambert, but they raised cash when credit for new loans for a new industry was not available. True, many of the early dot.coms are dot.gones today, but those who survived changed our world. The same patterns repeat in the bigger picture.

Economic experts will have different views about what causes business fluctuations. Alan Greenspan, head of the Board of Governors of the U.S. Federal Reserve System from 1987 to 2006, stated his greatest mistake was to underestimate the impact the new dot.com industry would have on the economy. But as traders and investors we have less interest in the cause of a major change approaching, and more interest in the fact one is coming, when, and how big of a change will it be? That is why we opened Chapter One by looking at the connections between world markets and different asset classes like foreign currency, interest rate instruments of short to long-term yields, and stocks. The big reversals in stock markets can ALWAYS be seen in the charts of several countries that give the same warning in their · charts. When the charts are in agreement, the entire world will experience a contraction, but it is just a question of when and what the trigger will be. Then, we dust ourselves off and carry on starting the cycle all over again.

One group of economists will not agree that business expansion and contraction is accurately measured by a nation's GDP.   They may argue it is the liquidity or availability of cash to loan to businesses causing a credit and debt cycle. This one is interesting, and we should take a look at it more closely.

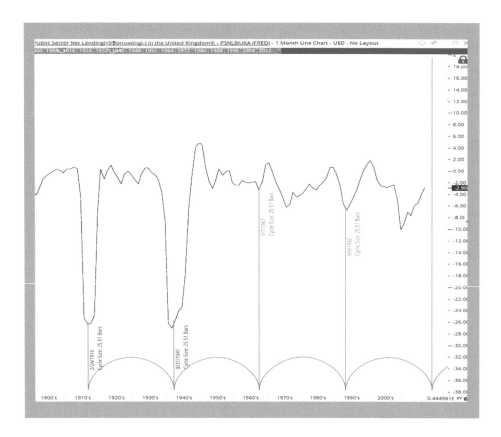

Figure 2.7
Public Sector Net Lending
(+)/ Borrowing (-) in the
United Kingdom from
January 1900 to
January 2016

Chart by Optuma

Figure 2.7 is a graph showing the public's Net Lending to Borrowing in the United Kingdom. Banks did not lend during the World Wars and every 25.51 bars, or about 25-years the graph takes another dip. The cycle is just manually being selected with this vendor's cycle tool. Is it valid? The data is from a reliable source, the St. Louis Federal Reserve in the United States, but we do not know if the data is clean. The two big drops that align with World Wars make sense in that they show extreme tightening by banks during periods of tremendous difficulty. But the cycle period is not valid because we do not know much about the data. Does the chart show a dataset that is consistent in how it is collected through its history? Questions like this just serve to say we need to fully understand what we will spend our time evaluating.

The line of thinking that measures the availability of credit is good. The data is available for different countries, and we can compare to see if easing or bank tightening is systemic for just one country or if it is across many countries. Some data like GDP does not help us much as the charts are visually a straight line on a rising slope. The datasets pertaining to credit and debt are far more interesting for a technical analyst who needs swings and movement within the data they examine.

Economic charts can be viewed as a behavioral science. For example, knowing what people are investing in and why they are borrowing is a consumer sentiment indicator. When the borrowed funds are flowing into real estate it might be because people view land as a lower risk asset class than others like stock or bond markets. Figure 2.8 shows a rising trend since 2017 in South Africa. They have been especially hit hard in the pandemic because of the fall of their South African Rand currency against world currencies. In addition, shipping costs in 2021 have exploded around the world. The nation with the highest increase in shipping cost in 2021 is South Africa. It is more expensive for them to buy anything outside of South Africa, it is more expensive to import goods, and inflation is beginning to accelerate making everything there more difficult. What are people thinking in South Africa? When a currency is in sharp decline people tend to favor real estate because their purchasing power is falling by holding cash. What if this trend is seen in many nations? That should raise a red flag that consumer sentiment is declining on a broader scale.

Figure 2.8
South Africa Commercial
Real Estate Loans to Total
Loans

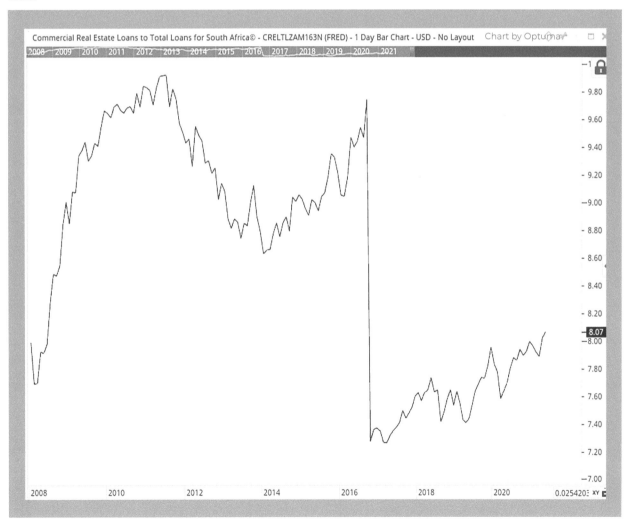

Figure 2.9 shows the Consumer Price Index (CPI) in Italy. The data set excludes prices from alcohol and tobacco. The 'vice' products rise when the public is stressed. That skews the data, so countries often separate the 'vices' from the totals as an optional compilation. Figure 2.9 shows green vertical bands to mark when Italy experienced economic recessions. Do not assume every country experiences a recession the exact same time or for the same duration. We can see periods in the data when the index consolidates sideways, and these coincide with the recorded recessions. On the bottom of the chart is a cycle of 47.65 periods. This is a 3.97-year cycle. Search 'Presidential Cycle to learn how the same cycle appears in other datasets.

Information given to us should always be confirmed when it is new to us. For example, Figure 2.10 tells us sales overseas are important for the retail market in Japan and are sensitive to currency fluctuations, but the two datasets do move in unison. If we shifted forward the red line representing Retail Sales by the same amount so that the red line low near 1992 aligned with the USDJPY low in 1995, the entire correlation would show a closer alignment. When we

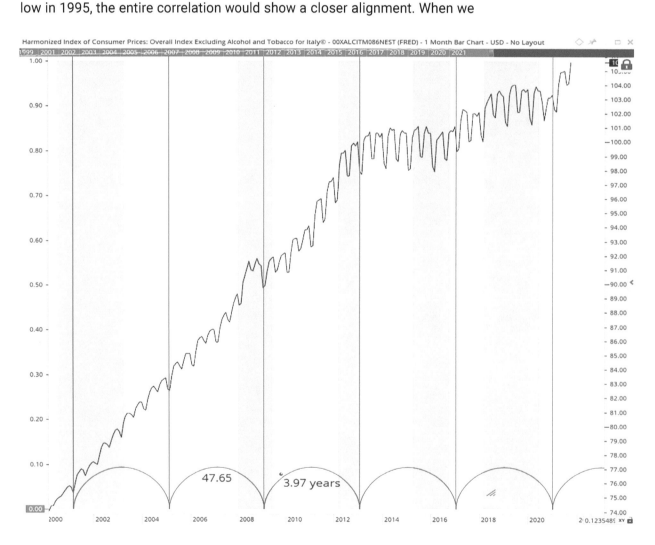

do this, it is called an offset. If we do not use an offset, as in Figure 2.10, we just know Sales lead the trend in USDJPY. If Sales leads, how can currency changes be the cause? We also have to consider what appears to be an inverse relationship in 1998. But if we know a timing offset is present across the entire chart, the sharp drop is a lead for the 2000 decline in USDJPY.

Figure 2.10
U.S. Dollar/Japanese Yen - bar chart -monthly
Retail Trade: Business Situation Activity: European Commission Indicator for Japan
May 1991 to November 2021

Chart by Opuma

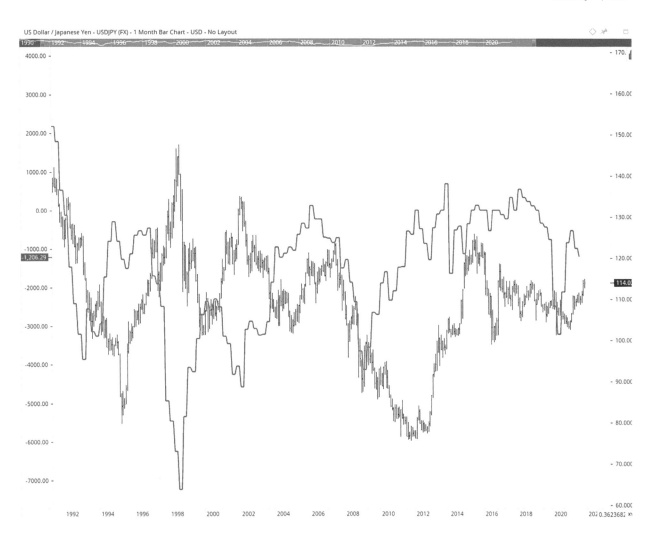

# IFTA

### Where Market Technicians from Around the World
## Speak the Same Language

## The Swiss Association of Market Technicians

**Meetings**
**Education**
**Networking**
**FX Research**
**SAMT Blog**
**Established 1986**

https://www.samt-org.ch/

SAMT

# UNDERSTANDING BUSINESS CYCLES

Cyclical business indicators are classified into three categories - leading, coincident, and lagging. They are classified based on the timing of their movements as compared to a business cycle. The charts in Figures 2.7 to 2.10 are just random charts where we do not know if the data being graphed leads or lags a business cycle.

Coincident indicators are broad series datasets that measure aggregate economic activity. Data for employment, production, personal income, manufacturing, and sales are all coincident indicators.

Leading indicators are so named because they tend to fluctuate in advance of the business cycle. Datasets pertaining to average weekly hours, new orders, consumer expectations, housing and construction permits, interest rate spreads, and stock prices are all viewed as leading indicators. It explains why the business news media devotes so much time to these report releases. However, leading indicators alone cannot provide the answers we seek. There are always several factors, and no single report will ever be the golden ticket to knowing where we are presently in a business cycle.

Lagging indicators are slow to fluctuate and the media will ignore them or view them to be inconsequential. Therefore the media was caught off-guard when a problem of growing supply-chain disruptions and exorbitant shipping costs lead to empty shelves in 2021. These indicators warn us of structural imbalances developing within an economy. Lagging indicators are those that define the cost of doing business, such as inventory-sales ratios, changes in unit labor costs, the average prime rate charged by banks, and commercial and industrial loans outstanding. Lagging indicators are not just about the costs of doing business; some consumer and social costs are lagging indicators also. For example, the ratio of installment credit outstanding to personal income, the change in consumer prices for services, and the average duration of employment. These indicators can help confirm movement in the leading and coincident indicators.

How often do government agencies change the components or composition of their indicators? Revisions are invariably a result of better statistics. Economists use statistical and economic tests to examine their databases. Generally speaking, they have six areas of study.

1. Conformity.
   This is perhaps one that is most troubling for a technical analyst. The data series must conform to the business cycle. But if you are selecting only those indicators that fit a perceived cycle, how do you know when external forces are building to warn a shift could develop?

2. Consistent Timing.
   Economists believe the data series must exhibit a consistent pattern over time as a leading, coincident, or lagging indicator.

3. Economic Significance.
   Simply stated it must make sense. Cyclical timing must be economically logical.

4. Statistical Adequacy.
   The data being collected must be collected and processed in a statistically reliable way.

5. Smoothness.
   It does not do anyone any good if the data is wild. Smoothness means the month--to-month movements are not erratic.

6. Schedule
   The data must be published on a reasonably prompt schedule. The word 'schedule' is not what economists use. They use the word 'currency' and it has nothing to do with foreign exchange. Therefore, I will use 'schedule' as my head cannot use 'currency' to mean anything other than Forex.

No quarterly series can qualify to meet these standards because they are not released in a reasonable schedule. You will find many monthly datasets fail regarding smoothness. In fact, there is no single ideal economic indicator that is viewed as the primary cyclical indicator.

How do economists work around this problem? They develop Composite Indexes with the goal to de-emphasize the volatility and behavior of individual indicators to highlight the cyclical patterns within the like categorized data group. Table 2.1 shows the individual leading indicators used to compile a Leading Composite Index. The composite index in Table 2.1 was developed by The Economic Cycle Research Institute (New York). From a post-war

| | Lead (-) or Lag (+) at Peaks (months) | | | | | | | | | Average Lead (-) |
|---|---|---|---|---|---|---|---|---|---|---|
| | Nov. 1948 | July 1953 | Aug. 1957 | Apr. 1960 | Dec. 1969 | Nov. 1973 | Jan. 1980 | July 1981 | July 1990 | or Lag (+) |
| Average weekly hours | -11 | -3 | -21 | -11 | -14 | -7 | -10 | -7 | 0 | -9.3 |
| Average initial claims | -22 | -10 | -23 | -12 | -7 | -9 | -21 | -4 | -18 | -14 |
| New orders, consumer goods | N/A | N/A | N/A | -13 | -3 | -8 | -10 | -2 | -2 | -6.3 |
| Vendor performance | -7 | -8 | -28 | -14 | -4 | 0 | -9 | -3 | +1 | -8.1 |
| New orders, capital goods | N/A | N/A | N/A | -13 | -8 | +8 | -10 | -3 | -7 | -5.5 |
| Building permits | N/A | N/A | -30 | -17 | -10 | -11 | -19 | -10 | -58 | -22.1 |
| Stock prices | -5 | -6 | -1 | -9 | -12 | -10 | missed | -8 | -1 | -6.5 |
| Money supply | N/A | N/A | N/A | missed | -9 | -10 | -24 | missed | -7 | -12.5 |
| Interest rate spread | N/A | N/A | -33 | -21 | -25 | -21 | -47 | -11 | -33 | -27.3 |
| Consumer expectations | N/A.. | N/A.. | -9.. | -2 | -10 | -15 | -15 | -2 | -18 | -10.1 |
| **Composite Index** | -5 | -5 | -20 | -11 | -8 | -9 | -15 | -3 | -6 | -9 |

| | Lead (-) or Lag (+) at Troughs (months) | | | | | | | | | Average Lead (-) |
|---|---|---|---|---|---|---|---|---|---|---|
| | Oct. 1949 | May 1954 | Apr. 1958 | Feb. 1961 | Nov. 1970 | Mar. 1975 | July 1980 | Nov. 1982 | Mar. 1991 | or Lag (+) |
| Average weekly hours | -6 | -1 | 0 | -2 | -2 | 0 | 0 | -1 | 0 | -1.3 |
| Average initial claims | -6 | +4 | 0 | 0 | -1 | -2 | -2 | -2 | 0 | -1 |
| New orders, consumer goods | N/A | N/A | N/A | 0 | -1 | 0 | -2 | -1 | 0 | -0.7 |
| Vendor performance | -7 | -6 | -4 | -11 | +1 | -1 | -2 | -8 | 0 | -4.2 |
| New orders, capital goods | N/A | N/A | N/A | -3 | -1 | 0 | -2 | +3 | 2 | -0.2 |
| Building permits | N/A | N/A | -12 | -2 | -10 | 0 | -3 | -13 | -2 | -6 |
| Stock prices | -4 | -8 | -4 | -4 | -5 | -3 | missed | -4 | -5 | -4.1 |
| Money supply | N/A | N/A | N/A | missed | -7 | -2 | +7 | missed | -4 | -3.2 |
| Interest rate spread | N/A | N/A | -4 | -10 | -15 | -8 | -3 | -22 | -21 | -11.9 |
| Consumer expectations | N/A** | -6** | +1** | -3 | -6 | -1 | -4 | -8 | -5 | -4 |
| **Composite Index** | -7 | -6 | -2 | -3 | -7 | -2 | -3 | -8 | -2 | -4 |

\* Lead time for individual indicators are preliminary. They have not gone through the normal review procedures.
\*\* Unofficial estimates.

Table 2.1
Timing at Business Cycle Turning Points, 10 Leading Indicators and Composite Index, 1948-1999.
The Economic Cycle Research Institute (New York); The Conference Board.
An indicator's performance, particularly leading indicators, is judged on the consistency of their timing.

period, the leading indicators have a better performance at cycle peaks than at troughs. Though data availability improved after 1960, there is a problem. The variability in the length of the leads is problematic.

This later point is precisely why Edward Dewey believed some economic business cycles are not true cycles. His definition required a stricter observance in the period length for a cycle. However, there are several economic cycles he does agree with, and we will address them shortly.

Leading indexes can lead cyclical downturns in the economy by eight to 20 months. Recoveries are often given a shorter warning by one to ten months. It is one of the challenges economists face.

The other challenge is the ratio between indicator categories. The ratio of a coincident index and lagging index is believed to anticipate business cycle peaks and troughs. When a sharp decline is seen in the ratio it signals a large increase in the costs of doing business. It is generally believed this occurs late in the expansion phase of the business cycle. However, the ratio cannot indicate the timing of a peak. As an example, from 1970 to 1990 the lead times varied from eight to 11 months in the United States compared to the actual peaks. That timing is not useful for asset management or trading. The capital risk exposure due to poor timing would be unmanageable. Economic business cycles provide macro awareness. We use technical analysis, which offers more timely signals, to develop our executable strategies.

What changes contribute to a meaningful warning that a recession is approaching? The inventory-sales ratio, for example tells us when inventories are rising faster than sales. That means inventory is building up on seller's shelves faster than the sales orders coming into businesses. We break this information down as we want to know the sectors that show the problem or if they all have rising inventories indicating a systemic problem developing.

Rising interest rates can be a problem as well because it suggests a squeeze on the availability of credit. Most countries today have interest rates near zero as we struggle with the economic shock from Covid-19. The day is coming when thismust change. In the United States we have rising inflation in 2021, yet the Federal Reserve is holding the benchmark rate near zero. How do you raise rates to counter inflation and not put a squeeze on business credit? Chartist do not address such a problem, but we can see tremendous vulnerability in charts and just know this goes on the shelf as one of the possible triggers that could cause a shock if mishandled. Technology stocks hate increases to rising interest rates and banks love it. The details the economists can debate.

At the Economic Cycle Research Institute (New York) the Conference Board examined the rough equivalents of indicators classified in the United States as leading the business cycle for 13 other market economies. While Table 2.2 shows, that as a group, these indicators exhibit leading behavior, the problem is that there are insufficient long-horizon cycles to make a conclusion. As technical analysts we require three times more data than the cycle period identified. Much of the information in this economic chart should be ignored. The message here is that the standards deemed acceptable by one discipline of financial analysts should never compromise your own standards.
When a Composite Index is constructed, economists use standardization factors to determine how monthly changes in each component contribute to the monthly change in the associated index. The factors are designed to give each component the same opportunity to contribute to the change in the

## Timing at Business Cycle Peaks and Troughs, Long-Range Gauges, 13 Countries

| Country | Number of Business Cycle: | | Average Leads (months) at: | | |
|---|---|---|---|---|---|
| | Troughs | Peaks | Troughs | Peaks | Overall |
| United States | 9 | 9 | -6 | -11 | -8 |
| Canada | 2 | 2 | -14 | -12 | -13 |
| Germany | 4 | 4 | -10 | -10 | -10 |
| France | 4 | 4 | -2 | -9 | -6 |
| United Kingdom | 3 | 3 | -13 | -20 | -17 |
| Italy | 3 | 2 | -11 | -12 | -11 |
| Switzerland | 4 | 4 | -15 | -13 | -14 |
| Sweden | 4 | 3 | -7 | -10 | -9 |
| Japan | 2 | 3 | -12 | -10 | -11 |
| Korea | 2 | 2 | -7 | -1 | -4 |
| Australia | 6 | 5 | -7 | -15 | -11 |
| Taiwan | 1 | 1 | -12 | -10 | -11 |
| New Zealand | 6 | 6 | -5 | -4 | -4 |

*Sources:* Economic Cycle Research Institute (New York); The Conference Board

Table 2.2
Timing at Business Cycle Peaks and Troughs, 13 Countries
The Economic Cycle Research Institute (New York); The Conference Board.

index. The factor is very small like 0.486. Always less than a value of one. But they serve to equalize volatility of the individual component and keep it current.

In the United States the factors being applied are reviewed every mid-December. The revisions are minor with little effect on the composition of leading, coincident, or lagging indicators. The process just brings them up to-date. When they feel an indicator is not current, they discontinue it. Sometimes I believe a popular dataset is discontinued for political reasons. Economic boards would never say that, but neither your vote nor mine matters in their decision. When an indicator is discontinued it usually means we need to ask an economist for their understanding of why it was discontinued and what the appropriate replacement has been named to take its place.

# U.S. BUSINESS CYCLE
# POST-WORLD WAR II (1945 TO 1991)

## U.S. Business Cycle Expansions and Contractions Post-World-War-II Period

| Business Cycle Reference Dates | | Duration in Months | | | |
|---|---|---|---|---|---|
| Trough | Peak | Contraction | Expansion | T-T | P-P |
| October 1945 | November 1948 | 8 | 37 | – | 45 |
| October 1949 | July 1953 | 11 | 45 | 48 | 56 |
| May 1954 | August 1957 | 10 | 39 | 55 | 49 |
| April 1958 | April 1960 | 8 | 24 | 47 | 32 |
| February 1961 | December 1969 | 10 | 106 | 34 | 116 |
| November 1970 | November 1973 | 11 | 36 | 17 | 47 |
| March 1975 | January 1980 | 16 | 58 | 52 | 74 |
| July 1980 | July 1981 | 6 | 12 | 64 | 18 |
| November 1982 | July 1990 | 16 | 2 | 28 | 108 |
| March 1991 | – | 8 | – | 100 | – |
| Average, 1945-1991 (9 cycles) | | 11 | 50 | 61 | 61 |

*Sources:* National Bureau of Economic Research; The Conference Board

Table 2.3
U.S. Business Cycle Expansions and Contractions Post-World War II.
National Bureau of Economic research; The Conference Board.

Table 2.3 accurately records how many contraction and expansion intervals occurred from 1945 to 1991 in the United States. The 'T-T' and 'P-P' columns record the number of months from trough-to-trough and peak-to-peak. They vary substantially and therefore Edward Dewey would argue that the business cycle is not a true cycle. However, there are cycles we should know because a great deal of study has confirmed their presence and we can verify their existence by objective computer analysis.

At auction I battled with three other fund managers to purchase a single original chart of the Dow Jones Industrials and Railroad Averages from 1932. I won. It is in Figure 2.11. The chart showed the work in progress by the analyst. What is so important about the year 1932? The Dow Jones Industrial Average bottomed after the Great Crash on July 7th, 1932.

But of greater importance, is that the chart shows the divergence at the bottom between Rails and the Industrials. The chart is the work of analyst Robert Rhea. Rhea wrote the first book about 'Dow Theory' in 1932. The Dow Theory was named after Charles Dow who originated the indexes. (It was William P. Hamilton who first used the Railroad Average and Industrial Average to confirm the direction of both indexes.)

In Figure 2.11 Rhea is also examining cycles and key price pivot points by hand. Rhea is given credit for calling the bottom in 1932 and wrote a letter called, 'Dow Theory Comments'. OK, back to the bank vault you go!

Figure 2.11
Original 1932 working chart of Robert Rhea, the author of the 'Dow Theory'. (1932)
Dow Jones Industrials and Dow Jones Rails - 1932 - daily (private library of Connie Brown)

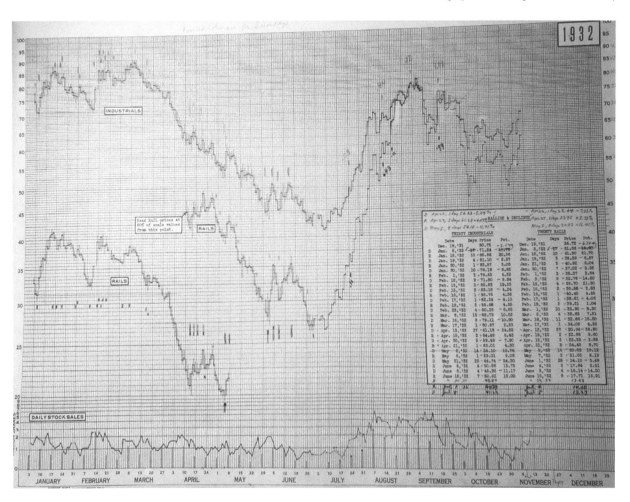

How did analysts detect cycles before computers? There are steps to know that we can do by hand that explain why we will then evolve to more sophisticated steps using a computer. The first step is to become familiar with cycles that are widely acknowledged. Then we can look at the methodology to help us make our own assessments.

Economists did not begin to classify economic cycles by periodicity until the mid-1800s. It is to the economist, Joseph Schumpeter, who briefly served as Finance Minister of German-Austria in 1919 and who emigrated in 1932 to the United States, that we owe the names and classification of business cycles in our dialogue today. He was a professor at Harvard University and became one of the most influential economists of the early 20th century.

The longest business cycle, the Kondratiev Wave, averages 54-years. Schumpeter named this cycle after the Russian Nikolai Kondratiev who first identified the cycle. We only know of Kondratiev's work through its having been smuggled out of Russia. Long story, he was imprisoned after releasing his findings; I recommend you read more about it. The Kondratiev Wave is

## BUSINESS CYCLES ACCORDING TO PERIODICITY:

- KONDRATIEV WAVE - 45-60 years

- KUZNETS CYCLE - 15-25 years

- JUGLAR CYCLE - a period of 7-11 years

- KITCHIN CYCLE - a period of 3-5 years

- 40-month and 56-month Cycle

## OTHER CYCLES TO STUDY:

- 90-Year and 45-Year Cycles (1080 and 540-months)

- 84-Year Cycle

- 56-Year Cycle

- 30-Year Cycle
- 20-Year Cycle
- 19-Year Metonic Cycle
- 11.5-Year Solar Sunspots Cycle

- The harmonic fractals of long-term cycles = 26-Years, 17 1/2, Years, and 13-Years. (Harmonic fractions are 1/2, 1/3, 1/4, 1/8.)

categorized as long wave theory. Professor Schumpeter attributed long cycles to technological innovation. Earlier in this chapter, we considered the rise of the dot.com innovators and the transportation changes that came when the railway systems were being built. These innovations changed business cycles and their impact extends over a very long period of time. The Internet is certainly a perfect example of Schumpeter's thinking that innovation is the driver behind economic change.

An example of a medium-range economic cycle is the Kuznets Cycle identified in 1930 by Simon Kuznets. Kuznets attributed his cycle of 15 to 25 years to immigration. Flows of people coming in/out bring changing needs for construction and infrastructure. That is why the Kuznets Cycle is also called the Kuznets Swing as it is a study of demographic changes. There is a field of specialization called Behavioral Economics. Demographic changes lead to our deeper interest in understanding  behavioral models of mass psychology. Modern day economists like Yale University Professor Robert J Schiller, University of Chicago Professor Richard Thaler, and London School of Economics Professor Paul Dolan, are names you would benefit from exploring.

Another medium or mid-wave cycle is the Juglar Cycle with a periodicity of 7 to 11-years. The cycle was identified by  French economist Clément Juglar and attributed to inventory and fixed capital changes. Economists view fixed capital as the physical assets required to produce a product where the asset is essential for the continued cycle of the production line.

Professor Schumpeter introduced the concept that the Juglar Cycle contained four distinct stages. Some economists view the Juglar Cycle to be 'The' Business Cycle.  The four phases are:

- Expansion - The first phase enjoys low interest rates and production increases. The rising demand and potential declining supply contribute to rising prices.
- Crisis - Multiple bankruptcies, Stock market crashes, clearly public sentiment swings to fear due to instability.
- Recession - The third phase triggers a drop in prices and in output.
- Recovery - Due to lower prices and incomes, businesses rebuild, productivity increases, aggregate demand increases, consumer confidence recovers, stocks recover.

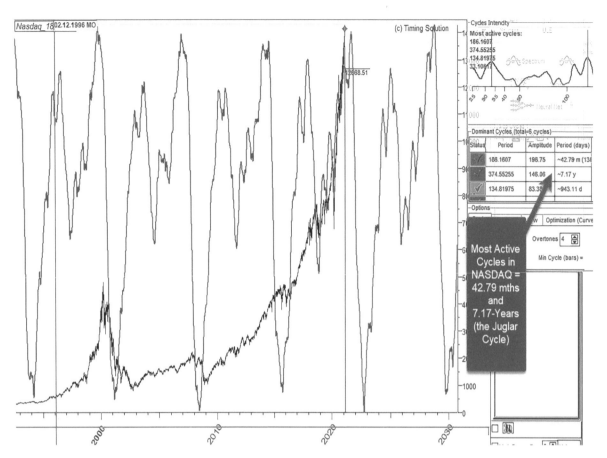

Figure 2.12
Cycle Spectrogram Analysis of the NASDAQ using daily data from 1996 to 2021.

Chart by TimingSolution

Computers are objectively extracting the cycles we just discussed. The analysis method is called spectrogram analysis. To define any cycle; we need to know the period; the length of the cycle, the amplitude (which tells us the strength of the cycle, and a phase which defines the epoch point that defines the starting angle of the cycle.

Figure 2.12 is a spectrograph showing the results for the daily NASDAQ 100. The computer is making thousands of computations regarding period, amplitude, significance, and a host of other statistical computations to help us find the most active cycles pulsing through the dataset. On the far right-side of Figure 2.12 is a small table that lists the most active cycles extracted by computer analysis. The first is a cycle of 42.79 months. The second is the Juglar Cycle showing 7.17 years. The graph displays the daily price data of the NASDAQ 100 with a red oscillating overlay line. The line is a composite cycle where the top four active cycles have been weighted and summed to create the single cycle.

In Figure 2.13 the criteria in the three columns are different than those in Figure 2.12, but the column to focus on is the third column showing the most active periods in the S&P500. The spectrograph running across the top shows the strength of a cycle period. The x-axis is the period, and the y-axis

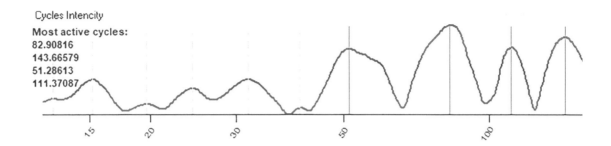

Cycles Intencity

Most active cycles:
82.90816
143.66579
51.28613
111.37087

Dominant Cycles (total=8 cycles)

Add manual

| Status | Period | Fitness | Period (days) |
|---|---|---|---|
| ✓ | 82.90816 | 49.02% | ~9.16 y |
| ✓ | 143.66579 | 39.46% | ~15.88 y |
| ✓ | 51.28613 | 37.64% | ~5.67 y |
| | 31.72506 | 17.70% | ~42.07 m (12 |
| | 15.2133 | 15.19% | ~614.08 d |
| | 12.5686 | 14.51% | ~507.33 d |
| | 24.45161 | 12.73% | ~986.98 d |

Figure 2.13
Cycle Spectrograph Analysis Identifying the Juglar Cycle
(~9.16 Years) as the Most Active Cycle
in the S&P500.

Chart byTimingSolution

is the amplitude indicating the cycle's strength. The highest peak in Figure 2.13 for the S&P00 equates to a cycle of approximately 9.16 years. The Juglar Cycle has once again topped the list.

You might have noticed the cycle shown as a red line in Figure 2.12 does not look like the theoretical sine wave. Let's shelve that observation for a moment because we cannot ignore the short-term cycle in the spectrograph in Figure 2.12 that tops the list as the most active. It is a cycle with a period of 42.79 months. This cycle has been studied extensively by Edward Dewey. It was known to be one of the cycles of interest to John. D. Rockefeller who founded Standard Oil. The cycle is known as the 41.6-month cycle, but modern-day spectrogram analysis tells us it has shifted slightly to include 41 to 45-months.

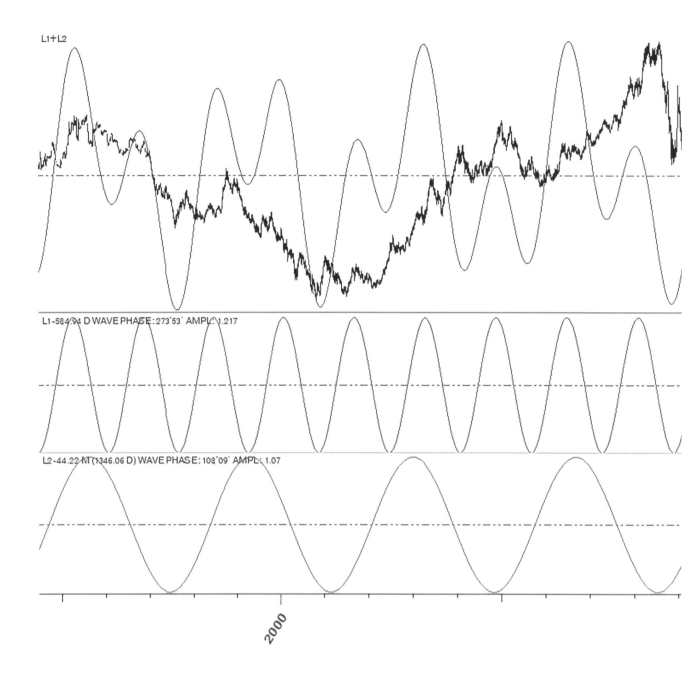

L1+L2

L1-584.94 D WAVE PHASE: 273°53´ AMPL: 1.217

L2-44.22 M (1346.06 D) WAVE PHASE: 108°09´ AMPL: 1.07

2000

Figure 2.14
Cycle Spectrogram Analysis for EURUSD - weekly
Chart by TimingSolution

The top window shows the weekly EURUSD prices from 1995 to 2021 and a composite cycle. The middle window shows a red cycle with a period of 584.94 days. The bottom window is a blue cycle with a period of 44.22 months. These two cycle periods were identified as being the most significant and active in the spectrogram analysis results shown in Figure 2.15. Regardless of the financial asset class examined, the 41 to 45-month cycle will often be identified as one of the most active cycles pulsing through the market. Figure 2.14 shows this to be true for EURUSD weekly

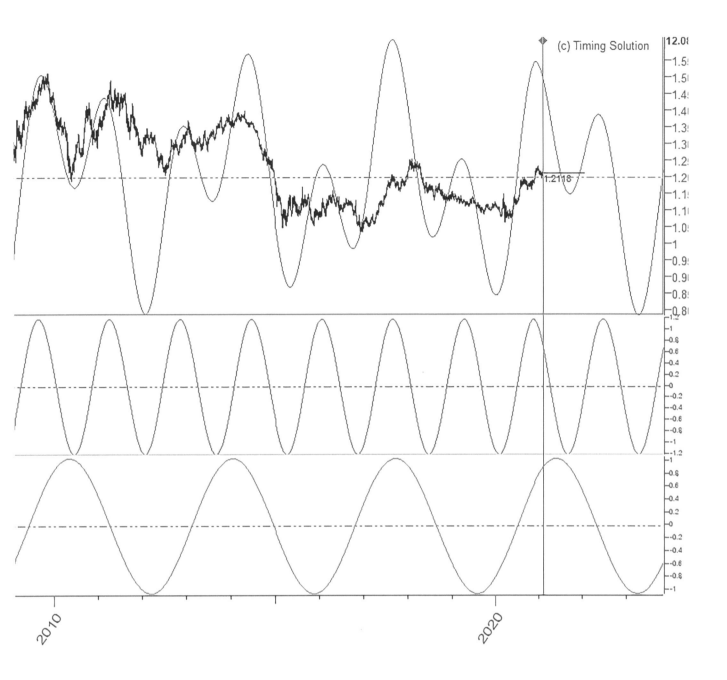

data. The two independent cycle periods must be combined to create one composite cycle. It is a simple process of summation. When cycle peaks and troughs from the two periods are in phase, they have a greater impact on price movement. In finance this is known as J.M. Hurst's Principle of Summation. The composite cycle in the top window is the Summation Principle in action. Most software designed for technical analysis only allows us to plot single cycles on a graph. It is much less effective than plotting one composite cycle as seen in the top window on the EURUSD data.

The 41 to 44-month cycle was extracted by spectrogram analysis in both the NASDAQ and EURUSD. It demonstrates Hurst' Principle of Commonality.

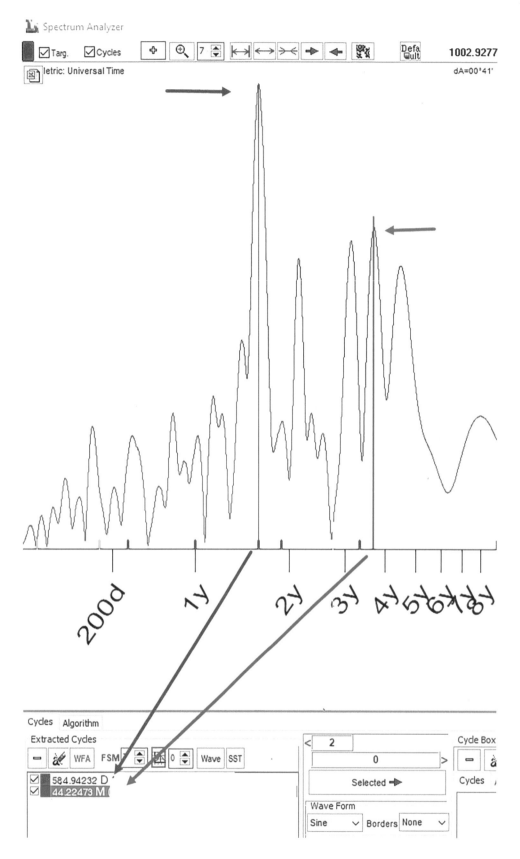

Figure 2.15
Cycle Spectrograph Results for EURUSD - weekly data from 1995 to 2021. The computer has extracted two cycles with periods of 44.22 months and 584.94 days as the two most active.

The spectrograph shows desired characteristics of high amplitude indicating strength, with narrow pulses up indicating the periodicity is specific to the time interval detected.

Chart by TimingSolution

## CLASSIC CYCLES
# THE EIGHT PRINCIPLES OF CYCLE ANALYSIS

J.M. Hurst is a legendary cycles analyst of financial markets. He was an aerospace engineer and was one of our pioneers in the field of computer research to study the nature of cycles in stock price action. Hurst authored the groundbreaking book, *The Profit Magic of Stock Transaction Timing*. The book made a significant impact on our industry and our understanding of market cycle theory.

Hurst defined eight Principles of Market Cycle Analysis,

- THE PRINCIPLE OF CYCLICALITY- Price action consists of a combination of specific waves and therefore demonstrates cyclical character traits.

- THE PRINCIPLE OF COMMONALITY- All asset classes (FOREX, Equity, Interest Rate, and Commodities) share price movements in common. For example, market lows tend to be more in sync than market highs. Therefore, analysis of multiple markets will help identify the most active cycles.

- THE PRINCIPLE OF SUMMATION - Cycles of different periodicity combine by a process of simple addition.

- THE PRINCIPLE OF HARMONICITY- The wavelengths of longer cycles are mathematical multiples of shorter cycles. (Harmonics.)

- THE PRINCIPLE OF SYNCHRONICITY- Cycle troughs of longer cycles will coincide with cycle troughs of shorter cycles that are related.

- THE PRINCIPLE OF PROPORTIONALITY- Cycle amplitude is proportional to wavelength.

- THE PRINCIPLE OF NOMINALITY- Hurst used an average period when harmonic ratios were grouped.

- THE PRINCIPLE OF VARIATION- Expect deviation to occur.

**LEARNING OBJECTIVES**

To become familiar with J.M. Hurst's Eight Principles of Cycle Analysis

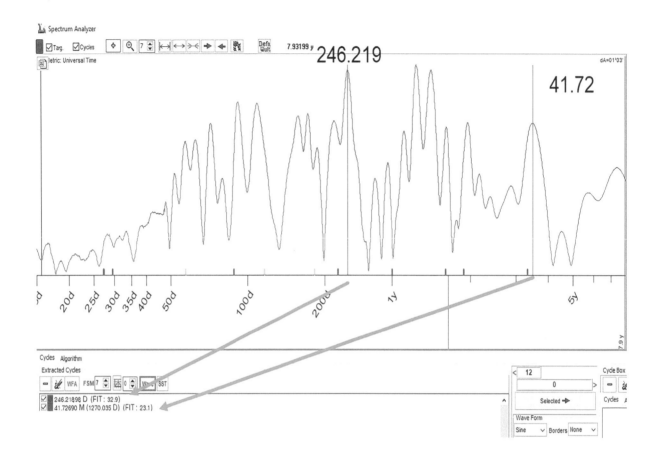

Figure 2.16
Cycle Spectrograph Results for S&P500 - daily data from 1995 to 2021.

The computer has extracted two cycles with periods of 246.22 days
and 41.72-months as the two most active.

Edward Dewey's ideal period was 41.6 making this study extremely
interesting that the cycle remains active in current market price
action.

Chart by Timing Solution

Some readers may wonder if the cycle is present in the S&P500 because it has a different composition weighting than the NASDAQ. A spectrogram analysis was conducted for data from 1996 to 2021. The computer extracted Dewey's ideal cycle. The study in Figure 2.16 shows a cycle with 41.72-months as the second most active cycle in the S&P500 Index. Dewey's ideal theoretical cycle was 41.6-months.

Edward Dewey believed the 41.6-month cycle had inverted after World War II and had been replaced by a new cycle of 52-months. It was not until 1970 that Dewey realized both cycles were present because the cycle periods were fractal multiple ratios of longer cycles that were well known. This is important. Edward Dewey wrote about his thoughts and opinion regarding the 41.6 and 52-month cycles in the Foundation for the Study of Cycles magazine, *Cycles;* January 1970. It is always more interesting to read the original dialogue of the original author than another analysts' summary. Forgive the quality of the microfiche copy. The article has been reproduced with the permission of The Foundation for the Study of Cycles in Figures 2.17 and 2.18. Dewey describes and introduces for you the fractal properties of cycle periodicity.

As we conclude Part One in our study of cycles, you can at this point read cycle charts prepared by other analysts. You have learned many of the key terms we use to describe cycles. We have covered a great deal of information together from economic theory to market technical charts.

Spectrogram Analysis has provided a good introduction to the field of data sciences that can objectively confirm some of the observations about periodicity recorded by our predecessors. We know we have a solid footing to build upon and grow farther in our understanding.

Part Two is where we will look at the methods and mathematics we use to create these cycle studies. Market analysis is always to some extent about cycles. Some indicators will have movement because of the hidden cycle attributes of the price data. The information we have explored together in Part One has prepared you for a journey that will likely continue an entire lifetime.

Figure 2.17
Edward Dewey's discussion regarding cycle dominance in 'Cycles', January 1970,
Foundation for the Study of Cycles. Reprinted with permission FSC.

4067

# Stock Price Cycles: An Exchange of Information and Ideas on the 52-Month Cycle

The May 1967 issue of *Cycles* carried a letter from a member which started an exchange of information and ideas between the letter writer and another professional investigator of cycles. An edited, but fairly complete version of this correspondence follows.

Also included at the end is a supplement written by Chapin Hoskins* to extend the scope of the discussion beyond the subject of stock prices.

MAY 1967 LETTER FROM PARNELL MCKENNA* TO *CYCLES*.

Although the method used is a bit unconventional and Standard & Poor's 500 stock index is used, I have a few observations that may be helpful in putting some light on the behavior of the 41-month stock market cycle in the postwar period, or at least may suggest an area to investigate

The upward trend in stock prices from 1949 through early 1966 at least, was not to be denied. Yet during the sus-

*Parnell McKenna of Wilmington, Delaware issues a market letter "Studies in the Movements of Stock Prices," and Chapin Hoskins is Chairman of the Trustees of the Institute for Trend Research at Hopkinton, New Hampshire.

tained advance it appears that both the 41-month and the 9.2-year cycles exerted their influence. As a result of this or for other reasons, there is a suggestion of a 52-month cycle.

While there has been time for only a few repetitions of this possible cycle, it does suggest the 51.25-month cycle alleged by Mr. Dewey in 1952, and may be worthy of examination from that point of view.

The trough in 1960 was judged to be a reversal and considered to be the time of a crest. On this basis, the periods between crests from 1952 through 1964 averaged 50.3 months. Troughs from 1949 through 1962 averaged 53.3 months apart. The average time, crest-to-crest and trough-to-trough works out to 52 months, while the median was 52.5 months.

While the suggestion by Lane, as reported by Mr. Dewey in 1954, that the 41-month cycle had reversed appears to have been reasonable at the time it was made, data presently available suggest that since 1949 the rhythm may have lengthened.

To go a bit farther, the indications that I have are that the last crest should be dated July 1964, and that November 1966 will be the date of the last trough.

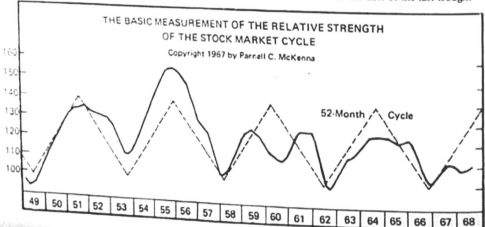

THE BASIC MEASUREMENT OF THE RELATIVE STRENGTH OF THE STOCK MARKET CYCLE

Copyright 1967 by Parnell C. McKenna

52-Month Cycle

## JULY 1967 LETTER FROM CHAPIN HOSKINS TO PARNELL MCKENNA

Your interesting letter in May *Cycles* mentions a 52-month cycle in stocks and others. We have watched the 52-month cycle and its fractions for a number of years, and I think we understand its place in the complex of stock market cycles.

[LATER]

If I were to write you all that we have learned about the 52-month and related cycles, it would take many pages. But perhaps I can make the basic points clear with not too many words.

A few basic points that should be kept in mind:

1) Any series is likely to be subject to more than one rhythm, and this is particularly true of a stock price index because it is an aggregate of stocks which represent many types of business activity.

2) The existence of more than one cycle results in conflicts of force. The most frequent result is that *one rhythm may dominate for a given period of time and then yield its dominance to another. This shifting of dominance is in itself rhythmic.*

3) *A phenomenon which is associated with shifting dominance is that in some series the major moves may be timed by one rhythm and the minor moves by another.*

*This last fact is particularly visible in stock prices, and since fractions of 52 months have dominated relatively short rhythms in stock prices for a number of years,* you need to understand something of the background of the apparent 52-month cycle.

As far back as written records go, there are evidences of cycles of 52 years and its fractions in human affairs. The obvious fractions are, of course, the 1/2, the 1/3, and the 1/4, or 26, 17 1/3, and 13 years.

Fifty-two years is 624 months. Its 1/3 fraction is 208 months, or 4 times 52. The 13 year fraction is 3 times 52. The 416-month cycle which is sometimes mentioned is 1/5 of 208.

*We are never surprised when we find evidence of a 52-month rhythm, or 26, or 78, or 39, in any series. Neither are we surprised when at certain times we find those lengths becoming subordinated.*

*The reality of a 52-month influence in stock prices shows itself in fractional movements which appear in short term rates of change though not necessarily in the price itself.* At October 3, 1931, a very sharp drop in the 13 week rate of change came to an end. Then 451 weeks later, at May 25, 1940, another sharp drop ended. Again 453 weeks after that was January 29, 1949, and 455 weeks thereafter was October 19, 1957. On each of these occasions, sizable declines ended in terms of rate of change.

You will note that those intervals average 453 weeks, and none of the three intervals differs from this by more than two weeks. *Other observations lead us to consider 452 weeks to be the true interval here. This you will find, is very close to twice 52 months.*

After the first of these lows there were six others in the next 107 weeks. After the 1940 low there were six in the next 104 weeks. Changes after the last two lows mentioned were similar.

All of these dates were important turning points in the rate of change, but, except in 1957, they do not mark the end of shakeouts in price.

*It is also a fact that rhythms related to 52 months do sometimes mark the ends of stock price declines, but the ends of bull markets reflect an entirely different cyclical rhythm.*

Just two more remarks to show the importance of the 52 month fractions. First, a 226 week compound rhythm dominated the rise and fall of the British pound in recent years, and the first great crisis of the Wilson administration was almost perfectly timed this way. Secondly, you will sometimes find that the ratio of an individual stock to the total market will follow this rhythm even though the market as a whole does not seem to be doing so.

This memorandum has not been as brief as I expected, and perhaps it is not as clear as I would hope. But it will supplement your own observations of a 52 month influence in the market.

## JULY 1967 LETTER FROM PARNELL MCKENNA TO CHAPIN HOSKINS

I wish to express my sincere thanks to you for having taken the time to summarize your findings concerning the 52-month cycle.

Frankly, I was not aware that there was a significant cycle of that length, and it was something of a surprise when it appeared that stock prices in the post-war period had been dominated by a rhythm of that length.

Yet it appeared so definite, and with such remarkable precision at market troughs, that it could hardly be disregarded. Your comments have provided considerable food for thought, and suggest further investigations on my part that may enable me to understand the cycle better.

Incidentally, I have been watching a short cycle in the Dow Jones Industrials recently. While I have not attempted to define it's length precisely, it appears to be about 52 1/2 market hours. This is perhaps the two week cycle noted by Mr. Dewey in "Putting Cycles to Work in Science and Industry." But then I suppose you are quite familiar with that one also.

I do appreciate your comments and again my thanks.

7

# PART TWO: CYCLE ANALYSIS METHODOLOGY

How do we identify a cycle? When we look at a chart of price data by visual examination, we first look for a visually apparent rhythmic fluctuation. A rhythmic fluctuation is defined by Edward Dewey as; "a pattern that repeats with a beat. Highs, lows, areas of strength alternating with areas of weakness. Whatever you see has to be averaged to obtain a possible average cycle length to start the analysis."

Figure 2.18 shows three cycles of different periods and all starting from different base-line dates. The yellow cycle is the longest with intervals of 158.51 bars in length. This is the period. The cycle has been further subdivided into quarters. The subdivisions are marked with vertical red dotted lines and the number of bars from the start of the 158.51 cycle are notated on the dotted line. When we

Figure 2.18
Gold Futures Spot - 2-day bar chart
Three rhythmic cycles selected by visual examination.
158.51 period (bars) from 08/17/2018,
128.67 period (bars) from 03/19/2020,
84.32 period (bars) from 04/02/2020.
The 84.32 period cycle (yellow) is further subdivided by 4. These subdivisions are marked by red dotted vertical lines. Subdividing the period of a longer cycle by 2, 3, and 4 are examples of harmonics within the fundamental cycle.

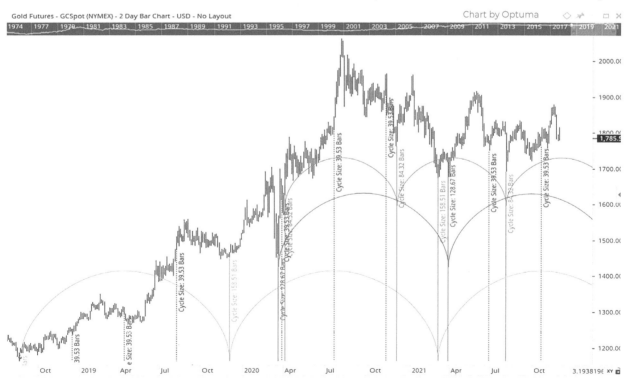

divide a fundamental period into half, thirds, and quarters, we are defining harmonic subdivisions within the longer cycle. If you examine these red dotted cycles in Figure 2.18, it  is clear the subdivisions are as meaningful for us as the longer fundamental cycle itself.

The second cycle begins from March 19, 2020. When I selected that price low to start the cycle, I did not have the harmonics

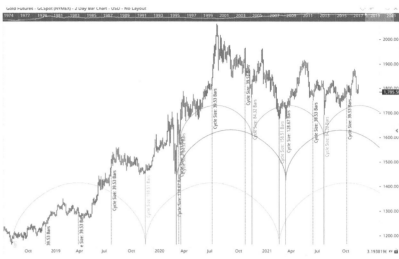

Figure 2.18
Gold Futures Spot - 2-day bar chart

(repeat from prior page)

marked for the longer cycle. But after adding the harmonic subdivisions of the longest cycle, it became clear the cycle in blue with a period of 128.67 is nearly an exact harmonic of the first cycle. The harmonic falls a couple of bars later, but it is interesting how close they merge.

In March 5, 2021 and March 26, 2021, the Gold market defines a price swing low near the same horizontal level. We call this pattern a double bottom. What is interesting is how the first low of March 5 coincides with the 158.51 cycle in yellow. The second price low near March 29 coincides with the 128.67 period cycle in blue. The way the market respected these two cycles is a classic way markets utilize cycles. The fact the two cycles are nearly in phase at the low exacerbates the market swing.

Now we need to critique the Gold chart in Figure 2.18. The chart demonstrates how many people in our industry use cycle tools. Pick a low, any low, and try to fit another low to the  software tool's low. In *Cycles*, Part One, the statement was made we must have three times more data than the cycle period of study. Look closely at Figure 2.18.  None of the cycles meet this criterion or you would see three complete cycles within the dataset. The beats may be valid, but then we would see that the cycle beats are continuations from the left side of the frame.

What we have now is a pretty picture that demonstrates the principles, but not a result that is analysis worthy or to be acted upon when the next  cycle lows occur. These selected baselines to begin a cycle must be in a rhythm to a wider look-back period to be considered significant.

However, the work we accomplished in Figure 2.18 has not been wasted. Three different rhythms have been detected in Figure 2.18. To remove the trend, we first need a simple moving average. The average takes 'x' number of closing prices and then we find their arithmetic average. As a new closing price enters the 'x' set of numbers, we drop off the oldest. That's all there is to a simple moving average.

It becomes a more involved discussion when you realize the oldest closing price causes a major deviation as it drops off, or when a big jump enters the number set we total. One consideration is to weight the data so the one out of step does not cause a big jump in the mean of the remainder. We also have other ways to handle a distortion when the new data is a deviation skewing the average we had been using. Some data must be smoothed first. These problems we will address another time. Stay with the simple moving average concept for now.

Consider a series of 17 numbers all recording the closing prices of 17 price bar. This data sample has a summed total of 1350. We then simply divide 1350 by 17. The mean or arithmetic average equals 79.41.

Something to think about here. What if seven of the 17 closing prices are all the same and have a value of 60? The distribution values of closing prices are skewed more towards 60. Now what should we do? This is called a central tendency and we calculate a median average to handle this condition. The median is found by ordering the set from lowest to highest and finding the exact middle. As example, ~~1, 2, 5, 6~~, 7, 8, ~~12, 15, 16, 17~~. We can then disregard the four lowest and four highest values. Now just average the two middle numbers 7 and 8. Divide by 2 and the median equals 7.5.

Another situation we may have to consider: is what if neither the arithmetic mean nor the median solves the problem because there are two central tendencies the numbers are grouping towards within your dataset? As an example, if 4 and 12 both make a strong case, then we need to test them both. two central tendencies the numbers are grouping towards within your dataset? As an example, if 4 and 12 both make a strong case, then we need to test them both.

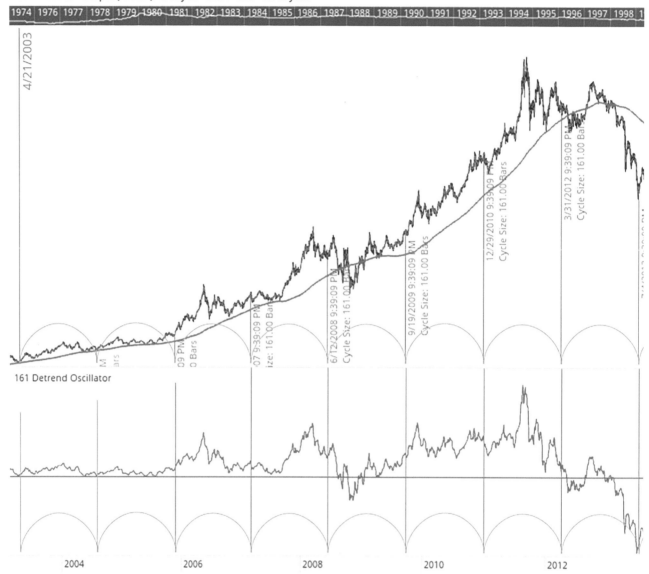

Figure 2.19
Gold Futures Spot - 2-day bar chart (February 2003 to November, 2021)
Using extended historical data than used in Figure 2.18, we see the rhythm of the 158.51
beat in Figure 2.18 is possibly closer to a 161-period rhythm.

In Figure 2.18 we made a visual examination of the data to select a rhythm. The longer cycle had a period of 158.51, though we did not have three complete cycles from which to judge our selection.

In Figure 2.19 we have price data in 2-day bars for Gold from February 2003 to November 2021. Again, using a visual examination of the rhythm, we find the 158.51 period suggested in Figure 2.18 was close, but a little short. The better period could be closer to 161.

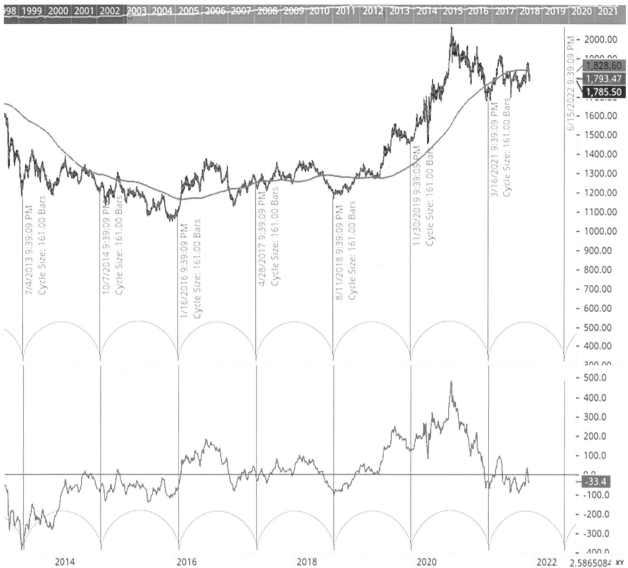

The top window frame contains the 161-period cycle in yellow under the 2-day bar chart for Gold. Running along the black price data is a simple 1-period moving average in red that serves to connect the closing prices. Now the important step. People in general fail this next step. We will add a second moving-average. Dewey uses the period or rhythm we obtained through visual observation. The purple 161-period moving-average is on the data in the top window that is added to the 1-period moving average. Here is what we are going to do with these averages.

Detrending is the spread, or differential, between the two averages. When the shorter period average is below the longer, the detrend line is negative. When the shorter is above the longer period average the difference is positive. This creates the oscillator movement as the averages separate, cross a zero line, then separate again. The amplitude is the degree of separation between the averages. Figure 2.19 graphs the blue detrend result in the lower frame of Figure 2.19.

Find the cycle marked July 4, 2013. The detrend plot shows an extreme low that price does not match. The price chart then retests this same price low December 24, 2013. The detrend low is significantly higher. We call this pattern bullish divergence. This is a warning a trend reversal is developing, though it may not be immediate. While Gold prices continue to trend downwards after a sharp bounce up from the double bottom and bullish divergence pattern, the detrend oscillator continues to rise because the spread is narrowing between the two moving-averages. Gold prices stay below the purple 161-period moving-average on price until February 4, 2016, when the short moving-average finally crosses back up through the longer average.

Divergence patterns are another benefit of using a detrend oscillator. For example, study the price reversal just behind the January 16, 2016 cycle beat. Price makes a new low and the detrend plot shows a positive divergence. The detrend oscillator not only helps to define the period rhythm but can communicate other signals common to all oscillators that we will study more closely in Chapter Five.

Notice the July 4, 2013, cycle beat and price low for Gold. You may want to return to Figure 2.4. The Annualized chart was a discussion about the computer's finding that July 4th was an important cycle low for the Dow Jones Industrial Average. Here we have found it again in Gold demonstrating Hurst's Principle of Commonality.

Many people do not know the correct period to use to create the second moving-average that is then used for the spread in the detrend oscillator. They tend to just use a 20-period average on everything. It is a harmonic of the 40-month cycle we discussed, but Dewey used a moving-average period that was equal to the rhythm. Therefore, we take these extra steps in the beginning, making a visual inspection to find the cycle that the market is actively respecting, because it is about probability. Also notice the cycle beat becomes more accurate after July 4th, 2013. When I selected the anchor date of April 21, 2003, I was very aware that the latter half cycle beats were more timely than those pulsing on the older data. It will never be exact because this cycle is not alone. The 161-period cycle falls near June 15, 2022. Is it a major price move into this down beat? We cannot answer with these methods alone. We just have an inflection point of interest on our chart and we only have a single cycle. We need to study the longer and shorter cycles to create a composite cycle like the one we developed in Figure 2.14 earlier.

I wonder if we did a spectrogram study, would the computer program find our 161-period rhythm? I cannot use a 2-day dataset because the computer can only analyze daily calendar days. The change is made and I save the data file from Optuma software. We then convert the data to *MS* Excel files. Be sure to save in csv format that is comma delimited. Now I can load this file into my cycle research software called TimingSolution. We are very curious what cycle periods the computer will extract.

The computer identifies periods of 176.194, 135.238, and 158.526. This puts our cycle period back to 158.5, the original period we used in Figure 2.18. The spectrogram analysis difference is likely due to our use of daily data and the computer then used a different moving average.

While our cycle from visual inspection was extracted through computer analysis, we totally missed the period the computer shows is far more significant. It is the 176.19 cycle period peak in Figure 2.20.

What did we learn? Manual inspection for market rhythms does not yield false results, but they may not be the best results we can obtain without the help of a computer. The 176-period and 592-period cycles have 2 harmonics included giving the modified sine wave pattern a 'wiggle'.

Figure 2.20
Gold Futures Spot - daily bar chart (February, 2003, to November, 2021)
Cycles extracted by Spectrogram Analysis -
1. 176.194 days
2. 135.238 days

In-between with a red arrow is the peak extracting the 158.526 -period cycle. A lower amplitude indicates it is not as strong as the 176 and 135-period cycles. The 176 peak is the strongest period that is less than a 1-year interval.

The manual visualization was correct, but not the most dominant active cycle that requires computer analysis.

Chart by TimingSolution

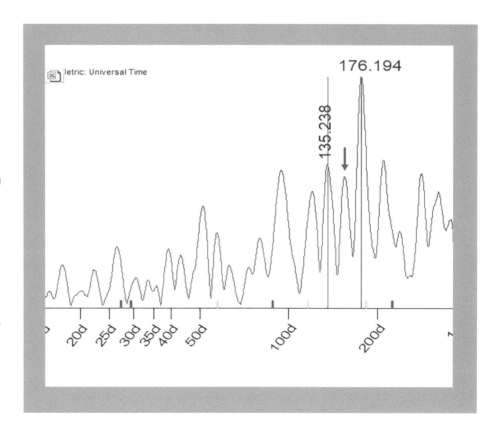

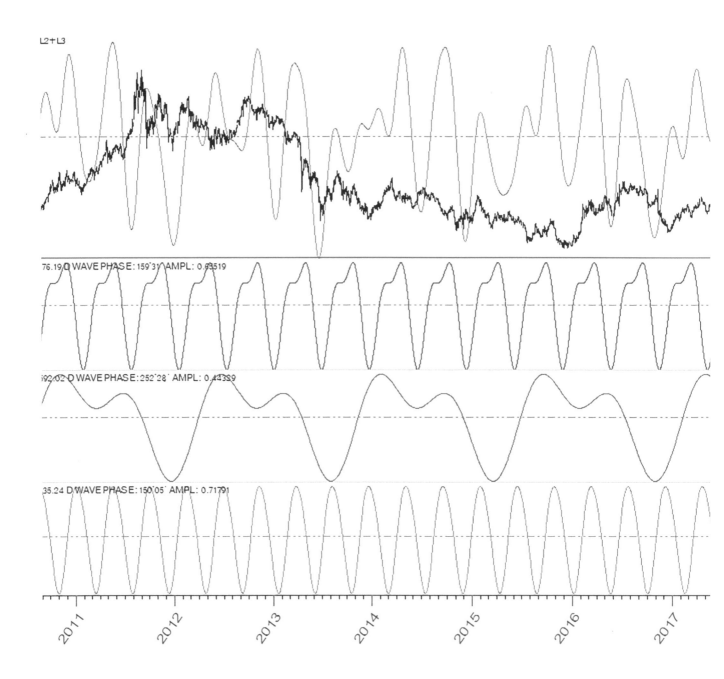

L2+L3

76.19 D WAVE PHASE: 159°31′ AMPL: 0.93519

592.02 D WAVE PHASE: 252°28′ AMPL: 0.44389

35.24 D WAVE PHASE: 150°05′ AMPL: 0.71791

2011   2012   2013   2014   2015   2016   2017

Two harmonics simply means a cycle, for example 24, is divide by 2 and 3. The cycle periods would be 24 (the fundamental), 24 divided by 2 equals 12, (the first harmonic), and then 24 divided by 3 equals 8 (the second harmonic). All three cycles, 24, 12, and 8 are then added using the Hurst Summation Principle. This creates the composite cycle with a wiggle in the middle frame in blue. All three cycles in red, blue, and green are added together to create the overlay cycle in the top frame on the Gold price data. The results are a good match, but not perfect. Longer-wave cycles are not in this composite cycle. Notice that in 2018 price and the composite cycle are in opposite positions. We call this a cycle inversion when price moves in the opposite direction of the cycle. Cycle inversions give evidence that we missed a longer dominant cycle.

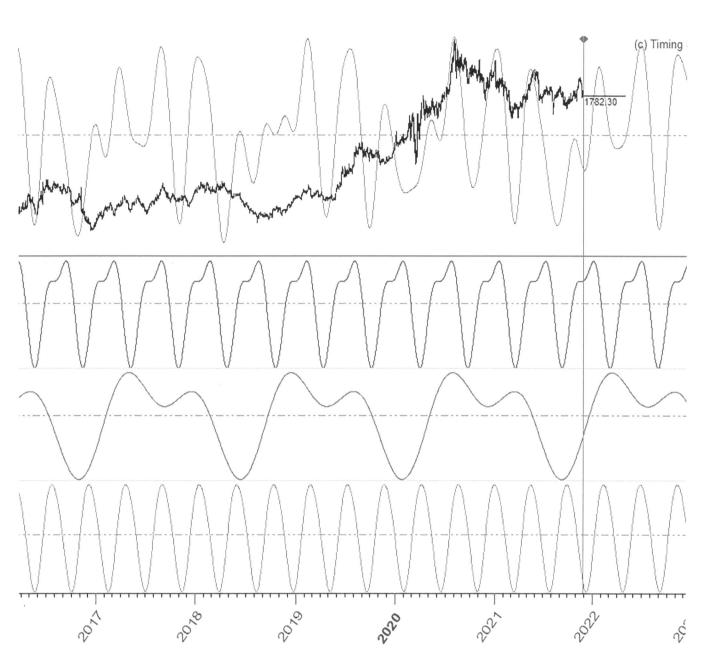

(c) Timing

1782.30

Figure 2.21
Gold Futures Spot - daily bar chart (analysis from January, 2000, to November, 2021.)
Cycle periods of 176.19, 592.02, and 135.24 are graphed below the price data top window. A composite cycle was then calculated by adding the three cycles together. The composite cycle is then plotted with price in the top window.

Chart by TimingSolution

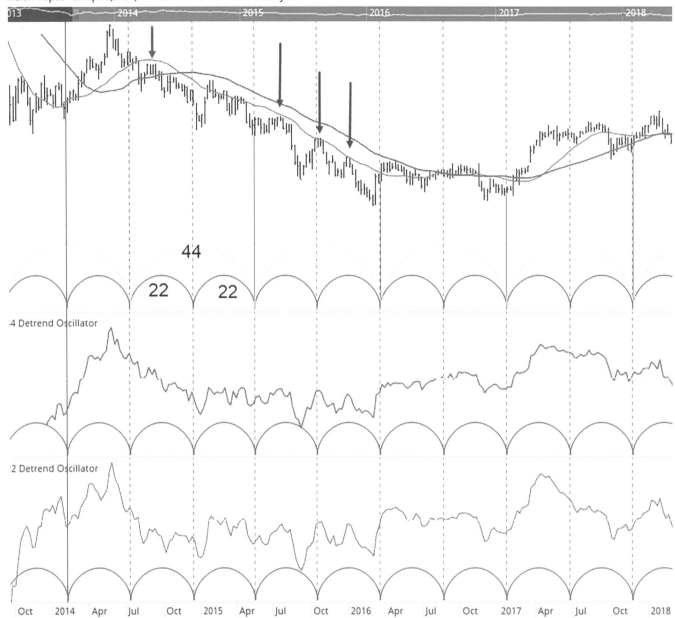

Figure 2.22
Indian Rupee -Futures SIRSpot (EFUT)- weekly bar chart
(August 30, 2013, to December 3, 2021)

Figure 2.22 is a weekly chart of the Indian Rupee Futures market. We will unpack this chart step-by-step as it is a solution to a problem you may also encounter. The first step was by visualization to find a rhythm. The lime-green cycle with a 44-period beat was selected and added below the price data. When I added this cycle to price the problem was first detected. The 44-period

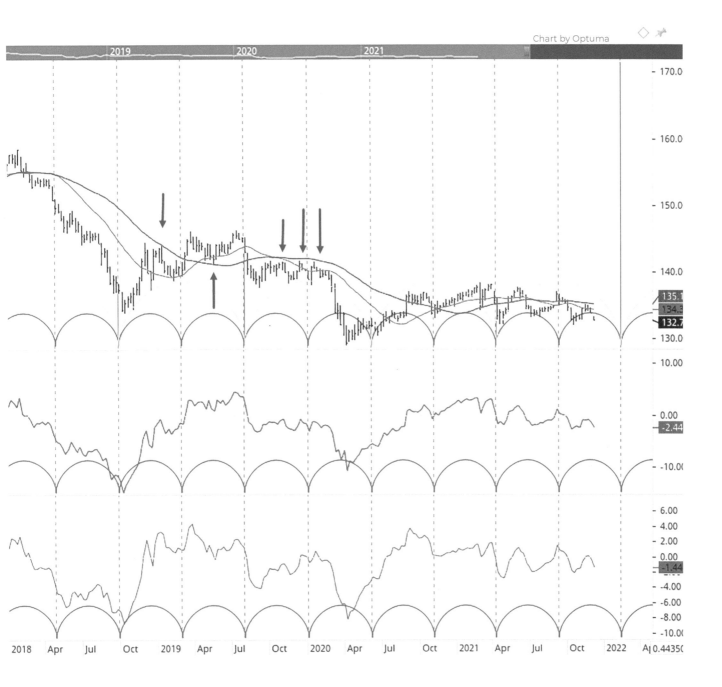

moving-average is the red line on price. It is rarely tested by price as support or resistance. This is one of the ways I test the cycle period selected. The second window under the price frame is the 44-period detrended oscillator.

When the trend is removed it is easier to study, but the detrend oscillator in the middle frame is very jagged. At first, I apply a simple 5-period moving-average of the 44-period detrend oscillator in an effort to smooth the oscillator. While often a solution, it was not the answer this time as the smoothing average

was too slow and shorter periods for smoothing were still much too jagged to be useful.

The next step was to halve the 44-period cycle using a harmonic half-cycle. It is under price and the detrended oscillator is in the bottom window.

The 22-period cycle was plotted with the 22-period detrend oscillator and transmitted to the middle and top chart windows. The half cycle harmonic of 44 periods tracks the price action extremely well. The key to problem-solving this market was knowing I could use a harmonic subdivision. The half-cycle must start on the exact same date as the fundamental cycle that began on September 3rd, 2013. The vertical dotted line transmitting up through all the layers to price shows that the 22-period is important. Arrows are on price mark points not to miss as you compare the price action to a 44 and 22-period simple moving-average on price.

A 22-period cycle is the 11-period Sunspot Cycle. Sunspot activity on the Sun correlates with magnetic storms that may project towards Earth. They impact crop yields of agriculture. You should read more on your own about this very important cycle. The first QR-Code on the bottom-left is the link to Wikipedia regarding Sunspots. The second scan on the bottom-right is a more informative discussion how the Sunspot Cycle impacts us on Earth. In my Gann book, *The Thirty-Second Jewel*, I documented hundreds of years in history where major wars track the Sunspot Cycle. Wars are often about resources or the control of them. If the resulting magnetic storms from increasing Sunspot Solar Flares on the Sun impact food availability on Earth, it could explain why there would be a correlation to a war cycle. Where are we at the end of 2021 in this cycle? Solar-flares are at the minimum and starting to rise. How do magnetic storms impact agriculture crop yield as magnetic storms increase? You need to research the answer to this as it is now important.

# THE TOOLS OF RESEARCH

**V**isual inspection to identify market rhythms is like fishing with a wooden spear when we could be fishing with a computer net.

Statistics is the discipline of learning from data. It helps us answer questions like, 'What cycle period is dominant?' with an answer that is a concrete numerical result. The key is knowing what data to collect, analyze, and then interpret so our answers are honest and meaningful. In Figure 2.19 we found that a 158-period cycle might actually be closer to 161-period. But through computer analysis we found it was the 161-period cycle that was the skewed answer. Data can be manipulated to find any answer, but the goal of statistics is to take data and help us make meaningful use of it as a verifiable truth.

Statisticians define data as a collection of observations. But does that not bring us right back to our visual observations of rhythms within market data? What is missing is the *process* of summarizing, organizing, and then interpreting the data. There are different descriptive measures to describe data such as the measures of center tendency and spread which we briefly touched upon. There is also a branch of inferential statistics that allows us to make a conclusion about a population sample so that we can consider a bigger question. A data sample is a subset collection from the population of interest. Let's say the population is Table 1.2 on page 61 of all the world's major Equity Indexes. The weightings within the indexes showed us Banks have the top weighting within the larger population of stock indexes. Data concerning just Banks would be a sub collection data sample within the total population of interest.

Statistics is about the process. Like a journey, to know the right Google road map to follow requires an idea of where we want to go. The process in statistics begins with knowing the question. It is best to have a clear and well-defined starting hypothesis, such as the cycle period-161, and then use a process to  confirm or challenge our assumption.

The process of
data collection
is the most
important step.

Once we have a clear question in mind that we want to answer, the next step is the data collection. If we have data, such as price data, we need to be confident we have reliable data. You may recall the explanation how vendors collect market data for the foreign exchange spot market. Most vendors have unreliable data because the number of contributors is too small. The largest data sample is being collected by Reuters and Bloomberg and it is not being shared with other vendors. Serious research in Forex requires access to one of these vendor's data libraries.

When the question being asked does not have an existing dataset, we have the added steps of designing a way to gather the data we need. That is not something at my level of expertise. Maybe I just rephrase the question to stay within my comfort level and ability. I view designing experiments to collect data an advanced skill.

Once we have the data, we can then analyze it, or better still have the computer do the grunt work for us. But we need to know the appropriate method to apply in each situation and an understanding of how the variables are being tested. The analysis can only be useful if the data we use has been carefully prepared. If the dataset contains an extreme value, like Crude Oil futures falling deep into negative price values in March of 2020, what should we do with that extreme value far from normal market price ranges? Statisticians have ways to help us.

Once we have an answer to our question, we would also like to know the probability of its occurrence. There are ways to test our conclusion to assess its statistical significance.

The first step is the most important step; the data. Sample data comes in different packages that determine which statistical method or process we should use.

Types of data:
1. A population parameter compared to a sample statistic.
2. A comparison between quantitative and qualitative data.
3. A comparison between discrete and continuous data.

In the first data type a population parameter is a measurement pertaining to the population, and a statistic is a measurement of the sample.

Qualitative data can be categorized and defined by a label or name. It does not count or measure anything. Labeled groups such as Generation 'x' traders, intraday traders, months of the year, all imply a group that is non-numerical.

Quantitative data is numerical. We must be counting or measuring something. I am not sure if the third type in my list should be listed as a separate data type, or better viewed as a subset of qualitative data. An example of discrete data would be the amplitude peaks in the spectrogram charts. The graph displayed a countable list of precise amplitude values indicating the various strengths of the cycle periods. Each peak could be rated.

In contrast, continuous data, like time on the x-axis, needs other language to define it such as monthly, weekly, or 2-day intervals. The measurement units clarify what data is being used or sorted in the continuous dataset. The 2-day bar chart is a fractional unit that occurs only in continuous data.

When markets are closed due to a shock event or the data has a gap, what do we do about this missing data? We cannot ignore gaps or compress the x-axis to remove a gap as it would distort the x-axis time series. Statisticians view missing data two ways. Random means the data can develop missing values in no particular sequence like some very thin currency cross-rates. Futures traded in Chicago for the Nikkei is often nothing but random gaps and spikes. The solution here is an easy one; use the actual Nikkei 225 data and not the exchange traded futures traded in off-hours. Data that is missing for a cause and reason can never be dealt with by changing the x-axis to remove the gap. The Dow Jones Industrial average was closed for several months at the start of World War I. Just know the cause why there is a price gap in our historical data.

What is most important is how data samples are collected. There are different methods.

In a population of S&P500 traders containing both men and women, we pick 100 people at random. This is a random sample; we know these traders all trade the S&P500 and any one of them could have won our golden selection ticket. The entire population had the same chance of being selected. We gave no consideration to the fact that a trader was male or female, traded from home or a large professional desk, or whether they were in Dubai or Chicago. Random is hard to do if you think about it. You have to plan in order to be random. As example, all traders are defined by a number. How do you pre-sort all the numbers before the selection process to be equally fair? How can you ensure the spinning drum does not have all the Chicago traders on the top? So random does not mean anything goes.

Let's say in our population of S&P traders listed by a number, we want to pick every trader whose number ends on the number 5. That would be a systematic data sample. We defined a systematic approach to collect the data sample in a certain way.

What if we take the S&P500 population of traders and separate them into two groups of male and female first? Then we take a random sample of 100 traders from each group? The two groups are called a cluster and the data sample is called a cluster sample. The cluster sample can be selected by random or systematic processes.

If we selected the first 100 traders signing into their account, that would be a selection of convenience. It is its own type of data sample.

Errors occur when our sample does not represent the larger population. If you happened by chance to select mostly Robinhood teen-aged traders in large numbers as the sample majority, would they represent the total population of S&P500 traders? I think not. Being a career S&P500 trader, I would say they better not! The inexperienced mob could skew any results being tested. Statisticians call this a sample error. The smaller the data sample, the bigger chance we have it may not represent the larger population. We have to pre-plan and think the process through carefully.

When we examined the spectrogram results showing cycle period to peak height or the period's strength, we were applying descriptive statistics. Visually we displayed a way that helped us consider the source data itself.

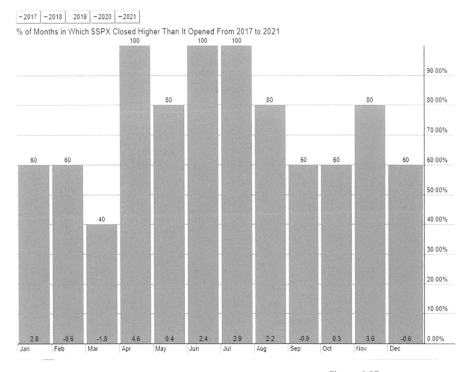

Figure 2.23
S&P500 - % of Months in
which %SPX Closed Higher
than it Opened
from 2017 to 2021.

(StockCharts.com)

A result that had no sharp and narrow peaks would have made us suspect that the data had issues. The results we viewed in Figure 2.20 visually gave us a better idea of how the data cycles were distributed as well. This is all descriptive information that we can use for further analysis.

When we are working with qualitative or categorical data, we often use a bar graph to visually display a table of data. Figure 2.23 is a bar graph. The months of the year are on the x-axis. The y-axis is the % of months in which the S&P500 closed higher than the opening price for that month. Descriptive statistics in action. The months of April, June, and July closed higher than the market opened in all five years of our study. The months of May, August, and November were also strong months for the S&P500. March was the weakest month within this 5-year time frame of our seasonal study.

Figure 2.23 should allow us to ask a new question. Does this pattern of market strength and weakness occur over the past decade?

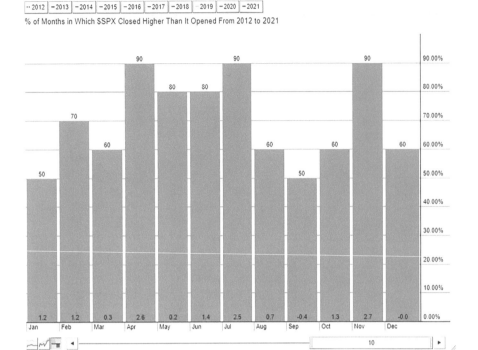

Figure 2.24
S&P500 - % of Months in
which %SPX Closed Higher
than it Opened
from 2012 to 2021.

StockCharts.com)

Figure 2.24 shows the distribution of strong and weak market months over a 10-year period. We see April, July, and November have been the months the S&P500 has closed higher than the price open for the same month. January and February are the weakest months.

Once we expand past a decade the bar graph flattens giving less information. That means we did not frame our question correctly. However, if we repeat the same study in blocks of 10-year units to compare decade to decade, we have a more meaningful study. An analyst well known for his work on seasonal decade comparisons for agricultural markets and stock indexes was W.D. Gann. A modern-day analyst viewed a leader in cycle analysis is Peter Elides. Elides attributed his life-long interest in cycle to Hurst whom we meet in Cycles: Part One.

When we have a qualitative variable like the names of the months, we always put this on the x-axis. The vertical axis is used to plot the scale that includes the full range that is possible. Figures 2.23 and 2.24 need the y-axis to accommodate all possibilities of 0 to 100%. The bar height displays the counts for each month, or category. The bar widths themselves will be equal for each month.

There is a market graph that uses a statistical display to evaluate market

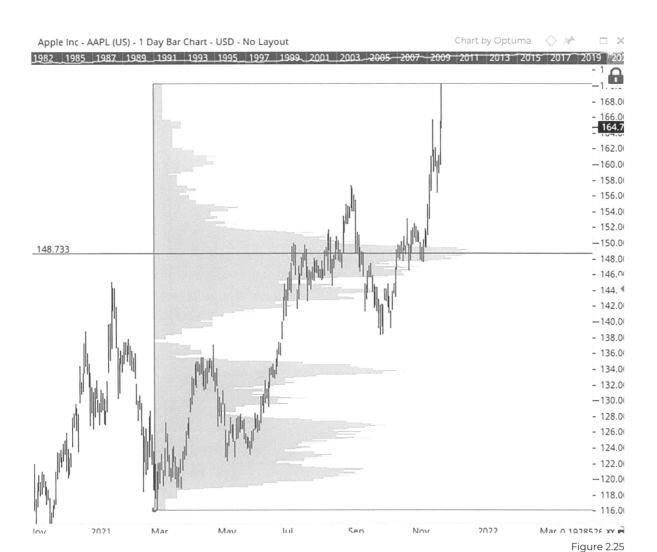

Apple Inc - AAPL (US) - 1 Day Bar Chart - USD - No Layout    Chart by Optuma

Figure 2.25
Apple Inc. (AAPL) - daily
Market Profile graph showing trade activity at a specific price level, over a defined period of
time. (March 3, 2021 to December 1, 2021)

activity. The method was developed in 1985 by floor trader J. Peter Steidylmayer and is called Market Profile. Price is on the y-axis, time on the x-axis. The number of trades accumulate at a specific price level over a fixed time interval. The graph in Figure 2.25 develops a distribution pattern that looks like a bell curve as trade volume activity is tallied for a selected time interval.

The bell-curve clearly shows the greatest trading activity occurred at a price level of 148.73 from March 3, 2021, to December 1, 2021. The 148.73 price is viewed as major price support. Steidylmayer applied statistics to create this distribution curve. He is comparing volume and price as tallied over time. This method is most often used for intraday charts where additional analysis about the distribution can be made every 30-minutes for example.

The Market Profile graph is a type of dot-plot. This type of graph is easy to read because we can see how the dots form stacks as compared to something else, in this case volume versus price. We can read the price where the higher frequency of trading volume takes place. We can easily see where the trading activity is centered and how the market builds a trend. It is just as easy to see where the activity fails and where the trading activity must accumulate to prepare for the next burst.

The bell shape can identify a normal distribution. Is trading taking place in the center of the curve or does the volume indicate the activity is not symmetric and more weighted to the top or bottom of the distribution period? High bottom activity would suggest the market is preparing to breakdown. More weighted to the top may suggest the market can break out of the current trading range.

The meaning of the word skewed is tricky. Imagine a bell-curve on a horizontal axis with the highest distribution on the far left-side of the graph. Does this mean the data is skewed left? No. Statisticians reference skewness based on the longer tail for the bell-curve. If the data is highest on the left, the distribution progressively declines towards the right with a long tail. Statisticians say the curve is skewed right. If the highest distribution of the bell curve is towards the far right, the data is skewed towards the diminishing tail and is skewed left.

There is another kind of graph statisticians often use to visualize data called a scatter plot. The graph is used to represent a relationship between two datasets. For example, a scatter plot is used to show the correlation between two funds, between a stock and an Exchange Traded Fund (ETF) of which it is a component, or between a fund and a benchmark index like the S&P500. In the first chapter we compared several international markets as chart overlays. Let us look at a real application using the weekly prices for the Australia All Ordinaries (XAO) and the French CAC 40 Index (CAC), to test their correlation and to resolve a specific question.

When the scatter plot slope trends upwards from the bottom left towards the upper right corner, the datasets have a positive slope depicting a positive correlation. When the scatter plot moves from upper left corner down towards the lower right corner with a negative slope, the correlation between the datasets is negative. Negative means an inverse correlation. A scatter plot that looks more horizontal with no angled slope is uncorrelated data.

# HOW TO CREATE A SCATTER PLOT DIAGRAM IN MICROSOFT EXCEL

1. In MS Excel cell A2 is the qualitative label such as the month, date, etc. Always check that the two datasets align. Next, use cell B2 for 'Series 1' quantitative numeric data. Cell C2 is the numeric data for 'Series 2.' Data series 1 and 2 will always be numeric values for the datasets to be compared.

2. Now create the chart. Select cells B2 to B14, and C2 through C14 . Drag your mouse or hold down the shift key for long columns. In the top menu tap 'INSERT' in the top menu. In the fourth box are the chart options. Select 'SCATTER' and then click on the style 'SCATTER.' The call-out will state that this chart type is used to compare at least two sets of data values or pairs of data. It will show the relationship between the sets of values.  That's the one we want.

3. After the scatter plot is drawn , click the chart. A '+' symbol appears outside the chart to the top right. Click it. Tap trend on the bottom of 'chart elements.' Then another menu. Click 'linear.' The line will be added to draw the slope. The example below shows that the two datasets have a positive correlation.

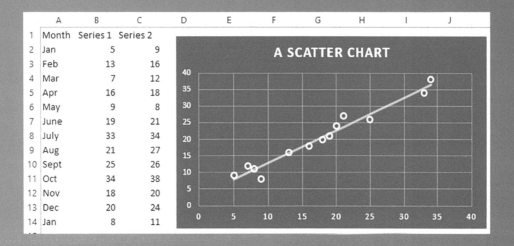

Figure 2.26
Australia All Ordinaries - weekly - line-on-close.

Statisticians need a question to answer before they can know the method and process to apply. I have a real question. At left is the weekly chart for the Australia All Ordinaries (XAO) stock market. See that sharp spike up into the 2000 price high? Well, the market I like to pair with the XAO is the French CAC 40. The French CAC 40 also spiked, but people trading stocks listed on the French exchange created an emotional bubble that significantly pushed their index higher than Australia's. You can jump ahead to Figure 2.29 to visually see what I am referring to here.

My question has to do with this emotional difference between the two mass crowds. How does this spread difference into the 2000 market high impact correlation? Can I study the longer horizon dataset, or should I only use the data that follows after the crash into 2003? Should I continue to compare these two markets in my chart overlay, or should I look for a replacement with a higher correlation over the longer time horizon? All these smaller subset questions evolve from the 2000 market bubble reaction of these two countries. What if I wanted to do a cycle study of the spread? It just raises more questions, and I don't know the answer to the primary question.

First step is to collect the data. I use Optuma Gann edition software.
The red arrow in Figure 2.26 points to the menu selection "Copy Data to Clipboard". The software gives no visual confirmation, but the data is captured, and it is so fast it is done instantly.

Second step is to open a new blank Microsoft Excel spreadsheet. Right click cell A1. The menu options show an upper and lower paste option. Tap the lower symbol for 'Special Paste.' Then do not mess this next step up: tap 'Paste as Unicode Text.' All your transferred data fills eight columns A through H. If you mess up everything is put in column A and the data is separated by a comma. In Microsoft Excel the charting feature needs to see data in separate columns and rows. The data we just pasted will collect for each week the Date, Time, Open, High, Low, Close, Volume, and Open Interest (OI). Even though the chart format is line-on-close, all the data is collected. If you have averages and indicators, that comes over too. So just be sure you have a clean chart.

I then make a mistake. I change the display over to be just the French CAC chart. Then repeat steps 'Copy Data to Clipboard,' 'Special Paste' by tapping cell J1, and in pours the same data for the CAC. The problem I see is that the dates do not align for the two datasets. I start to delete the weeks causing the misalignment. That's when I notice a new properties option circled in red in Figure 2.26. 'Date to Load From.' Back to the XAO and then select 07/08/1988 which is the start of the shorter dataset.

| | A | B | C | D | E | F | G |
|---|---|---|---|---|---|---|---|
| 1 | Australia All Ordinaries | | | French CAC 40 | | | |
| 2 | Date | Close | | Date | Close | | |
| 3 | 7/8/1988 | 1612.6 | | 7/8/1988 | 1368.96 | | |
| 4 | 7/15/1988 | 1623.6 | | 7/15/1988 | 1316.43 | | |
| 5 | 7/22/1988 | 1636.2 | | 7/22/1988 | 1300.54 | | |
| 6 | 7/29/1988 | 1611.7 | | 7/29/1988 | 1320.55 | | |
| 7 | 8/5/1988 | 1641.4 | | 8/5/1988 | 1324.48 | | |
| 8 | 8/12/1988 | 1623.5 | | 8/12/1988 | 1295.32 | | |
| 9 | 8/19/1988 | 1640.6 | | 8/19/1988 | 1310.02 | | |
| 10 | 8/26/1988 | 1595.6 | | 8/26/1988 | 1281.27 | | |
| 11 | 9/2/1988 | 1546.2 | | 9/2/1988 | 1286.12 | | |
| 12 | 9/9/1988 | 1545.5 | | 9/9/1988 | 1301.6 | | |
| 13 | 9/16/1988 | 1559.9 | | 9/16/1988 | 1365.21 | | |
| 14 | 9/23/1988 | 1551.1 | | 9/23/1988 | 1387.59 | | |
| 15 | 9/30/1988 | 1551.6 | | 9/30/1988 | 1418.13 | | |
| 16 | 10/7/1988 | 1525.9 | | 10/7/1988 | 1439.31 | | |
| 17 | 10/14/1988 | 1551.6 | | 10/14/1988 | 1437.36 | | |
| 18 | 10/21/1988 | 1595.3 | | 10/21/1988 | 1457.19 | | |
| 19 | 10/28/1988 | 1581.5 | | 10/28/1988 | 1496.83 | | |
| 20 | 11/4/1988 | 1570.4 | | 11/4/1988 | 1505.24 | | |
| 21 | 11/11/1988 | 1558.2 | | 11/11/1988 | 1492.53 | | |
| 22 | 11/18/1988 | 1493.3 | | 11/18/1988 | 1472.49 | | |
| 23 | 11/25/1988 | 1506 | | 11/25/1988 | 1472.96 | | |
| 24 | 12/2/1988 | 1451 | | 12/2/1988 | 1468.25 | | |
| 25 | 12/9/1988 | 1471 | | 12/9/1988 | 1497.19 | | |
| 26 | 12/16/1988 | 1447.3 | | 12/16/1988 | 1476.63 | | |
| 27 | 12/23/1988 | 1484.1 | | 12/23/1988 | 1539.99 | | |
| 28 | 12/30/1988 | 1487.4 | | 12/30/1988 | 1573.94 | | |
| 29 | 1/6/1989 | 1478.3 | | 1/6/1989 | 1642.99 | | |
| 30 | 1/13/1989 | 1517.9 | | 1/13/1989 | 1643.23 | | |
| 31 | 1/20/1989 | 1517.9 | | 1/20/1989 | 1643.87 | | |
| 32 | 1/27/1989 | 1542.6 | | 1/27/1989 | 1677.32 | | |
| 33 | 2/3/1989 | 1511.7 | | 2/3/1989 | 1693.48 | | |
| 34 | 2/10/1989 | 1509 | | 2/10/1989 | 1690.15 | | |

Sheet1 ⊕

Ready

Left
Figure 2.27
Australia All Ordinaries - weekly closing prices in column B.
French CAC 40 closing prices in column E.

Right
Figure 2.28
Column D was deleted to put the two data columns next to one another. The scatter plot was created showing the correlation of the two markets.

Special paste into cell A1. Repeat for the French CAC 40 and select the same start date to load into Optuma to create the chart. Then copy and special paste into MS Excel. Now my dates all align as they start on the same date and end together on the last date of 12/3/2021 on the same row.

Now about all these columns of extra data I do not need. Delete all unwanted columns by tapping the column letter and delete. Allow the remaining columns to shift left. Figure 2.27 shows you the spreadsheet up to this point. I double check the date alignment and can then delete column D.

Next step is to create the scatter plot. Starting from cell B1, while holding the shift key down, highlight to cell C1746. Go to the top ribbon menu. Select 'Insert' and select the chart option circled in red in Figure 2.28. Then select the first

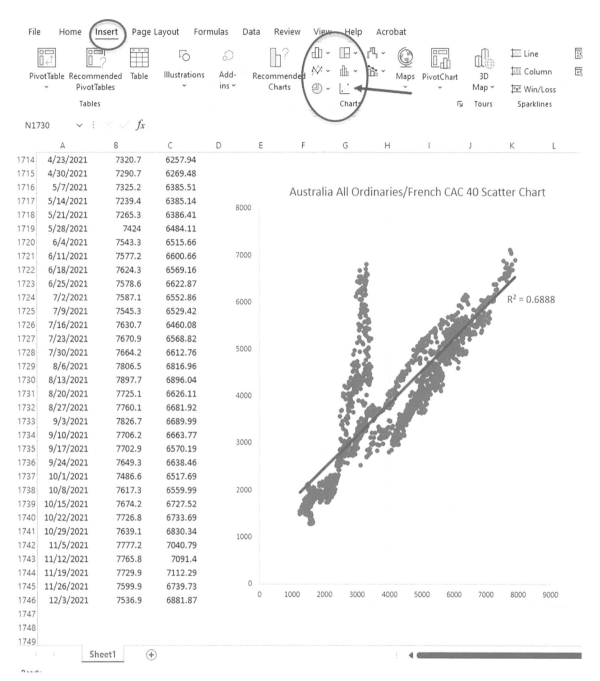

| | A | B | C | D | E | F | G | H | I | J | K | L |
|---|---|---|---|---|---|---|---|---|---|---|---|---|
| 1714 | 4/23/2021 | 7320.7 | 6257.94 | | | | | | | | | |
| 1715 | 4/30/2021 | 7290.7 | 6269.48 | | | | | | | | | |
| 1716 | 5/7/2021 | 7325.2 | 6385.51 | | | | | | | | | |
| 1717 | 5/14/2021 | 7239.4 | 6385.14 | | | | | | | | | |
| 1718 | 5/21/2021 | 7265.3 | 6386.41 | | | | | | | | | |
| 1719 | 5/28/2021 | 7424 | 6484.11 | | | | | | | | | |
| 1720 | 6/4/2021 | 7543.3 | 6515.66 | | | | | | | | | |
| 1721 | 6/11/2021 | 7577.2 | 6600.66 | | | | | | | | | |
| 1722 | 6/18/2021 | 7624.3 | 6569.16 | | | | | | | | | |
| 1723 | 6/25/2021 | 7578.6 | 6622.87 | | | | | | | | | |
| 1724 | 7/2/2021 | 7587.1 | 6552.86 | | | | | | | | | |
| 1725 | 7/9/2021 | 7545.3 | 6529.42 | | | | | | | | | |
| 1726 | 7/16/2021 | 7630.7 | 6460.08 | | | | | | | | | |
| 1727 | 7/23/2021 | 7670.9 | 6568.82 | | | | | | | | | |
| 1728 | 7/30/2021 | 7664.2 | 6612.76 | | | | | | | | | |
| 1729 | 8/6/2021 | 7806.5 | 6816.96 | | | | | | | | | |
| 1730 | 8/13/2021 | 7897.7 | 6896.04 | | | | | | | | | |
| 1731 | 8/20/2021 | 7725.1 | 6626.11 | | | | | | | | | |
| 1732 | 8/27/2021 | 7760.1 | 6681.92 | | | | | | | | | |
| 1733 | 9/3/2021 | 7826.7 | 6689.99 | | | | | | | | | |
| 1734 | 9/10/2021 | 7706.2 | 6663.77 | | | | | | | | | |
| 1735 | 9/17/2021 | 7702.9 | 6570.19 | | | | | | | | | |
| 1736 | 9/24/2021 | 7649.3 | 6638.46 | | | | | | | | | |
| 1737 | 10/1/2021 | 7486.6 | 6517.69 | | | | | | | | | |
| 1738 | 10/8/2021 | 7617.3 | 6559.99 | | | | | | | | | |
| 1739 | 10/15/2021 | 7674.2 | 6727.52 | | | | | | | | | |
| 1740 | 10/22/2021 | 7726.8 | 6733.69 | | | | | | | | | |
| 1741 | 10/29/2021 | 7639.1 | 6830.34 | | | | | | | | | |
| 1742 | 11/5/2021 | 7777.2 | 7040.79 | | | | | | | | | |
| 1743 | 11/12/2021 | 7765.8 | 7091.4 | | | | | | | | | |
| 1744 | 11/19/2021 | 7729.9 | 7112.29 | | | | | | | | | |
| 1745 | 11/26/2021 | 7599.9 | 6739.73 | | | | | | | | | |
| 1746 | 12/3/2021 | 7536.9 | 6881.87 | | | | | | | | | |

option 'Scatter.' Click the spot where you want the chart in the spreadsheet and presto. Done. Tap the chart. The '+' sign appears just outside the chart border top right. That gives you a few options. Click 'Trend' on the bottom. Then 'Linear' to add the line. I also wanted a value added. It is in Figure 2.28 as $R^2$= 0.6888. Just shelve that for now until we discuss it.

The scatter plot in Figure 2.28 looks like a side view of an alien hand turned up with a long thumb sticking straight up. It is that 'thumb' that caused my concern. The scatter plot shows that the slope angle is a positive correlation. But we already knew that from just looking at the two datasets charted as an overlay. How strong is the correlation? The best way to answer this question

Figure 2.29
Australia All Ordinaries - weekly - line-on-close. (Black)
French CAC 40 - weekly - line-on-close. (Red)

is to calculate a correlation coefficient. Microsoft Excel will automatically create the value R-squared.

$R^2$= 0.6888 in Figure 2.28. R-squared is a statistical measure of how close the market data are to the regression line. This number is also called the coefficient of determination. In this example, the result is 68.9 percent on a scale from 0 to 100%. Zero would mean none of the variables can be explained by the comparison market. We will take the time to develop a fuller explanation in the next chapter.

Figure 2.30
Australia All Ordinaries - weekly - line-on-close. (Black)
French CAC 40 - weekly - line-on-close. (Red)
The spread (blue) between the two markets. The original red and black lines opacity in Figure 2.28
was reduced so the blue spread plot is easier to see.

We know the stock markets in Australia and France both rallied into market price highs in 2000. Figure 2.29 shows us that traders and investors in the CAC 40 were far more emotionally involved in the bubble event than in Australia. We know what caused the exuberant rally, the dot.com craze, but correlation is not causation. Correlation is a measure of linear relationship only between two variables and can never reveal cause. In this case we just happen to know the cause even though the scatter plot does not.

My question concerns the stronger move up in the French market relative to the rally in Australia. Does this destroy the correlation of the two markets? The answer is no. Why? Because both markets moved in the same direction together at the same time, though by a different multiple. The French CAC 40 had a higher Beta than the Australian XAO market. The key here is that *the markets were moving in-sync*.

A scatter plot is a graphic portrayal of a correlation. A correlation is just a linear association between two variables. A positive correlation means as one variable increases, the other variable increases. A correlation coefficient can range from -1 to +1. It will tell us the strength and direction of the correlation. A perfect correlation is positive 1.0. It means you can perfectly predict the other variable by knowing one of the variable's score. A negative correlation means as the score in one variable increases, the other decreases. A perfect score is negative 1.0. You will never see perfect scores in real data.

Outliers are the most common reason a correlation coefficient result can throw off. The data we considered into the 2000 market highs is not considered to be outlier data. If we have an isolated price that is just sticking out there on its own, that will impact a false correlation coefficient, but the data in 2000 was mirrored by both markets, though the beta, market reaction, was greater in the French CAC 40.

Another reason the correlation coefficient may not give an accurate representation of the correlation to a population is that the range may be too small or restricted. If I had tested the correlation from only the 2003 market lows, the correlation would have been even higher. But that range would have been misleading by ignoring the question raised about the rally into the 2000 market high.

A third reason the correlation coefficient may mislead is the fact that the two datasets may have a non-linear relationship. The overlay with a visual examination helps us avoid this particular problem.

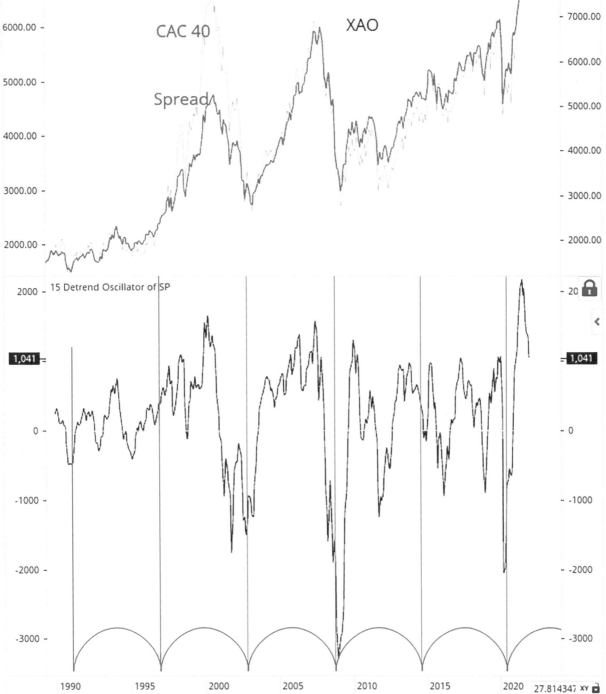

Chart by Optuma

CAC 40

XAO

Spread

15 Detrend Oscillator of SP

27.814347 XY

Figure 2.31

The spread of the monthly Australia All Ordinaries and French CAC 40 has been detrended. (15-period black line lower frame) The detrended spread was then used for cycle analysis. Cycle = 70.66 bars.

# REVIEW

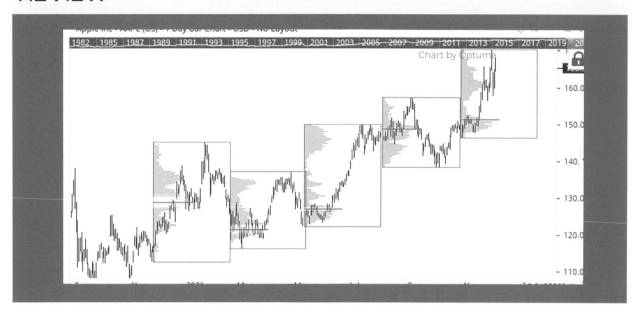

### 1. Market Profile is a chart technique that utilizes statistics. What statistics plotting method is being applied?

Market Profile creates a type of distribution curve. In practice the plotting analysis includes standard deviation within the distribution to help evaluate market activity at key price levels within a time interval.

### 2. A distribution bell-curve plotting a heavy accumulation on the far right-side of the chart is skewed in which direction?

Skewness is a reference to the irregular long tail on the distribution plot. Therefore, in this example, the distribution curve is skewed to the left where the long tail developed from the bell-curve on the far right.

### 3. Can scatter plots identify a cause why markets have a correlation relationship?

Never. Scatter plots can only measure a linear correlation between two datasets. Scatter plots could be used to test the correlation between two markets, a stock within a sector, a fund to a benchmark index, a commodity to an interest rate instrument - any two datasets with a linear relationship.

We apply statistics more frequently than many realize from chart methodology to testing.

### 4. What is detrending and why do we use this methodology?

Detrending allows us to remove trend in price action for further analysis that is easier to evaluate from a differential oscillating above and below a zero line. A detrend oscillator requires a 1-period simple moving-average to connect closing prices, and then a second simple moving-average with a longer period. The spread between the two averages is plotted below the price data. When the slower moving-average has a positive spread to the 1-period moving-average it will plot above zero, negative below zero. Zero is a line where the averages cross above or below one another.

### 5. A correlation coefficient can be read in a range of -1.0 to +1.0. Explain how to interpret these values.

A positive correlation means as one variable increases, the other variable increases. A perfect correlation is positive 1.0. It means you can perfectly predict the other variable by knowing the other variable's score. A negative correlation means as the score in one variable increases, the other decreases. A perfect score is negative 1.0. Perfect scores are only theoretical and actual results will be within the range. We are interested in values higher than 0.5 or less than -0.5

### 6. A summary of introductory terms used by statisticians:

Descriptive statistics is used to organize and summarize data.

Inferential statistics draws conclusions about a population based on information from a sample.

A sample is a subset of a population. A statistic is a number that represents a property of the sample.

Parameter describes a population.
A parameter is a numerical characteristic of the whole population that can be estimated by a statistic.

How accurately a statistic estimates a parameter depends on how well the sample contains the characteristic of a population

Probability is a mathematical tool used to study randomness. It deals with the chance of an event occurring. A common test to determine probability is called chi-square. (Pronounced Ky (like My))

**3**

CORRELATION COEFFICIENTS CAN TELL
US THE STRENGTH AND
DIRECTION OF THE RELATIONSHIP

# CHAPTER THREE

# Correlation

## HOW TO OBJECTIVELY MEASURE MARKET RELATIONSHIPS.

Chapter Two introduced scatterplots using Microsoft Excel so we could objectively answer a question about the correlation between two specific datasets. This would have been useful in Chapter One when we discussed several market comparisons. But for many readers the use of overlays is new and describing a visual comparison offered a good first step. For some readers the charts may have raised additional questions. We will go back to some of those same market comparisons now to create a more objective understanding of how one market moves in relation to another.

I never trade a market without knowing that there is a comparison market or stock to lean on. It increases my probability of being right, it adds a depth that a single market cannot give, and it clarifies what the heck is going on when the patterns are clear in the correlated market, but not in my S&P500! Watching multiple global markets will always warn when a global crash is on the horizon. You will not know what the trigger will be, but you will see all the warnings when the balloons are ready to pop.

Correlation can be seen by visual inspection using an overlay of two markets, but we need something more concrete when we start asking, "Which one is better?", or "How strong is the association between these two markets?" If we had a measurable value, we could then make further comparisons to see if there are better pairings to chart together.

The real question we need answered is how to determine how well the two markets tend to change together. That is tradeable information. By using a correlation coefficient, we will be able to describe both the strength and the direction of the relationship for our two markets. If two markets had a near perfect inverse correlation, we would be happy with that as well.

Microsoft Excel automatically calculated an R-squared value. This explains the variance of one variable relative to the variance of the second. Variance measures the variability. It can only tell us the degree of the spread or how far apart prices are from each other and from the center line of the distribution. Was this automatic offering by Microsoft the best measurement for us to use?  For example, our result in Figure 2.28 was 0.6888. This means approximately 69% of the observed variation can be explained by the variance in the other market. Is a high number good? R-squared seems to be of great debate within the statistician community. High is not necessarily good and low is not necessarily bad. I am not a statistician and need values that are easy to interpret. I want a high number to mean the right market comparisons have been paired together in my chart. Simple. There is one type of correlation coefficient statisticians all agree upon that we should use for linear relationships like our market comparisons. It is called the Pearson coefficient.

Two markets are viewed to have a linear relationship when a change in one market is associated with a proportional change in the other.  Notice the word proportional. This might become a problem again for Figure 2.28 because the French CAC 40 moved significantly higher relative to the Australian market into the 2000 market highs. The Pearson correlation coefficient will untangle this problem for us. The Pearson coefficient is a true measure we can use to show how well one market will increase or decline by a similar amount relative another market.

When the value is near zero the relationship is non-existent or random. We mentioned before that a +1 is a perfect positive relationship and -1 is a perfect inverse relationship.  We will never see a perfect correlation, but we are not looking for perfection, our goal is to quantify less than perfect relationships as that's our real-world environment. Generally, ignore or pass on results when r= -0.5 to +0.5.

The Pearson correlation coefficient will take the mean rather than a variance

| | A | B | C |
|---|---|---|---|
| 1 | Australia All Ord | | French CAC 40 |
| 2 | | r= | 0.8299 |
| 3 | Date | Close | Close |
| 4 | 7/8/1988 | 1612.6 | 1368.96 |
| 5 | 7/15/1988 | 1623.6 | 1316.43 |
| 6 | 7/22/1988 | 1636.2 | 1300.54 |
| 7 | 7/29/1988 | 1611.7 | 1320.55 |
| 8 | 8/5/1988 | 1641.4 | 1324.48 |
| 9 | 8/12/1988 | 1623.5 | 1295.32 |
| 10 | 8/19/1988 | 1640.6 | 1310.02 |
| 11 | 8/26/1988 | 1595.6 | 1281.27 |
| 12 | 9/2/1988 | 1546.2 | 1286.12 |
| 13 | 9/9/1988 | 1545.5 | 1301.6 |
| 14 | 9/16/1988 | 1559.9 | 1365.21 |
| 15 | 9/23/1988 | 1551.1 | 1387.59 |
| 16 | 9/30/1988 | 1551.6 | 1418.13 |
| 17 | 10/7/1988 | 1525.9 | 1439.31 |
| 18 | 10/14/1988 | 1551.6 | 1437.36 |
| 19 | 10/21/1988 | 1595.3 | 1457.19 |
| 20 | 10/28/1988 | 1581.5 | 1496.83 |
| 21 | 11/4/1988 | 1570.4 | 1505.24 |
| 22 | 11/11/1988 | 1558.2 | 1492.53 |
| 23 | 11/18/1988 | 1493.3 | 1472.49 |
| 24 | 11/25/1988 | 1506 | 1472.96 |
| 25 | 12/2/1988 | 1451 | 1468.25 |
| 26 | 12/9/1988 | 1471 | 1497.19 |
| 27 | 12/16/1988 | 1447.3 | 1476.63 |
| 28 | 12/23/1988 | 1484.1 | 1539.99 |
| 29 | 12/30/1988 | 1487.4 | 1573.94 |
| 30 | 1/6/1989 | 1478.3 | 1642.99 |

Shee ... (+)

Figure 3.1
Cell C2 shows the result
for the Microsoft Excel Pearson correlation
function used to
measure correlation between
the weekly Australia All
Ordinaries and French CAC 40.
(July 1988 to December 2021)

to create the value we seek. The Pearson correlation formula is: correlation(r)= ((the mean for the first variable) - (the standard deviation for the first variable)) * ((the mean for the second variable) - (the standard deviation for the second variable.)) This result is then divided by (the number of data rows minus 1) * the standard deviation for the first variable * the standard deviation for the second variable. Standard deviation is the average distance from the mean that is used to measure the spread from a normal distribution. What is a normal distribution? Remember the bell curve? Where all the data wants to cluster under the bell in the middle of the graph is the norm.

The only thing we have to be extremely careful about is to ensure all the dates align within the two columns. Easy to make an error here. Also be sure none of the prices are missing in either market.

In Microsoft Excel use the Pearson function. In the cell where you want the result, type =PEARSON(B4:B1747,C4:C1747) The B4 is the cell where my Australian All Ordinaries closing prices begin on 07/08/1988. The B1747 cell is my last closing price on December 3, 2021. Cell C4 to C1747 is the corresponding set of closing prices for the French CAC 40.

At the top of the Microsoft Excel menu is 'Help'. Tap that and search 'PEARSON correlation' if you need more information. The top part is on the next page in Figure 3.2.

Now the result. r= 0.8299 If 1.0 is a perfect positive correlation, then comparing the Australia All Ordinaries to the French CAC 40 is a great pairing we will keep.

Figure 3.3 is comparing markets from Chapter One charts in Figure 1.17 and Figure 1.29. The first comparison is the CADJPY (Canadian

# Help

← ⌂  🔍 pearson correlation

## PEARSON function

This article describes the formula syntax and usage of the **PEARSON** function in Microsoft Excel.

### Description

Returns the Pearson product moment correlation coefficient, r, a dimensionless index that ranges from -1.0 to 1.0 inclusive and reflects the extent of a linear relationship between two data sets.

### Syntax

PEARSON(array1, array2)

The PEARSON function syntax has the following arguments:

- **Array1**  Required. A set of independent values.

- **Array2**  Required. A set of dependent values.

### Remarks

- The arguments must be either numbers or names, array constants, or references that contain numbers.

- If an array or reference argument contains text, logical values, or empty cells, those values are ignored; however, cells with the value zero are included.

- If array1 and array2 are empty or have a different number of data points, PEARSON returns the #N/A error value.

- The formula for the Pearson product moment correlation coefficient, r, is:

$$r = \frac{\sum (x - \bar{x})(y - \bar{y})}{\sqrt{\sum (x - \bar{x})^2 \sum (y - \bar{y})^2}}$$

  where x and y are the sample means AVERAGE(array1) and AVERAGE(array2).

Figure 3.2 - Use Microsoft's Excel Help to search "PEARSON correlation". That will give you more information if needed.

Dollar/Japanese Yen) with Crude Oil futures from January 7, 2000, to December 3, 2021. Results from -0.5 to +0.5 are poor results. The result r= 0.4821 falls in this range. But do not ignore these two markets! Why? The study does not know they are not used by a trader every single week. We use this market pairing at critical pivot levels ONLY when other indicators such as oscillators are telling us something major could be on the horizon. For this reason, technical analysis requires thought and is not a black box in my opinion.

Figure 3.3 -
Pearson Correlation study

$f_x$  =PEARSON(K5:K524,L5:L524)

| F | G | H | I | J | K | L | M |
|---|---|---|---|---|---|---|---|
|  | CADJPY | Crude Oil |  |  | SPX | S&P/ASX 200 |  |
|  |  |  |  |  |  |  |  |
| w/April 24, 2020 | **r= 0.4821** |  |  | to 12/17/2021 | **r=** | **0.9257** |  |
|  |  |  |  |  |  |  |  |
| Date | Close | Close |  | Date | Close | Close |  |
| 1/7/2000 | 72.31 | 24.22 |  | 1/6/2012 | 1277.81 | 4108.5 |  |
| 1/14/2000 | 73.04 | 28.02 |  | 1/13/2012 | 1289.09 | 4195.9 |  |
| 1/21/2000 | 72.74 | 28.2 |  | 1/20/2012 | 1315.38 | 4239.6 |  |
| 1/28/2000 | 74.02 | 27.22 |  | 1/27/2012 | 1316.33 | 4288.4 |  |
| 2/4/2000 | 74.43 | 28.82 |  | 2/3/2012 | 1344.9 | 4251.2 |  |
| 2/11/2000 | 75.09 | 29.44 |  | 2/10/2012 | 1342.64 | 4245.3 |  |
| 2/18/2000 | 76.54 | 28.45 |  | 2/17/2012 | 1361.23 | 4195.9 |  |
| 2/25/2000 | 76.15 | 30.35 |  | 2/24/2012 | 1365.74 | 4306.8 |  |
| 3/3/2000 | 74.27 | 31.51 |  | 3/2/2012 | 1369.63 | 4273.1 |  |
| 3/10/2000 | 72.86 | 31.76 |  | 3/9/2012 | 1370.87 | 4212 |  |
| 3/17/2000 | 72.55 | 30.91 |  | 3/16/2012 | 1404.17 | 4276.2 |  |
| 3/24/2000 | 73.21 | 28.02 |  | 3/23/2012 | 1397.11 | 4270.4 |  |
| 3/31/2000 | 70.89 | 26.9 |  | 3/30/2012 | 1408.47 | 4335.2 |  |
| 4/7/2000 | 72.35 | 25.04 |  | 4/6/2012 | 1398.08 | 4319.6 |  |
| 4/14/2000 | 70.94 | 25.57 |  | 4/13/2012 | 1370.26 | 4322.9 |  |
| 4/21/2000 | 71.71 | 25.88 |  | 4/20/2012 | 1378.53 | 4366.5 |  |
| 4/28/2000 | 73.07 | 25.74 |  | 4/27/2012 | 1403.36 | 4362.1 |  |
| 5/5/2000 | 72.74 | 27.29 |  | 5/4/2012 | 1369.1 | 4396 |  |
| 5/12/2000 | 72.94 | 29.62 |  | 5/11/2012 | 1353.39 | 4285.1 |  |
| 5/19/2000 | 71.45 | 29.89 |  | 5/18/2012 | 1295.22 | 4046.5 |  |
| 5/26/2000 | 71.27 | 30 |  | 5/25/2012 | 1317.82 | 4029.2 |  |
| 6/2/2000 | 73.06 | 30.35 |  | 6/1/2012 | 1278.04 | 4063.9 |  |
| 6/9/2000 | 72.49 | 30.2 |  | 6/8/2012 | 1325.66 | 4063.7 |  |
| 6/16/2000 | 72.55 | 32.33 |  | 6/15/2012 | 1342.84 | 4057.3 |  |
| 6/23/2000 | 70.53 | 32.25 |  | 6/22/2012 | 1335.02 | 4048.2 |  |
| 6/30/2000 | 71.64 | 32.5 |  | 6/29/2012 | 1362.16 | 4094.6 |  |
| 7/7/2000 | 72.88 | 30.28 |  | 7/6/2012 | 1354.68 | 4157.8 |  |
| 7/14/2000 | 72.69 | 31.4 |  | 7/13/2012 | 1356.78 | 4082.2 |  |

Figure 3.3 in columns K and L show the weekly closing prices for the S&P500 and the Australian S&P/ASX 200 from January 6, 2012, to December 17, 2021. The result shows r= 0.9257. Yikes, near perfection. But not so fast! I did write that one of the ways you can get a false result is by having too little data. There are less than 600 data points in this weekly series. Results like this should flag you there is something off and you need to think about your process carefully. The result is squirrelly because I picked a swing from 2012 into current prices that is nearly a perfect overlay in the chart. I deliberately selected this range to give you a misleading result. If an investor did not know better, you could be sold a false result in a prospectus document as a reason to diversify. That is not how we are using this information.

Let's go back to the first comparison in Figure 3.3 of CADJPY (Canadian Dollar/Japanese Yen) with Crude Oil futures from January 7, 2000, to December 3, 2021. Crude Oil futures the week of April 24, 2020, made the historic free-fall towards -$40 dollars. What do we do with an anomaly like that negative data value? The answer is given by a close examination of the closing price for this week. The close was $16.94. The weeks prior to and after April 24, 2020 are $18.27 and $19.78 respectively. The $16.94 closing price is not an outlier value within the closing prices. The correlation study never sees the historic extreme low. We do not have to delete that particular week from both series, or make a manual adjustment such as delete then duplicate the prior data point to smooth the series.

I also encountered another situation you may experience. I made the same study for the Saudi TASI market with Crude Oil futures. I used the same time range from January 7, 2000, to December 3, 2021 as tested with CADJPY. However, setting up the data was a pain. The Saudi TASI data will not align with Crude Oil trading weeks and will step out of sync. You must delete the Crude Oil weeks the TASI market does not trade due to religious holidays. As there were so many weeks within the range of a dataset, I knew I needed a longer look-back time interval. My data only starts in 2000 for TASI. The test for a weekly dataset was abandoned. I could have used daily data, but the manual date alignment issue would be time consuming. A test between the Toronto TSX and Crude Oil would solve the data issue and answer the same questions.

I think you have what you need to make a correlation study using two markets of your own choosing. Just don't blindly accept the result you obtain. It does require consideration how you use the chart and further consideration how the result can be interpreted.

**4**

CROWDS ARE PREDICTABLE &
FORM REPEATABLE PATTERNS

CHAPTER FOUR

# Market Patterns

"THE CROWD IS ALWAYS DOMINATED BY CONSIDERATIONS OF WHICH IT IS UNCONSCIOUS. A CROWD IS AS EASILY HEROIC AS CRIMINAL FOR ITS LOWERING OF INDIVIDUAL INTELLIGENCE"

Gustave Le Bon, (1841 - 1931)
*The Crowd; A Study of the Popular Mind.* (1896),
Pantianos Classics

The mental unity of a crowd is a unique force.

A crowd will strip you of your individual identity. It will not matter if you were raised to follow a certain religion, what your family heredity may be, or if you were born to a high or low social class. It will not matter if you were educated at Oxford University or a community school, and it will have no regard if you have a strong political identity or not. As part of the crowd, you will be willing to drop all these personal traits in order to become part of the assembly that forms a singular minded mass crowd.

Traders will understand this better than anyone, more so than an analyst crunching quantitative data, that market dynamics are driven by crowd psychology. It is the trader at home watching their monitor who understands that what is unfolding from day to day is the push and pull forces of the crowd. Do not get in the way when the stampede starts to run. Traders need to understand crowd dynamics if only for the purpose of their own self-preservation.

Let me frame for you how we will explore this subject together. First, a demonstration by a trader on the battlefield. Second, a more in-depth discussion about crowds and types of crowds. Then another demonstration in very short-horizon price action to show how crowd dynamics apply as a fractal pattern in all time horizons. We will repeat this sequence as needed.

Traditional discussions in technical analysis books will segregate patterns into categories that do not explain the sentiment that creates these patterns. For example, we can give you a description of continuation and directional signals, but they do not explain how a trader would read them. We also tend to isolate trading signals from market psychology. As a trader with more than 30-years' experience, I know it is not about a collection of isolated pattern labels. Trading is about understanding the ebb and flow from the tide of crowds. Ask yourself continuously, "Why is the crowd doing this or that?" "What mathematical relationship are these movements derived from and how can those connections forecast the next move the crowd makes?" Yes, each market swing has a mathematical relationship between the past pivots and future pivots. We will look at this in a later chapter. Ask yourself, "Why do similar price patterns form at critical market points and what do they mean?" "Why do crowds clearly develop repeatable patterns in fractal time horizons?" Patterns of human fear and greed never change. Individuals may change; but crowds do not. I talk to my monitor to ask, 'What are you people doing next?' Stranger yet, you will be able to use technical analysis to forecast the behavior of the crowd before they even know their next move.

How can this be? Technical analysis is about building an arsenal of tools and methods to help us read the actions of the crowd. In the hands of an experienced trader the way technical analysis is applied is very different than the way analysts and researchers use the same methods and formulas. We must all do our homework to know our place in the bigger picture. But then the front-line, battle-hardened traders takeover.

The funds and big players cannot move very quickly. They must trade the big picture. They also have very deep pockets and hunker-down when things get ugly with the expectation that things over time will be better and will prove them to be right. With massive resources they can afford to sustain deep drawdowns of unrealized losses. That is up to a certain point. Then they want out of the burning barn all at the same time. This is especially true near pay-day, which is the end of each calendar quarter. A massive price spike down exhausts the selling pressure and a market reversal forms what we call capitulation. The bar marked 'C' in Figure 4.1 is capitulation. The market moves back up towards 4454 marked 'D'.

Why is there such a strong move up from 'C'? The traders who are short

Figure 4.1
December 2021 S&P500
Mini Futures Contract -
(ESZ21) - daily

In the middle frame is
the Composite Index by
Connie Brown. The lower
frame is George Lane's
Slow Stochastics.

Chart by TradeStation

are in trouble and see their profits decline or losses increase with every tick higher. The move up is a short-squeeze. It is a panic move. The traders who sold the S&P500 late are being forced out and must buy to cover their short positions. But then, just as price briefly penetrates above resistance at 4454 (D), the market free-falls to new lows at 'X'. This is often the case following a capitulation price bar. The top at 'D' has no new buyers stepping up to the plate. We do not need a volume indicator to know that the buyers have hidden under a rock to just watch what happens next. For the rally to be successful, new buyers would have to step in as the market exceeded resistance at 4454. They do not.

The price bar at 'D' is recognized as a failure and the bearish crowd knows

it. The price bar at 'D' is called a key reversal directional signal. But it is not confirmed until the next bar that fails just *under* 4454. That is all we need to realize that this pattern failure means weakness and the wolf-pack is all over it to sell aggressively. Why? We know the market cannot return above this line drawn at 4454 in a rally that becomes a *bull trap*. Therefore, sellers want in as close as possible under the line so we can place stops just on the other side of 4454 with minimal risk. The farther the market falls below 4454, the greater the risk to the short-seller as the stop placement cannot move down as rapidly.

Without knowing the critical levels, you are just winging it as a trader. We will address this later because as much attention should be given to where the market is going as to where it should not be trading.

In Figure 4.1 the market falls towards 4250 and develops four bars retracing the same range above 'X'. This is the sign that the selling pressure in the crowd is exhausted. The rally then resumes and runs to the new price highs at the top of the chart. There are several ways for us to know this is a market top, but we need to focus next on the decline towards the lows marked '1'.

The price action at '1' in the red circle shows you how the bearish crowd does its darnedest to push the S&P500 futures down through a horizontal support line at 4498.47. The line is in the middle of a narrow band of Fibonacci retracement that creates a confluence zone of support. We will discuss how these support levels are created in Chapter 5. The support levels were calculated nine days earlier before the market decline began. We can calculate the critical levels of support that a crowd of market participants will use as a cliff.

Three times they try to break the 4498 area. The horizontal Fibonacci target zone intersects with a green moving-average I added to the price action. The averages in all my charts will be simple moving-averages with periods of 13, 33, and 88. The green average is the slowest so it will be the 88-period moving-average. Why use these particular periods for moving-averages?

When the moving-average bisects a horizontal Fibonacci confluence zone of support or resistance, I have two different methods which confirm one another. The average is a short-cut to a method W.D. Gann developed called the Square of Nine. We will not go into that method here, but these three averages save much time, and you see the application in Figure 4.1. It tells me the middle support zone at 4498 is more important than the other two levels in the chart at 4542 and 4454. Now we see the battle unfolding near 4498 and the sellers are losing.

If 4498 were broken, the next support zone at 4454 is where the market would fall, but the back-and-fill price action in circle '1' shows the selling pressure is exhausted again. Heaven help the sleeping trader sitting on a huge short position, but the market rarely gives just one warning. In Figure 4.1 the bottom oscillator is George Lane's Slow Stochastics. We will study oscillators in detail in the next chapter, but you have a general idea now how to read a detrend oscillator, it is the same concept for most oscillators.

The stochastic oscillator in the daily chart creates a trough at point '2'. But what you will not find in technical analysis books is the green arrow pointing from '2' to the oscillator trough on the same horizontal level
made in early October of 2021. Not only are these oscillator troughs on the same horizontal level, but the price action above the 'Oct' x-axis label creates the same back-n-fill price pattern action that is followed by a strong rally. Same pattern on a different day in the current market at '1'. Cover all short positions ASAP before the crowd runs you over! They are getting ready for a repeat performance.

Figure 4.2 is a 120-minute view of what happens in the December 2021 S&P500 futures. The two swings into the chart's price lows create a double bottom pattern. This is a directional signal. A directional signal means you must take immediate action. Smart traders have a method to help them. The 120-minute bar chart has a pivot price high labeled '3'. The pivot connects to an extending blue line. The trick is to know the correct angle at which to draw this line. It is a trend line, but not a conventional trend line. The analyst will start the blue line from the top price or second pivot nearer to 4720. A line drawn by an analyst will be drawn with the purpose of connecting the sequence of lower price highs within the decline. Convention says it takes three tests of the line to confirm a trend. That's academic theory. Convention will not help a trader one bit. This is the wrong angle to use.

The trader will read the price action and start much lower at pivot '3'. Why? The line truncates the thin narrow spikes up that we call key reversal patterns. We need to look at how this trend line was drawn in clearer detail.

Figure 4.3 captures the same 120-minute chart as in Figure 4.2. The bars have more space added between each, so they are easier to examine. Now listen up traders. Thirty years of trading experience will make you change your ways. Start the trend line from the strong bar in the first black circle. Figure 4.2 starts from the pivot price highs, but mass crowds leave breadcrumbs on the road that create a string of mathematical milestones. It means we can calculate what happens next as the crowd develops swings from these markers. No, I know, you have not read about this before, so we will go slowly, and I know it is hard to change old ways.

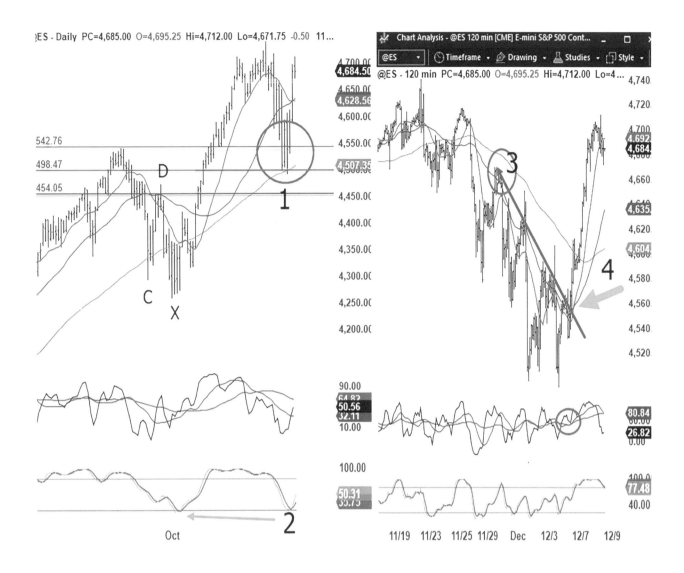

Figure 4.2
December 2021 S&P500 Mini Futures Contract - (ESZ21) - Daily Left, with Fibonacci
confluence support zones.
December 2021 S&P500 Mini Futures Contract - (ESZ21) - 120-minute Right

In the right-hand middle frame is the Composite Index by Connie Brown. The lower
frame is George Lane's Slow Stochastics.

Chart by TradeStation

**Strong bars and gaps are the most important internal formations the crowd leaves behind.** In Figure 4.3 the trend line starts from the top of the strong bar that starts a strong move down within the first black circle. Then extend the line so it just touches the bar marked by the first black arrow pointing down. This is a serious failure. Extend the line using this angle to see that the red trend line truncates two bars in a blue circle. The blue circle is a key reversal pattern we called a directional signal. As traders, we want to truncate the key reversal because everybody lost money in it. The buyers were overrun and forced out, the weak sellers panicked and covered their short positions when the market passed through the red line. You do not want to use price action where everyone lost money.

Then extend the line further. Notice the second black arrow where the market begins to create a series of four price bars that fail just under the red line. In the third circle buyers try to run the market through the trend line, but they fail, causing another key reversal directional pattern under the green 88-period simple moving-average. It is an early warning that the buyers are out there, but they were too early. Market prices drop to a new low. Now this is important. In the last swing down no price bar closes below the close of the lowest price bar in the decline between the blue and black circles. The sellers failed because all they can do is retest the prior low to the left causing a double bottom. What is essential is to see that the market then passes up through the red trend line, pulls back, pushes through a second time, then *tests the top of the red trend line* at the black arrow pointing up. In Figure 4.2 this position is marked with a green arrow and the number '4'. Buy it. Stop placement? Just below the red moving-average for low risk. Let the short squeeze begin!

There are numerous signals in the averages. We will go into detail in the next chapter but do observe the spread of the averages. Study if the spread is positive where a shorter-period average is tracking higher than a longer period average. Notice if the oscillator in the frame under price is using the averages as support.

Progress! You are beginning to read the behavior of a crowd in the price action and not thinking like an analyst. Analysts are historians. What I mean by that is that analysts discuss and focus on what was. Traders focus on what will be, andask of every indicator how it can help us right now. So many professionals I have taught will point out divergences maybe months ago and how the market reacted long ago. Can that tell you something about what will happen tomorrow? If not, I am not interested. Everything we use is a probability to determine what is to come.

Figure 4.3
S&P500 Mini Futures
Contract - (ESH22) -
120-minute

The frame under price
is the Composite Index
by Connie Brown. The
third frame is a 7-period
detrend oscillator. The
bottom, or fourth frame,
is George Lane's Slow
Stochastics.

The formula for the
Composite Index you can
download from a QR-Code
in Chapter 4 - Oscillators.

Chart by TradeStation

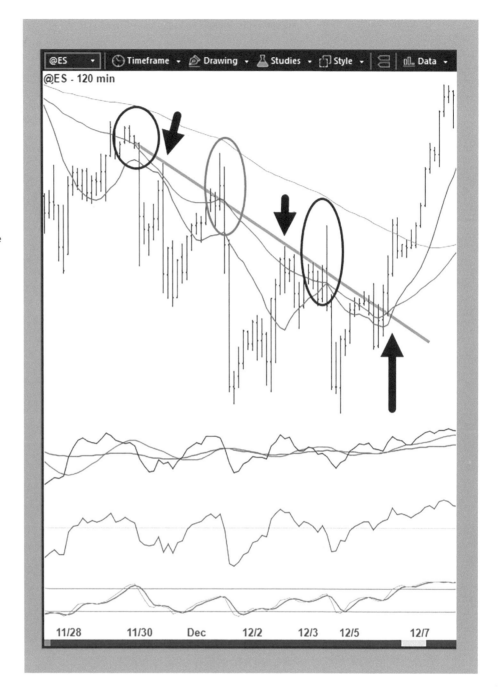

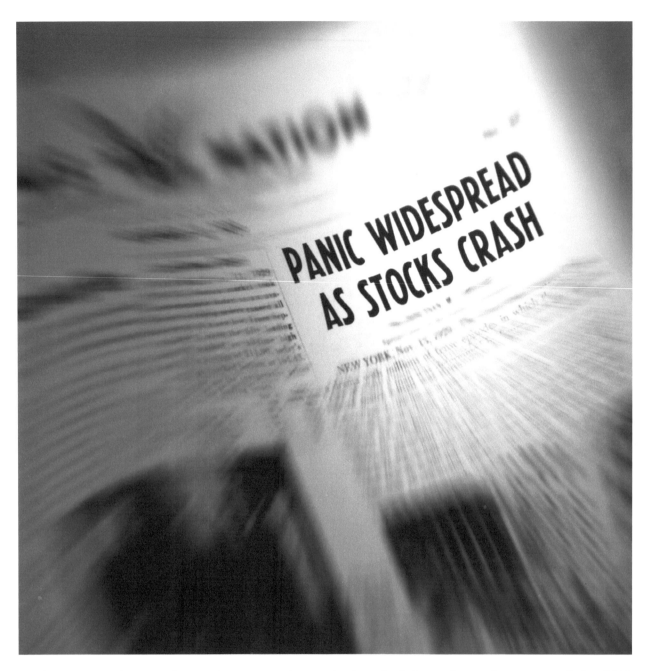

Nothing upsets the crowd more than uncertainty. The Covid-19 crash was a panic to stock food and toilet paper. The smart money ran as fast as they could into 4-week T-Bills. Treasurydirect. gov is the safest 'money under your mattress' location. Safer than a bank as T-Bills are backed by the U.S. Government's ability to tax its citizens. Banks are only as safe as the firm or person they loaned *your* money to. FDIC insurance? Forget it, they don't have the cash to cover all the FDIC insurance offered. In 2008 FDIC was raised to cover deposits up to $250,000 in American banks. It was to halt a run-on banks maybe hours away. It might as well be $1 million, but consumer confidence reversed on $250,000. That's a shell game with consumer sentiment.

Gustave Le Bon studied the character of crowds in a most interesting period in history. His studies of 1896 were on the cusp of the Industrial Revolution, a time when the old was being destroyed to make room for the new. Whether the new was a good or bad thing is still debated today. But without question his work called *The Crowd* has many interesting observations.

Le Bon states it is difficult to describe the mind of crowds with exactness, because it varies according to "the nature and intensity of the exciting causes to which crowds are subjected." But he makes an interesting observation that the point at which a gathering becomes a crowd is when it becomes an organized single mindedness entity. That is the point at which the individual is stripped of his or her unique identity and is transformed into the unconscious mind of the crowd. Their individual IQ drops, their ability to apply sound logic and reason is greatly diminished, and their ability to take action against the will of a crowd is near impossible.

The greatest single fear for a crowd is the fear of being left out. In extreme cases the crowd creates a bubble forcing prices upwards to heights without any aversion to risk. There are several examples in history which you should research and be aware of.

1. (1637) The Tulip Bulb Fever - The perfect study for what happens when a perceived new investment class goes very wrong.

2. (1720) The South Sea Bubble - The South Sea Company shareholders assumed that a U.K. Government loan paid an annuity, but it was a sham. One of the investors caught in this collapse was Sir Isaac Newton.

3. (1720) France's Mississippi Company Bubble - Perhaps America's first run on a bank. The problem in a word; speculation.

4. In the 1800s England had nine panics. They are documented in the writings of a German economist living in England and an American in the U.S.A. who together showed us the tight connections between markets in various countries even then. See Chapter One, *The Thirty-Second Jewel.* (Brown.)

5. The Crash of 1929. The best book to read is *The Day the Bubble Burst,* by Gordon Thomas and Max Morgan-Witts. This is a serious page turner, and you will not be able to put it down. It is a social history and relates the stories of the key players during the Crash. It is a free audio book on Amazon.

Figure 4.4
Pinduoduo Inc. (PDD) - weekly

Chart by TradeStation

We do not need to examine a price chart to understand what followed when the Tulip Bulb mania of 1637 burst the crowd's exuberance. We can find the same outcome in every chart that has a bubble burst. The market spikes up in a parabolic manner, then when a bubble bursts, the crowd panics pushing prices down to the origin where the market began to move up.

Pinduoduo Inc. is a Shanghai corporation that operates an e-commerce platform in the People's Republic of China. They sell products that would have been a consumer magnet as the Covid Pandemic restrictions and lockdowns developed: food and beverage, childcare products, personal care items, sports and fitness goods. All desirable products you would want to order online and have delivered directly to your home.

As the lockdowns became more firm and urgent, so too did the crowd's conviction that Pinduoduo stock would advance and they piled int. The shares ran up from levels below $40 to more than $200. Then the composition of the unconscious crowd began to change. Crowds do not feel pain. But individuals do feel pain and the more individual shareholders felt the pain of their mounting losses, the more people would shift their consciousness to self-preservation and a run for the exit door. Then China began to cram-down on stocks they deemed out of control, but this came well after the bubble burst. This new uncertainty made the crowd further destabilize. Market bubbles always look the same and this chart is still working towards $40 where the rally began.

Now this is where it gets interesting. I mentioned earlier that crowds leave a footprint that creates a measurable mathematical grid within the market data.

The first marker of importance to recognize is the presence of a strong, long price bar. The second important formation is a gap. Now we have different kinds of gaps. Gaps in the middle of a move are called running gaps. When they are near the start of a move, they are called break-away gaps. A gap that is near the end of a long price swing is an exhaustion gap. For this exercise, we do not care what kind of gap it may be, only that a gap can be seen in the chart. In Figure 4.4 the first black arrow is pointing up to the start of the longest bar in the entire chart. The second black arrow is pointing down to the price bar that fails at a small gap just to its left. I drew a line connecting these two important chart points.

Now we are going to go step-by-step through several charts to examine how this angle created in Figure 4.4 will occur several times throughout the entire chart defining a grid pattern of support and resistance.

Figure 4.5
Pinduoduo Inc. (PDD) - weekly

Chart by TradeStation

Figure 4.5 has a second line that is a gold color. It is a copy from the first red line. It is parallel so both have the same angle. That is the important part of this exercise. Always retain the exact same angle.

The two black arrows in Figure 4.5 point down to the top of two strong bars. One is within the rally and the other is the top where a serious failure occurs under the yellow line near 140 within the stock's decline.

Look very carefully and you will find after the large decline from the top that this same line is used as support before a bounce towards 160 develops. You will have to hunt this one out in the chart, so you begin to search for these subtle internal hidden readings. If you cannot find it now, just focus on the two black arrows as these demonstrate how the same angle is being utilized by this stock.

Next, we want to repeat these steps by copying the yellow line to anchor it to two new points within the price action. Figure 4.6 shows two black arrows pointing to the price bar highs where a new parallel line is drawn. Now look at the data of the higher yellow line. The black arrows show the line became resistance. But several bars above the line had price lows at the line using it as support. This stock is utilizing the same angle in the composition of its movements up or down.

We will repeat these steps once again.

Figure 4.6
Pinduoduo Inc. (PDD) - weekly

Chart by TradeStation

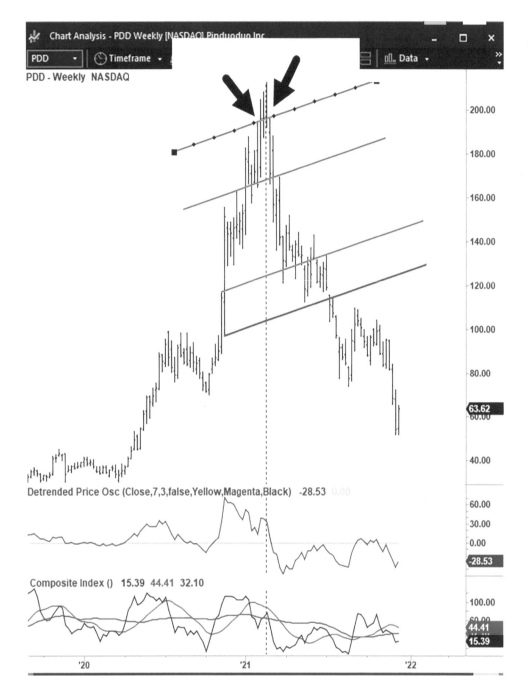

Figure 4.7
Pinduoduo Inc. (PDD) -
weekly

Chart by TradeStation

Figure 4.7 shows two black arrows pointing down to the tops of two price bars near the price high in the chart. Again, we found two critical bars related to price highs of the bars failing under this repeating angle.

Now what you did not know is that the true order in which the lines were drawn was the reverse of what we just discussed. The first line I drew was the top line in Figure 4.7. The larger decline had not begun.

As I know the angle to use, *I only need a single point from which to project the line*. I just had to know what bar in the rally to use as the anchor for each line within the rally. All the angles are projected from strong bar tops, or the low from the longest bar. Had there been a gap within the rally, I would have projected this same angle from both the bar high into the gap, and the price low after the gap. It defines a narrow channel.

As a trader I do not use conventional trendlines as they give infrequent trade signals. But internal angles are invaluable. Now one last chart. The black arrow in Figure 4.8 is the price pivot used to project this last parallel line. The green and red arrows show you the market reaction and its respect to the same angle a year later.

Extra bonus if you can see the very small gap near the chart bottom under this lowest red line. It confirms that the angle first drawn near the market top was the correct angle to use.

Figure 4.8
Pinduoduo Inc. (PDD) -
weekly

Chart by TradeStation

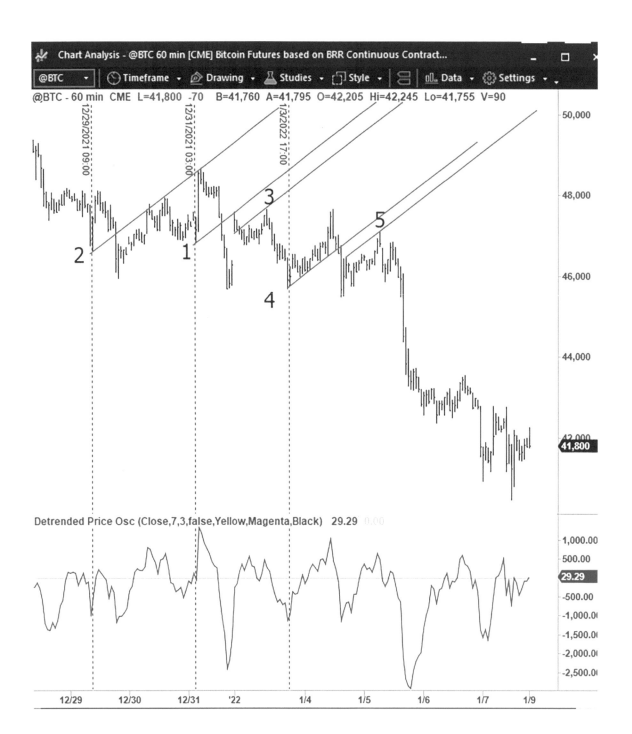

Figure 4.9
Bitcoin Futures - 60-minutes
7-period Detrend Oscillator beneath Price.

Chart by TradeStation

Figure 4.9 is a 60-minute intraday chart of Bitcoin Futures. I did not want you to think this discussion only applies to longer horizon charts. These methods apply to all time horizons.

Another example of utilizing drawn angles helps us continue the prior discussion. This time I am not using pointers, so you need to study the chart more closely. The first angle drawn on this chart was line '1'. The angle was selected by using the price low leading to a strong bounce up. The second point is the price high for the bar just above the gap.

To confirm I have selected an angle the market is respecting, a parallel line is created and moved higher than the one first drawn. When the line is moved higher it is discovered the same angle repeats from point '2' and is respected by the intraday market action at the swing high that started from '1'. Such a precise angle marking key price swing lows and a high tells me this is the correct angle to use again.

The price high at '3' is a failure on the resistance line that was started from a single price low, the price low in the bar over the gap. Don't forget gaps have very important geometric properties. Here the market is unable to retrace back to the line marked '1'. The rally into line '2' retraced the full distance. At '3' the market is weaker.

Bitcoin declines and creates a small key reversal. The parallel line is projected from point '4'. Price action shows line '4' is used as support for several bars and then an attempt to bounce up to the horizontal level created at point '3'. Not only does it fail, but a strong key reversal develops. When we see two long bars forming the key reversal, some will call this pattern railway tracks. If I changed the screen to be a 120-minute chart the two bars would merge to be a single key reversal. Same pattern, just a question of time horizon being viewed.

The market declines and breaks through support defined by line '4'. The first retracement is very shallow and defines a key reversal. As it starts to pullback line '5' is drawn. The market tries to rally and stops dead on pivot '5'. Now this is important. Once again, the market is displaying weakness because the bounce up cannot reach the resistance defined by angle '4'. The market fails and attempts a weaker bounce.

A complete trend reversal follows with a sharp decline. As a seller where would I put stops? Above pivot 3 and 5 having sold both when they failed. The entire series of swings from '2' to '5' are coiling in narrowing ranges. Look at '4', the horizontal level is tested three times. The failure at '5' is serious. Sell as the risk for bears is very low. Put stops above line '4'.

It was Gustave Le Bon who explained that a crowd is not an average of characteristics of its individuals, but a new mindset. He also said it is like combining a base and acid and creating something new altogether with its own characteristics. He believed it was the unconscious traits of human psychology that formed the traits of the crowd. These are deep- seeded emotions of which each individual is likely unaware.

R.N. Elliott wrote that "human emotions ...are rhythmical". We know from our cycle work that rhythms have a mathematical basis and this may explain why geometry can be seen in the price action of Figures 4.4 to 4.9.

The emotions of a mass crowd are not only rhythmical but form repeatable patterns in price swings. The patterns can be found in all time horizons as they have fractal properties. The patterns of a crowd in monthly charts are no different than the patterns they form in a 3-minute chart. The reason is that human emotions are strikingly similar regardless of time horizon. The emotions in longer time horizons are likely augmented, but in nature have similar patterns for emotions in lesser time horizons.

Price patterns created by the emotions of a crowd is a specialized discipline of technical analysis. It was first identified by R. N. Elliott. He called his observations of repeating fractal patterns within price data the Elliott Wave Principle. Had it not been for the writings of Robert Prechter Jr., we may have lost this valuable information that taught us how to map crowd psychology.

I have observed that many people who think they are experts apply the Elliott Wave Principle without any understanding that these waves have proportion and rhythm. There are specific rules that must be followed as they are recognizable patterns. Mapping emotions of a crowd is a discipline. But way too many people just make it up and wonder why they do not have the results they expected. Let me explain more clearly for you.

Rather than running through the fourteen building blocks of the Elliott Wave Principle, we will learn the *emotions* that fit the crowd as a market trend develops. This is far more important than learning how to count all the little twists and turns that send people crazy by the method.

What is most important is to develop an understanding of why crowds form repeating and recognizable patterns that help us map where in the emotional cycle the crowd is positioned currently relative to a bigger picture. It is incredibly surprising just how predictable we can be.

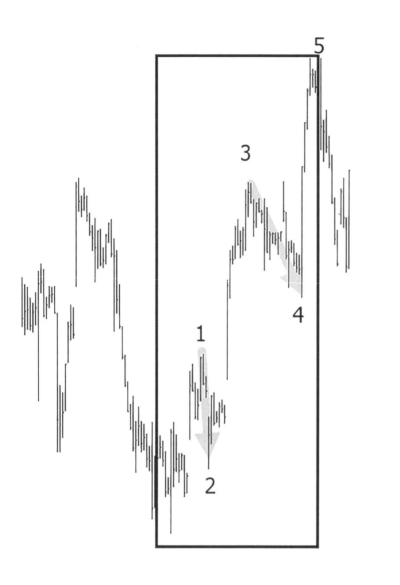

Figure 4.10
Mapping the
sentiment of
a crowd.

Chart by TradeStation

The chart in Figure 4.10 is an American stock. There is a price rally contained within a black rectangle that runs to the top of the frame. Start from the bottom left corner. There is a new price low with a pattern we have meet before called a key reversal. It is a directional signal. The developing swing up runs to a price high marked '1'. The emotions behind this first move up is one of doubt. Only the early smart money wants to buy because the crowd will be convinced this bounce should be sold. The prior trend or swing down looks strong and convincing; the crowd is thinking that surely it is not a complete decline.

The bears sell and push the stock down to '2'. Another key reversal signal develops at '2'. Miss that key reversal and you are dead meat. The second swing down is where the crowd believes the prior trend down is back in control, but the decline fails to challenge the old low. The very next price bar to the right of '2' fills a small gap that is seen in the second swing down. The evidence is building that the sellers are about to get run over. For four bars the stock just builds a small consolidation cliff. Then the gap up. Now experienced traders will not even flinch when that gap forms as we want to aggressively buy it. Why? A market that has any strength to the upside will not fill that gap so stops are placed under the gap and we want in as close to the gap as possible. You have to have a floor-trader mindset and the reflexes of a cat. Just jump in as any hesitation means you will be fighting for a position when the funds run the stock up. Be very aware of the spread between bid and ask. But this is part of the trade execution in the final chapter.

We have seen this move before. It is when everyone is on the same side of the market.
1. The early buyers' want to buy more shares to add to what they bought in the first swing up.
2. The crowd that thought the old trend down would resume are scrambling to take positions off the table as their profits from the decline are fast disappearing. They are forced to buy.
3. The cautious who were sitting out the pullback to '2' to see what happens, suddenly know they are late to the party and must scramble now to buy.

Everyone is buying into the top marked '3'. Finally, a pause because some people want to bank profits. But this pullback is always interesting. The crowd is thinking that they were late to the party and that if there were an opportunity to get in, they would. The rally does not end at '3'. The swing up is very strong as it has long bars- and don't forget the gap which we would call a break-away gap. Market swings that look like this need to bring the laggards into the net.

From '4' a rally runs straight up like a rocket. That is not a healthy swing up from '4' in a fifth wave position. It should be weaker than the move that develops from '2' to '3'. This swing from '4' to '5' is very strong. How could we collect more information about this move into '5'?
One way is to add volume data under the price action. The volume in the move from '2' to '3'

should be greater than the volume in the swing up to '5'. If the fifth swing up looks like the one in Figure 4.10 and has less volume, it means the rally has fewer buyers. That's a warning.

What happens after '5'? A sharp pullback towards the prior pivot marked '4'. The entire pullback from '3' to '4' is in a range we call the vicinity of the fourth wave. It is the natural target for a move that has just completed five swings, or waves.

Now what if the volume in the move from '4' to '5' is greater than the volume in '2' to '3'? Yikes, you better buy. This pattern of emotions for a crowd are fractal. That means the price high at '5' may only be the first five waves within a larger developing five-wave structure. When the next set of five wave swings unfold, they would be even stronger. They would be followed by another pullback, and then a fifth wave that subdivides into five smaller swings like in Figure 4.10 would top the move.

Now this is where I need to get my teacher ruler out. So many of you just map swings and fail to study the internals of a swing. Every move marked 1, 3, and 5 will have its own internals of 5 smaller swings. That's why we say that the emotions of a crowd have fractal properties. The entire rally in Figure 4.10 is called an impulse wave. It is comprised of three smaller impulse waves punctuated by two corrective waves. The corrective waves have red arrows, and the impulse waves have pale green arrows.

Crowds create swings with proportional attributes. Look at the character the crowd developed in the first and third swings. Study the number of bars required to define the first and third swings. Be aware of the time required and the price range of each swing. After the fourth swing, or wave we call it, there must be a fifth wave to follow.

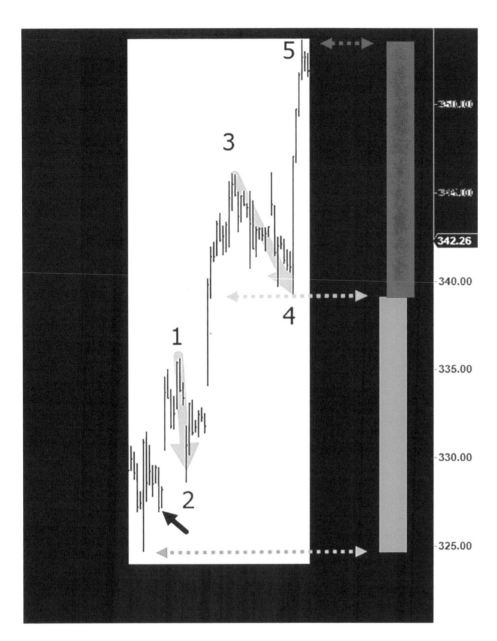

Figure 4.11
A price projection
technique from
a hidden marker.

Chart by TradeStation

That is why I say that understanding how to read the emotional developmental stages of a crowd is more important than learning how to label it. Do you need to know what to call the corrective pattern in wave 4? Not at first, but it does have a pattern name; an expanded flat.

Therefore, I am not going into a detailed discussion about the Wave Principle, as you are better off learning to recognize how crowds develop the same patterns over and over again to begin. The only thing you need to add are a few simple rules. Wave '4' cannot break the top of wave '1', wave '2' cannot break the start of wave '1', and wave '3' cannot be the shortest. That does not mean it has to be the longest, wave '3' just cannot be the shortest in length compared to the first and fifth waves.

Now look closely at Figure 4.11. For years I have had a fast way to target an incomplete developing five-wave trending move. I created a green bar to the far right. Normally it is on my chart, but you would not be able to see what I am doing very well, so it is off to the side. The measurement is from the start of wave '1' up, at the chart bottom, to the small pullback near the middle of wave '3' with a bright green dashed line. That small pullback is often the midpoint of the developing rally. Follow the bright green line left. Use this point to make a price projection. The green  bar measures the price range and likely midpoint of the rally. Then copy/paste the same bar. (Now red.) Move the red bar up to the top of the green bar. That's the first price target the crowd is aiming for to end wave '5'. Turns out this time, like so many other times, it was exact, and the stock then has to make a larger pullback seen to the right of the black rectangle in Figure 4.10.

Do not be confused by this measurement. I am not using the price low marked '4'. It is of no consequence if '4' stopped at the bright green dashed line or not. But you are learning something else about crowd dynamics... fourth wave pullbacks love to cluster together. The green line points to an internal pullback within wave '3'. We label that small pause wave iv of 3 when you start learning how to mark the fractals within the trend. But for now, all you need to see is it is the first pause after the longest bar up.

This is a very simple price projection method viewed as a rough estimate only. In Chapter Six we will cover how to develop very precise levels that do more than forecast market movement. The method you use should be able to assist with market entry and exit, stop placement, where the market should not trade,  and precise support/resistance levels so we know the correct leverage or position size to trade. We will cover all this in Chapter Six and then apply it in Chapter Seven.

Before we move on, there is one more thing to bring to your attention in Figures 4.10 and 4.11. Do you see that wave '2' requires about half as much time to develop as wave '4'? This happens so often it is a guide on what to expect. If wave 2 is swift and is over quickly,  then expect wave '4' to be more involved and consume a longer time frame to develop than '2'. If '2' takes a while to develop, '4' will take less time and be less complex. This is called the guideline of alternation.

Do crowds make other types of price patterns? Yes. There is a charting method called candlesticks. It has a full vocabulary of patterns with names like 'hammer', 'engulfing patterns', 'piercing line', 'morning star', 'falling three methods", 'hanging man', and 'dark cloud cover'. There are many more that describe crowd behavior. Names of patterns are different for favored analysis techniques taught in the East and West, but their meaning does not change. Reading chart patterns is a universal language.

At right is the Spring/Summer 2021 cover chart of our semi-annual IFTA Magazine. It shows a daily chart for Microsoft Corporation (MSFT). The pattern developing between the red lines is a battle between buyers and sellers called a contracting triangle.

People who do not trade just view this as a continuation pattern as the prior trend should resume. But the problem is where do you buy? Once you have been run over a few times by this pattern you get smarter. You do not trade it! Grab a coffee and watch the battle unfold.

The only place to safely buy is when the market breaks out of the pattern. That means the experienced trader knows not to buy at 'E'. Why? The low at 'E' might in fact develop its own contracting triangle. At least we know this chop will end before the price action reaches the apex of the contracting lines. The safe place to buy is after MSFT has broken through the red line and then pulls back to test the top of the trend line. That is the action point to pull the trigger. Then MSFT cannot re-enter the contracting triangle pattern. The swift price moves up from the pattern is called a thrust and a common resolution.

Convention says to measure the length of travel from 'A' to 'B' and add that to 'E' to define the price target. While this method is accurate this time, it is inconsistent, and I rarely do this. We will be using a different method that gives more consistent price targets in Chapter Six.

This pattern has a few variations on the same theme. Five swings that expand so the red lines diverge is an expanding triangle. When the triangle moves one red line to the horizontal it is still a triangle.

What if the pattern resolves in the opposite direction? In this case the price action breaks down through the lower red line. Normally the market tries to test the underside of the lower line and traders will sell it like crazy. That would be a pattern failure and failures are important because the crowd is often surprised and caught on the wrong side of the market. These patterns do require patience.

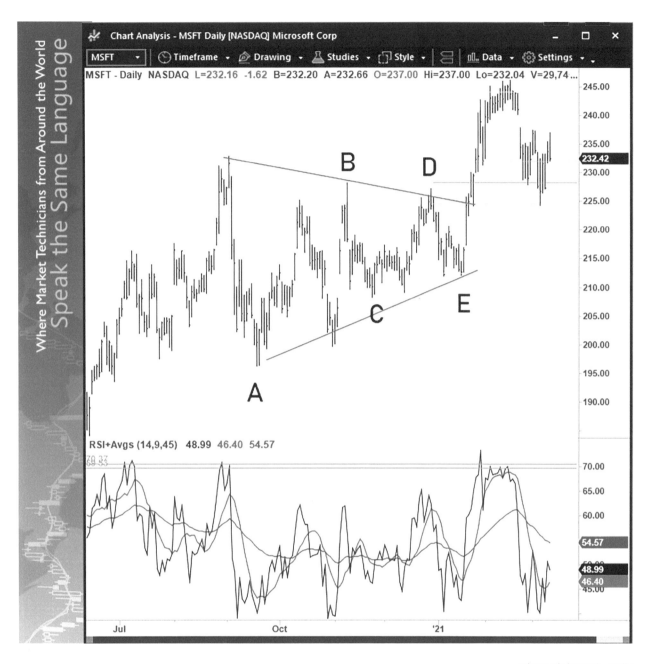

Microsoft (MSFT) - Daily
Cover Chart for the IFTA Magazine
Spring/Summer 2021

Chart by TradeStation

The patterns a crowd defines are indeed very rhythmical based on the chart examples we have been discussing. But the last pattern confirms an observation Le Bon made in his book *The Crowd* on page 73. He states crowds have leaders. He explains that whether animals or men, individuals place themselves under the authority of a chief. I would add 'or a chief mindset.' The triangle pattern is a battle over leadership within the crowd. In a market context that means a battle for control between the bears and bulls. Do not be foolish and step in the middle.

Le Bon goes on to describe how public crowds demonstrating in the street, gravitate to the strongest agitator. The crowd then surrounds that person, forming the nucleus mindset of the organization. A crowd is a servile flock that is incapable of survival without a master. But caution here. The leaders or leading mindset has no conscious regard to fact or reality. Everything outside of the crowd's collective mindset is invisible to them. There is nothing you can do to influence the crowd until individuals begin to feel pain. Then the unconscious mind begins to awaken them, and individuals then begin to peel away from the crowd.

In Figure 4.12 is the stock GameStop (GME) in a daily time horizon. The crowd was an organization of novice inexperienced young traders living on a new trading platform called Robinhood. With an evil fascination I watched their posts when the bubble burst. They believed if everyone bought more, they would push the stock to the moon. Same as any bubble burst, be it tulip bulbs or land being sold under the Hudson River, the pattern that follows is the same. These traders were shuffling the chairs on the deck of the Titanic, and I watched with an evil grin. Ye' young traders are about to learn a valuable lesson; you cannot stop a crowd stampeding for the exits.

The big gap in the crash is the point of recognition. They were dying and some posts showed millions of dollars had been lost over-night, but they still refused to let go of the falling anchor. Some lost their college savings and more. Sad. It was a serious bloodbath and the grin was wiped off my face. This would be a life-changing event for some students. But then a weaker crowd tried it again! The market washed them out. A third time an even weaker crowd tried to lift the stock 'to the moon'. That was their technical target. The crowd was indeed unconscious and like sheep followed the calls of their hypnotized leaders on social media. You would think they would have learned, but no, just off the chart they try again and fail. Lessons learned for some that would never heal in a lifetime. They were taught a hard lesson that the market cannot be bullied to move as you want it to move. Impose your will upon it and die. But learn what the market is telling you and you can stay in-sync and succeed.

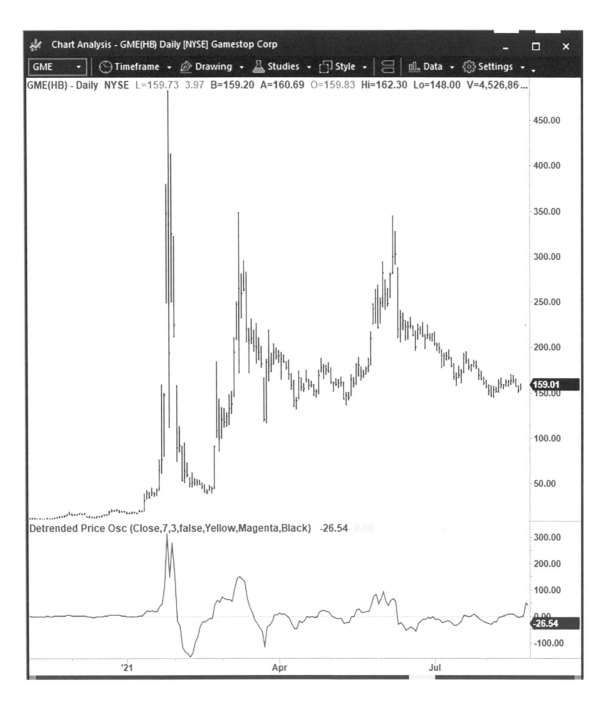

Figure 4.12
GameStop Corporation (GME - NYSE) - daily
Chart by TradeStation

You should Google other patterns called *flags* and *pennants* that are described in every book about technical analysis, but like triangles, do not trade their internals. They are just signs the larger trend is taking a pause. Wait until price breaks outside of their consolidation patterns.

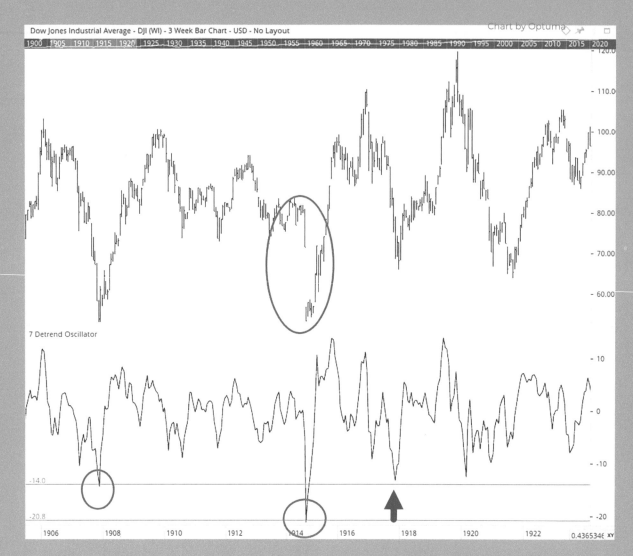

**Figure 4.13 - Dow Jones Industrial Avg - 3-week**

When markets crash, it is fascinating to see how they recover. What I mean by this is that former crash oscillator extremes are used as building blocks to create a new upwards trend. We will use the same oscillator we used to evaluate cycle rhythms. Figure 4.13 is the Dow Jones Industrial Average (DJIA) from 1905 to 1922. The oscillator under price is a simple 7-period detrend oscillator. We will use this oscillator in a different way than we did for the cycle analysis.

November 1907 the DJIA forms the first extreme displacement in the detrend oscillator. Draw a horizontal line. World War I caused the NYSE to close from July of 1914 to December 1914. When it opened all the fear that was building during closure caused a massive selloff. The detrend oscillator makes a new extreme low that was lower than the crash of 1907. Make a note to self what

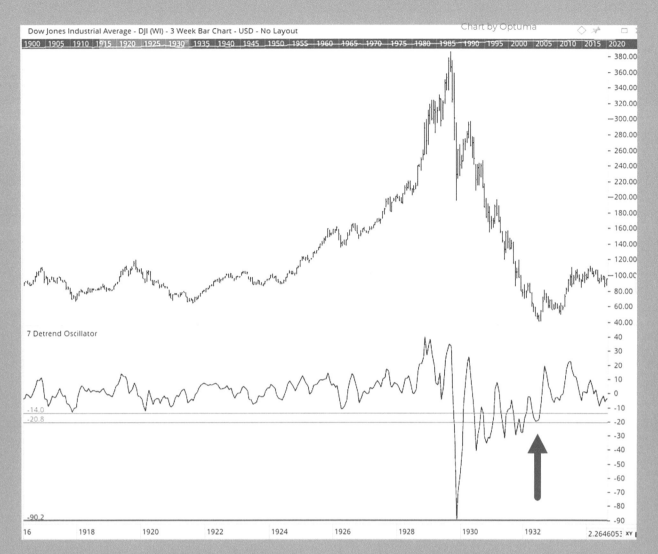

**Figure 4.14 - Dow Jones Industrial Avg - 3-week**

happens when a market is closed. All selling is exhausted at the reopening. Draw a new horizontal line on the oscillator extreme made December 12, 1914.

There is a pullback into the same horizontal line from the extreme recorded for the 1907 crash. The purple arrow points to October 27, 1917. The old crash extreme level is used as support.

Figure 4.14 is the 1929 Great Crash. A new extreme low in the detrend oscillator is recorded with a red horizontal line. Here is what is fascinating. The bottom of the crash does not occur until the detrend oscillator tests the same extreme displacement as was recorded for the WWI shock.

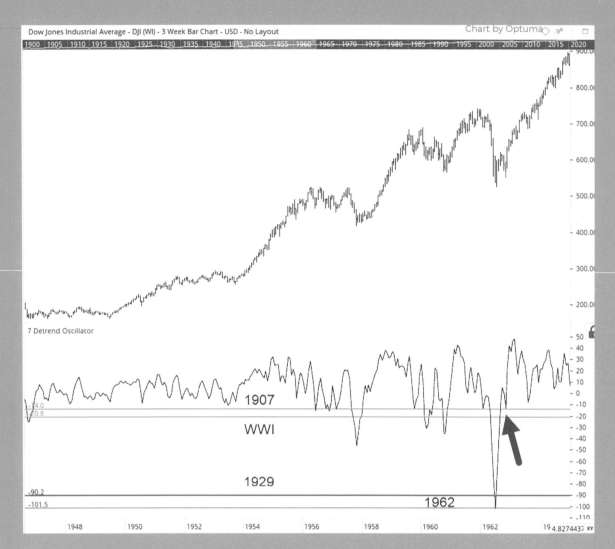

**Figure 4.15**
**Dow Jones Industrial Avg - 3-week**

The extreme low created in 1929 in the detrend oscillator is not challenged again until 1962 in a market decline called the Kennedy Slide of 1962. From the 1962 crash price low there is a small bounce off the lows and then prices try to make a new low but fail. The detrend oscillator has a purple arrow showing you that the oscillator is using the crash horizontal line from 1907 as support. It marks the true start of the recovery rally.

Before moving on be sure to record the new oscillator extreme with a blue horizontal line that is just below the red line recorded for the 1929 Crash.

Continuing with the same exercise for marking the detrend oscillator extremes that form at crash lows, we have a marginal new low in 1974 compared to

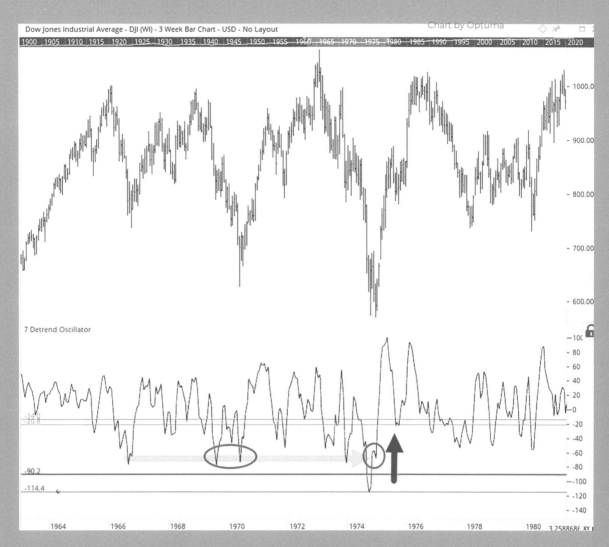

**Figure 4.16**
**Dow Jones Industrial Avg - 3-week**

1962. All I did was move the blue horizontal line down slightly from where it was set in Figure 4.15 at the 1962 oscillator low.

Figure 4.16 is developing important history in the detrend oscillator. There is a horizontal light purple arrow. A red circle above 1970 shows a double bottom which the oscillator formed on the purple line. The plum line is tested four times developing a history of probability at this level. From the 1974 oscillator extreme the oscillator moves up and develops a very small 'V' that is highlighted for you in a small red circle. This is on the same level as the light purple line. The market is telling you important things happen at this detrend amplitude. Pay attention! Miss that signal and the market rallies with conviction. It then pulls back. The oscillator at the purple arrow pointing upwards again uses the 1907 and WWI lines, now a support zone, to launch the next leg up in the rally. Old extreme levels in the detrend oscillator that were made by a crash are always important.

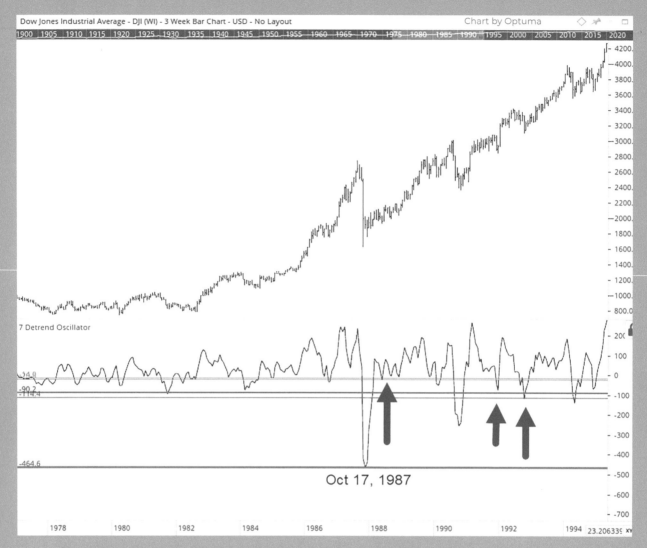

**Figure 4.17**
**Dow Jones Industrial Avg - 3-week**

Then we experience the October 1987 crash. New amplitude displacement in the detrend oscillator. The market does not begin a recovery rally until the oscillator passes up through the 1907 and WWI support zone. It pulls back and tests the top of the 1907 and WWI lines. The market takes off and the support zone is tested a couple times.

To the right are two more purple arrows pointing upwards. This highlights where the oscillator uses the 1929 and 1974 horizontal zones as support.

The range has expanded with the new detrend oscillator extreme for 1987. Now the two lines from 1929 and 1974 are compressed as a target zone.

If you scan left you will find that the 1929 extreme red line is used as support, as is the zone from the 1907 and WWI extremes several times.

In 2008, the new detrend oscillator extreme is mapped with a bright green horizontal line. Notice

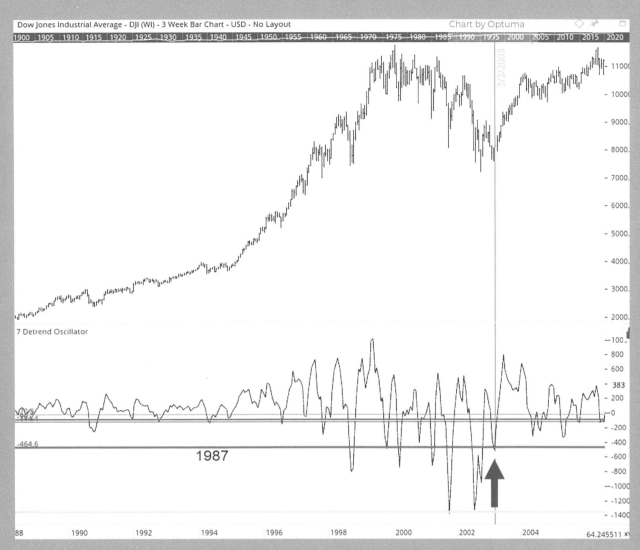

how the 1929 red horizontal line has now merged as a support confluence zone that contains the levels, we marked for the 1907, 1929, WWI, and WWII extremes.

Figure 4.18 shows that the 2008 low develops a double bottom as the green horizontal line is tested a second time in June of 2002. The oscillator bounces upwards and pulls back to the red line we recorded with the 1987 crash. Again, a prior crash oscillator low is used as the building block to begin a new trend after a shock wave down. A purple arrow points upwards to this test.

Now the big question. What did March of 2020 look like in this oscillator?

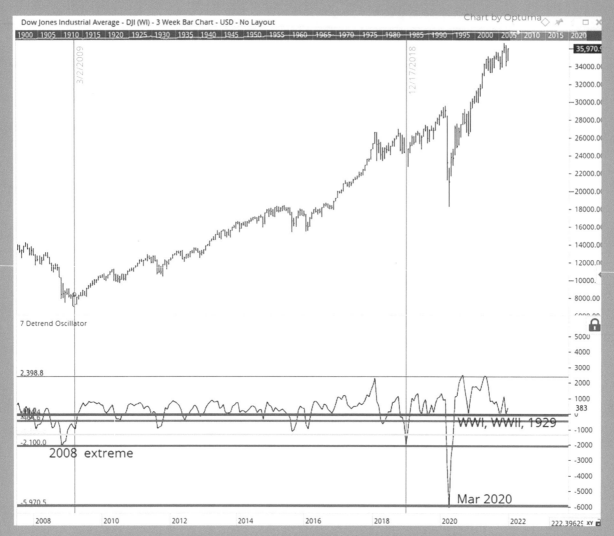

**Figure 4.19**
**Dow Jones Industrial Avg - 3-week**

Figure 4.19 shows you the new extreme in 2020 that developed in the 7-period detrend oscillator. This amplitude far exceeded the 2008 low and any other we have recorded in the DJIA since 1907. The 2008 extreme is the blue line. From the March 2020 extreme oscillator low, the oscillator soars upwards. It pulls back and then tests the 1907, WWI, WWII confluence horizontal line three times. The first is above the 'WWI' label and the second and third times are a double bottom on the line above the 'WWII' label.

What do we know from this series of charts? That someday a crash will push the detrend oscillator to new lows well below the March 2020 extreme. We also know the market will build and test support levels marked as amplitude displacements from former crashes.

A detrended oscillator from the spread of two simple moving-averages is a very powerful tool.

The 7-period detrend oscillator has been used for cycle analysis as well as to record sentiment extremes of a crowd, and later I will show you how it can be used for entry/exit trading signals. This often overlooked oscillator is going to be the answer to your questions about how to trade fast-falling markets in Chapter Seven.

There is one more method to share with you that we often use to monitor the extreme sentiment swings within the crowd. The method requires an understanding of standard deviation. We will take a side trip to build a base understanding about standard deviation and then we can see how it can be applied to price market data.

The mean value is calculated by adding all the data points, such as the closing prices for a fixed range, and then dividing by the number of data points. The volatility bands we will examine all use the closing prices.

What we want to know is the variance of each individual data point to the mean value. Variance is calculated by subtracting the mean from each data point, squaring each of these results, and then taking another mean of these squares.

The standard deviation is then calculated as the square root of the variance. When the data stays within a narrow range the standard deviation will narrow. If the crowd becomes extended beyond normal activity it is very evident, as the bands widen showing volatility is increasing.

The most well-known application in finance was developed by John Bollinger called Bollinger Bands. But there is a second formula that is lesser known that I favor called Stoller Bands. It was developed by one of my mentors Manny Stoller. Manny was my boss when I worked on the 104th floor of the World Trade Center. He worked on the 105th floor. We both experienced the first bombing of the South Tower, but we had left the Trade Center just before 2001.

Manny's formula gives a specific signal that Bollinger Bands will not develop. We need to take a look at both methods for plotting volatility bands on price data and then you may then be interested to research the bands from either gentleman on your own. The formula for Stoller Bands is in my book '*Technical Analysis for the Trading Professional*'. There are several ways to download this title from the Internet without charge in PDF format. Bollinger Bands are well documented if you just use Google or Bing.

Figure 4.20 Bitcoin/ US dollar (XBTUSD) shows a type of price envelope called Bollinger Bands. The mean period is 20 (green line) and use 2.0 for the standard deviation band envelopes. Use 10-period simple moving-average (SMA)and 1.5 standard deviation for short term intraday charts.

The bands adjust to price volatility. Bollinger Bands are exceeded by prices in strong trends. This is seen in the rally in Figure 4.20. While it means the trend is strong, I personally need boundaries that are rarely exceeded. It is the reason I do not use this popular setup. All volatility bands will narrow during intervals of narrowing price range activity as the calculation is a measure of momentum. Momentum will be more fully explained in the next chapter.

Figure 4.20
Bitcoin/US dollar - XBTUSD
- 2-day Bar Chart with
Bollinger Bands

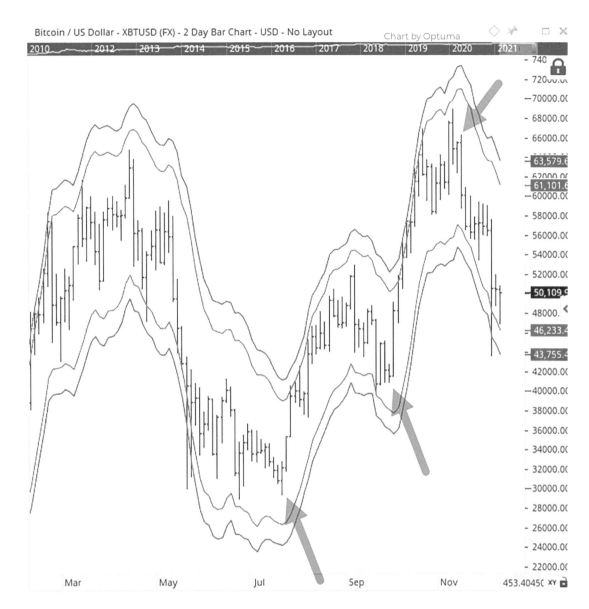

Figure 4.21
Bitcoin/US dollar - XBTUSD - 2-day Bar
Chart with Stoller Bands

Figure 4.21 shows the volatility bands called Stoller Bands. Stoller used a 6-period mean. The envelope is an inner band from a 1.5 standard deviation. The red outer envelope is a 2.0 standard deviation of the mean. The mean itself would track in the middle of the envelope but it is not shown. These bands rarely exceed the upper 2.0 standard deviation boundary compared to Bollinger Bands in Figure 4.20.

I use envelopes for analysis purposes only. Never for trailing stops. They solve a problem when the price action looks impossible. I recall a boss who once

asked for an analysis of the Italian Lira/Thai Bhat currency cross. Adding volatility bands helped to develop a picture of how the crowd moved prices within the bands and to what extreme they were positioned at the time. The Lira is now part of the Euro so the exact problem would not occur today. But if my analysis is correct, the Euro will break apart in the future and the German Dmark will return along with the Lira and a host of other former currencies.

Stoller Bands will develop a signal worthy of notice. Once the price action runs to the bottom or top of the band, the signal is the retest attempt that never pushes to the band and falls short. There are three signals that illustrate for you the pattern I am referencing with plum arrows in Figure 4.21.

You will find Bollinger Bands offered in all software packages for technical analysis. I gave the formula for Stoller Bands to Optuma so they are in their menu of tools. Look under 'Averages>Stoller Bands'. If your program does not have Stoller Bands just add them manually.

One last thought; the average to use for Stoller Bands is 6. The default in Optuma is incorrect as they use 5. Using 6 is just a little smoother and sets the correct displacement. You will also need to change their default setting to 1.50 in the 'first factor' and 2.00 in the 'second factor'. If you use Bollinger Bands, the starting period for the mean should be 20. Software defaults are just that ... vendor values. You should know the correct settings to use as vendors rarely do.

We have looked at many patterns developed by mass crowd psychology. The ones I study every moment of a trade are the swings we call Elliott Wave patterns and their fractal properties in longer time horizons down to very short time horizons. Wave position is a road map of the crowd. But one can use oscillators to create these road maps of crowd psychology. Oscillators can be used in many different ways and there are different kinds of oscillators. This will be the focus of our next discussion.

# 5

TRADING THE MOMENTUM
OF A MASS CROWD

# CHAPTER FIVE

# Oscillators

## OSCILLATORS ARE SO MUCH MORE THAN OVERBOUGHT OR OVERSOLD INDICATORS.

**N**ow we are getting into the really good 'stuff'. We will be building our resources for trading. I know you will look at oscillator indicators in a new light after this discussion. Grab your trader's hat as we are about to shift gears.

Where do we begin? Actually, we already did when we began to study the extreme amplitude displacements in a detrended oscillator in the Dow Jones Industrial Average from 1900 to 2021. But wait, you may be thinking, we did not look for any divergences between the oscillator peaks and troughs relative to price. Exactly! Oscillators are more than divergence signals though many think that is their only purpose.

Oscillators like Stochastics, MACD, the Relative Strength Index, and the Composite Index, all move in different ways relative to the same price data. We need to know why and how each has their own place in our toolbox. Most people ask, 'What oscillator is best?' Not the right question to ask. There is a clear need to understand the strengths and weaknesses of each oscillator before you decide what will be best for you.

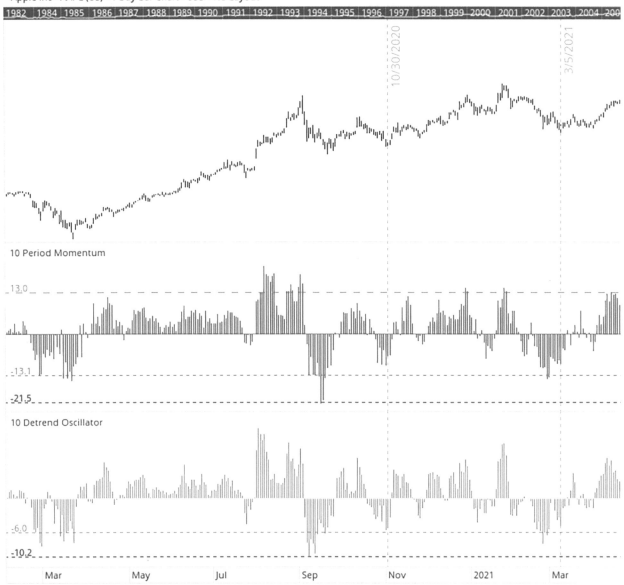

The detrend oscillator plots the spread of two simple moving-averages (SMA) on the closing prices. The resulting detrend oscillator is an unbound oscillator without range limitations in Figure 5.1. This is the same oscillator we have used before, but it has been plotted as a histogram rather than a line. This will make it easier to compare it to the histogram in blue.

The oscillators we are about to discuss are called momentum oscillators. Momentum measures the velocity of price changes, rather than the actual price. As an example, a 10-period momentum indicator will take the current price, and compare it to a price from 10-periods earlier. A momentum oscillator is the current price divided by a previous period. The quotient is multiplied by 100. The result is an indicator that oscillates around 100. What it tells us is how much the current price has moved relative to the period being compared, in this case,

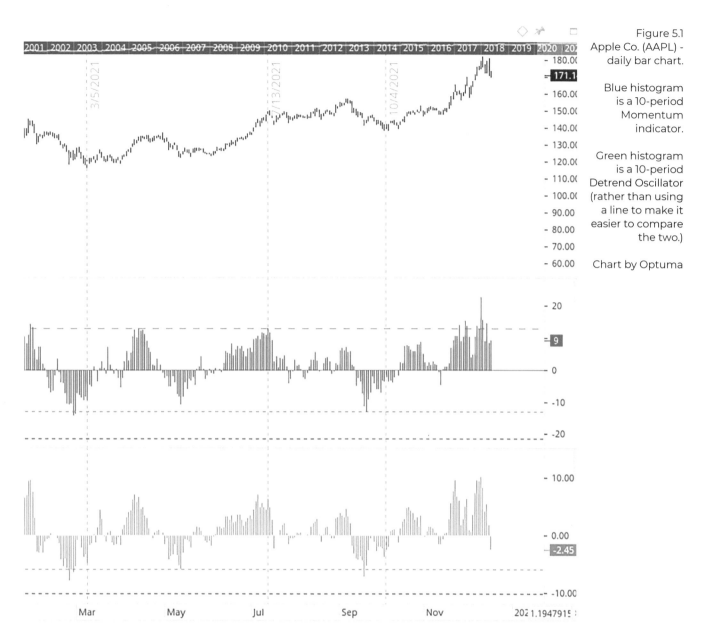

Figure 5.1
Apple Co. (AAPL) -
daily bar chart.

Blue histogram
is a 10-period
Momentum
indicator.

Green histogram
is a 10-period
Detrend Oscillator
(rather than using
a line to make it
easier to compare
the two.)

Chart by Optuma

from 10-periods ago. The more rapid and wider the change in the spread comparison, the more volatile the price movement is becoming.

Take a moment to study Figure 5.1. The extreme low is marked with a dashed red horizontal line. An internal green horizontal line connects where amplitude displacements tend to repeat. Study price and the different oscillator formations at these displacements very closely in the two indicators. The 03/03/2021 vertical line near the page center is the same date on page left and right. Does the Detrend turn up before the Momentum histogram? Yes. Are there other like amplitudes closer to the zero line that the market uses as support or resistance?

Now examine the oscillator tops and study how AAPL reacts to these resistance levels.

## Normalized Oscillator
# RELATIVE STRENGTH INDEX: J. WELLES WILDER JR.

Welles Wilder was an American mechanical engineer who developed several technical analysis indicators now viewed to be foundation indicators by our industry. His indicator called the Relative Strength Index is the most widely used oscillator in the world based on survey feedback conducted by organizations and media focused on analysis.

Some formulas are cumulative and when they were plotted by hand would mean taping new graph paper to old charts to accommodate new extremes. George Lane explained, "soon we had chart paper running all over the walls." Analysts like Wilder and Lane found the solution was to reduce their oscillators to a percentage. These oscillators then moved within a fixed range of zero to 100, and used 50 as their center line. We describe this reduction to a percentage as creating a normalized oscillator.

All normalized oscillators have the same problem; they will lock-up at the top or bottom of their scale range when markets are in a melt-up or meltdown market condition. If the normalized oscillator is about to move 50% from 50, it moves a far greater distance from the center line than it would if it moves 50% from a starting level at 90. Therefore, analysts and traders must know if the indicator they are using is normalized or not, and then they should use a second oscillator that is unbound and free to run to an unrestricted extreme for comparison.

Our exercise in Chapter 4, to examine the DJIA market crashes with the 7-period detrend oscillator, was teaching us much more than how to make a historical examination of oscillator extremes. We learned how to use an oscillator that was an unbound oscillator for support and resistance.

In Figure 5.1 the two histogram indicators clearly defined horizontal levels of attraction. This is extremely important for all oscillators, yet the instruction you will read on the Internet will state oscillators are unable to provide trend analysis guidance. Not true! We just need to keep it clear in our minds what kind of oscillator we are discussing, normalized or unbound, then, I'll do my part to help you understand how each function.

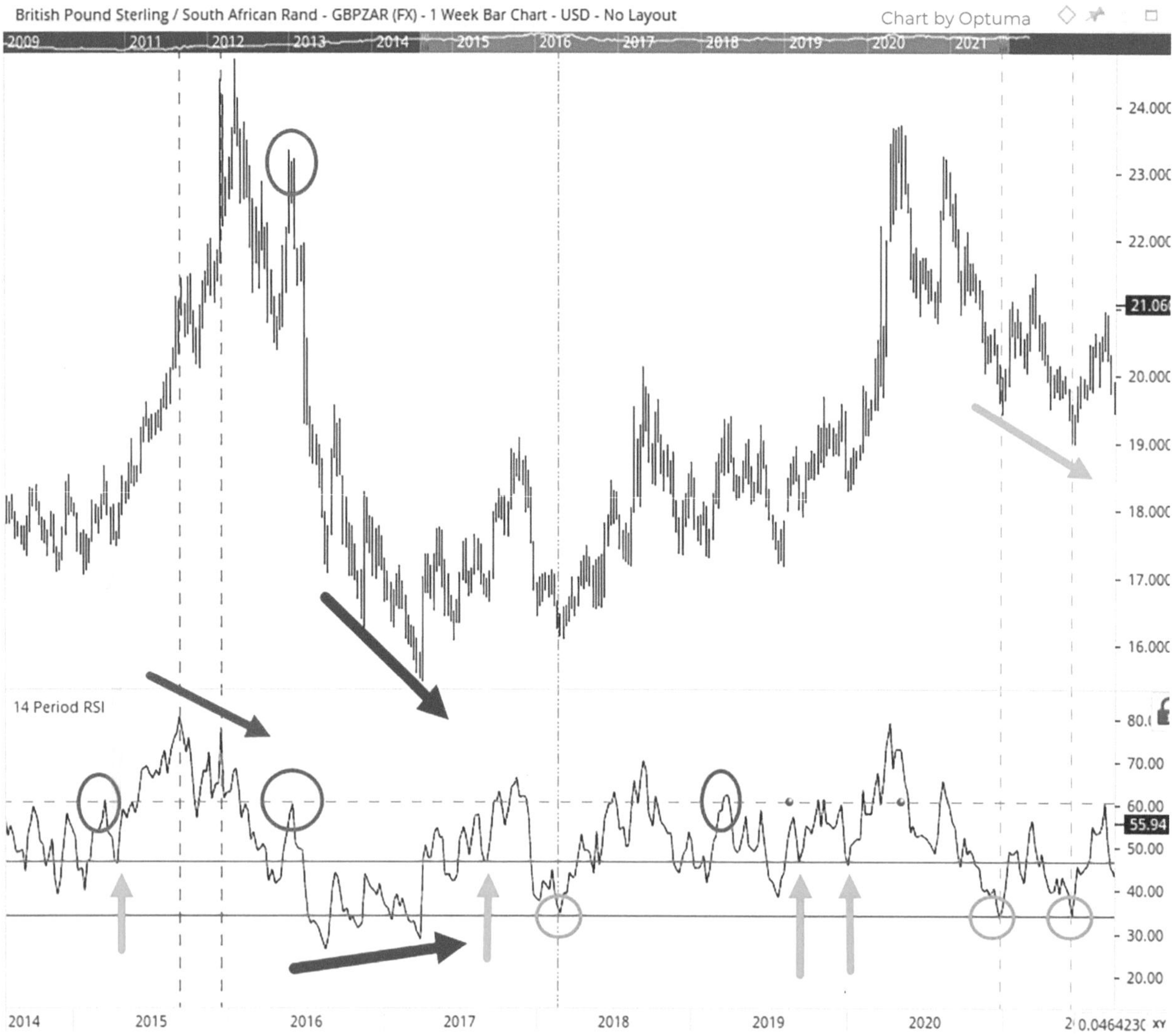

British Pound Sterling / South African Rand - GBPZAR (FX) - 1 Week Bar Chart - USD - No Layout

Chart by Optuma

14 Period RSI

Figure 5.2
British Pound Sterling / South African Rand GBPZAR - weekly bar chart
Bottom - 14-period RSI

Start with small steps as most people I teach have never trained their eye to see internal details within oscillators. The internal oscillations at repeating horizontal levels are more important than the divergence patterns as they are far more frequent and aid trading execution.

The chart in Figure 5.2 is a weekly GBPZAR currency chart. No particular reason this market was selected except to broaden my chart examples in the book. The method of reading price and RSI is the same in a 2-minute chart as in a 6-month chart. Each time horizon will favor different repeating horizontal oscillator levels, but they give the same message.

The first, and for some, the only pattern known in oscillators is divergence between the price action and oscillator. Classic bullish divergence is marked in Figure 5.2 with two purple arrows. The lines actually converge, not diverge, but we call this divergence regardless as it is a bad generic term burned into our vocabulary.

While we have the example, the price decline directly above the purple arrow, is a known behavioral pattern of crowds. Lower price lows with lower price highs in a narrowing range is a termination wedge. The selling pressure is being squeezed out of the crowd. It is an Elliott Wave Principle pattern that is widely known as a warning a trend is exhausted. The trend reverses before the wedge pattern touches the apex of the narrowing boundaries. The bullish divergence between price and the 14-period RSI adds further evidence that the selling pressure was declining.

Read this chart from left to right.

Three horizontal lines have been added to the RSI swings. One is a green dashed line and the others are red. Create the levels the oscillator defines rather than using vendor default lines.

The green dashed line was drawn from the far left oscillator peak in a small red circle. Why? The second red circle at the same amplitude displacement is where the downtrend for Sterling is fully recognized.

Notice a light green arrow pointing up to the price pivot that begins the rally. A red line is drawn. Oscillator peaks, or troughs, that align with significant price action are important. Divergences are not the only significant formations. In fact, the most valuable signals in oscillators will come in the middle of the range.

Traders read oscillators for the purpose of predicting what will occur in the next bar to enter the chart. In contrast, analysts are historians! "Well, we have divergence over here." Yes, and the market rallied maybe four years ago. Can that tell you anything what will happen next? Having taught both traders and analysts for many years, I can say that their mindsets are very different. Look at the vertical red dashed lines that align oscillator peaks to price in the rallies. It is divergence between RSI and price, but the market ran you over when it made another market high. The correct signal is the oscillator peak in the second red circle under a well-defined resistance level.

Important lesson: the first momentum extreme is the end of the crowd's third wave. There will be a pullback and the laggards will nearly always press the trend back to the old high or low to create the fifth wave. The oscillator will be weaker and have lower volume. Momentum indicators pick-up the dwindling price momentum forming divergence. So where is the real place to reverse a position or see that the uptrend is in trouble? The red circle on the RSI EXACTLY under the green horizontal line that marked the strongest start of the uptrend. Whoosh, the market fails and starts a free-fall. Lesson two: the most dangerous or strongest signals will come after divergence patterns. There will be many examples to help you.

Past the purple divergence lines, we come to a small green arrow pointing up. Scan left and right as there are four green arrows all pointing to RSI reversals on the same level. Study the corresponding price action. People say oscillators cannot be used for trend analysis. This is not true. The oscillator pivots on the same red horizontal line are perfect market entry signals. You will understand the remaining notations within the chart.

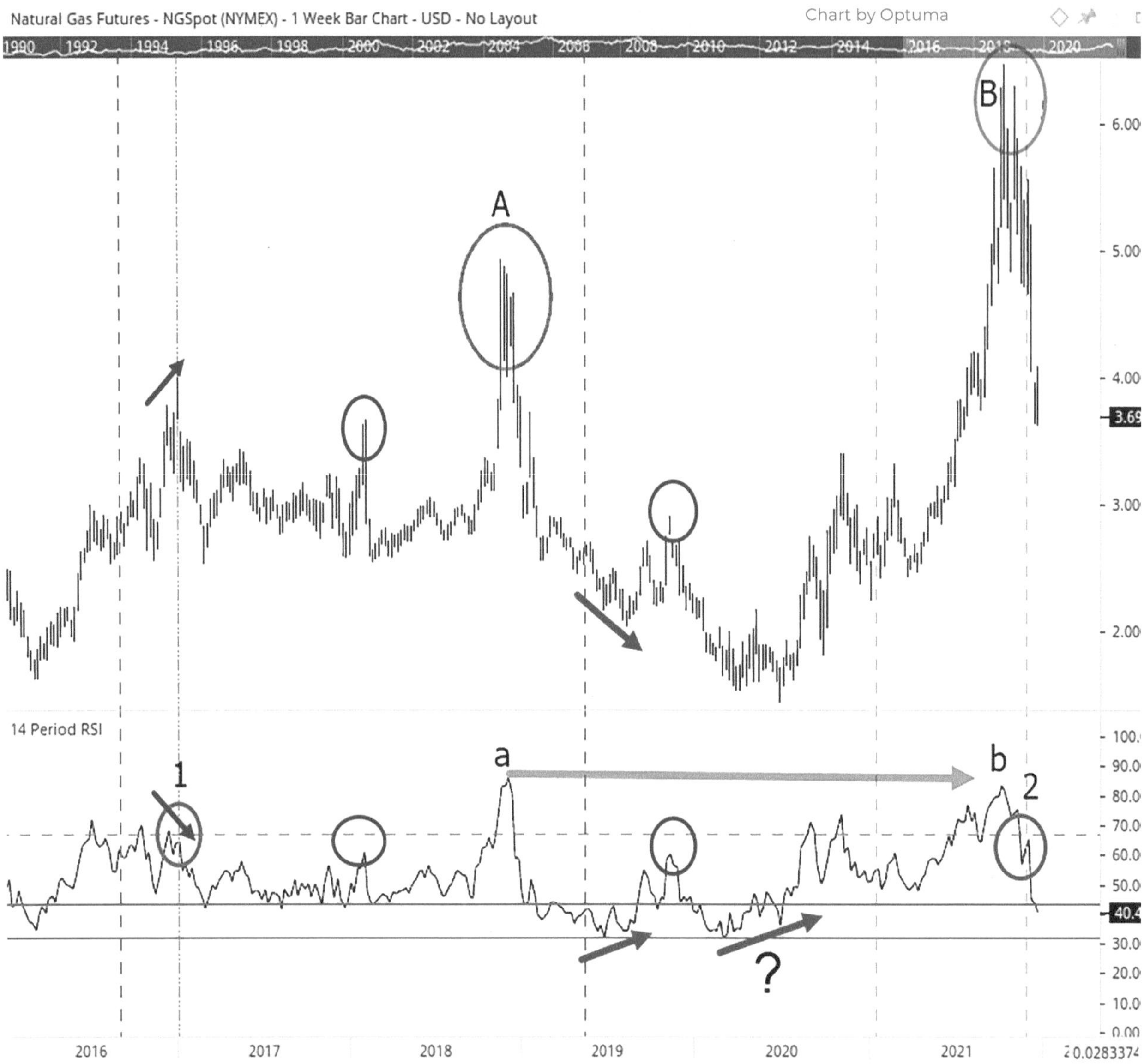

Figure 5.3
Natural Gas Futures - weekly bar chart
Bottom - 14-period RSI

Now that you have my pattern of working through charts, let's keep going from left to right in Figure 5.3 showing weekly Natural Gas futures.

Begin far left at peaks '1' in RSI in a red circle. There is a purple line over price and RSI indicating bearish divergence. Is this really divergence? I like the fact the divergence is a tight narrow 'M' in RSI, but it is not a divergence relationship when you look more closely and also compare RSI to the aligned closing prices. Should we always use the closing prices? Yes. But it is rare that we have to check as it is not often this close. The green dashed horizontal line is drawn from the RSI peak marked '1' because it is the second time the oscillator topped near this level.

Moving right in RSI, we see a purple circle that shows a significant price spike up to create this RSI peak. The rally fails leaving behind the scares of a major key reversal in price. From this RSI peak you would draw a horizontal line. As it is close to present line I did not add it to the page. But scan right and the second purple circle on RSI matches the extreme price pop that also fails in 2019. It demonstrates for you how past events in price with the oscillator position should be marked. They often repeat in later trends as being critical.

Follow the chart right to the price top in a red oval marked 'A'. Below this peak the RSI peak is marked 'a'. Draw a horizontal line from 'a'. In 2021 the market top 'B' in a purple oval will correspond to the RSI peak marked 'b'. The RSI peak at 'b' is the same displacement as RSI peak 'a' in 2018. We walked through testing extremes on the DJIA using an unbound detrend oscillator; here we have a normalized oscillator displaying similar characteristics at extremes. Lesson three: amplitude extremes always mean something significant and will be revisited.

Above the 2019 date label, bullish divergence is marked with red arrows in price and the RSI. This is where the lower red line on RSI began. It was extended left and right, and we see the 2015 market bottom nearly bottomed RSI at the same level.

Then we come to the second red arrow under RSI.  It has a question mark. The question for you is this: Is this bullish divergence? The answer is yes. Not a trick question. But there are three troughs, a tight  'W' and a single 'V' that define two divergences above the lower red line on RSI. The trend reversal signal is after the divergences when RSI lifts through the second higher horizontal line on RSI. The last signal is '2' on RSI. It is the true sell signal as it fails just under the green dashed line in RSI. Reaction in price is a third wave decline.

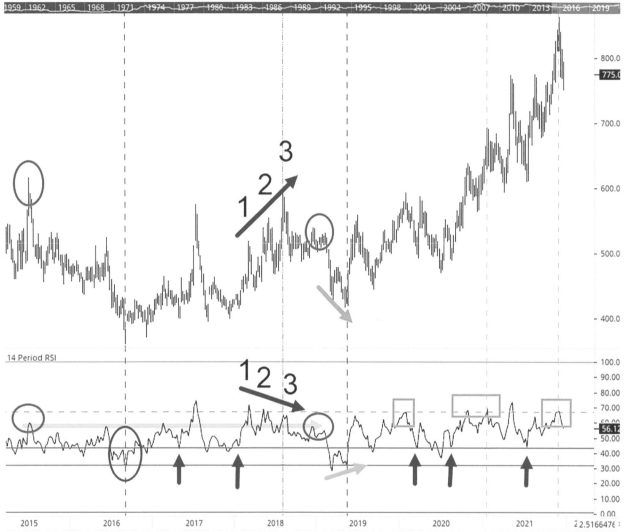

Figure 5.4
Wheat Futures - weekly bar chart
Bottom - 14-period RSI

Just so you do not begin to think all these discussions only apply to financial charts, a weekly chart for Wheat is shown in Figure 5.4.

On the far left is a small red circle over an RSI peak and the corresponding price action in the chart. Very significant market reversal. What pattern is it? A key reversal we know is a directional signal. Draw a horizontal line from this RSI peak across the RSI window. I used a wider semi-transparent purple line. The line defines several price reversals with RSI failing under this same line, but the line moves across to end at a purple arrow that marks where the Wheat market fails under this same level at significant RSI peaks circled in red. The corresponding red circle in price shows again how major moves are triggered from these internal range signals within RSI.

We must move back as we skipped a few signals. In RSI there are two purple arrows pointing up in 2017 and 2018. From these two RSI lows I drew the thin red horizontal line. Why? They mark significant price reversals. But, once RSI pops up from the second purple arrow, look at the roadblock RSI hits. The green dashed line. Bearish divergence, but to time this decline correctly you must use more than one time horizon. Then trade when the signals agree in both time horizons. This concept was first taught to me by Alex Elder and is called 'tri-screen' trading. Over the years I used only two side-by-side and found the time horizon should be in the ratio of 4 to one. For example, a 60-minute chart on the right will always be paired with a 15-minute chart on the right. It explains why some charts in the book have odd numbers of days or weeks. I only captured one half of the pairing I normally use. Both charts must then confirm one another. The swings in price marked 1 through 3 do not break down until RSI fails under the horizontal semi-transparent purple horizontal line. The RSI signal under the purple line is circled in red.

As we move right Wheat prices fall sharply into the green arrows under price and RSI marking bullish divergence. Notice the "W" formation in RSI is on a lower red horizontal line where the 2016 price bottom developed. What follows is a short-squeeze. But the first swing up from the marked divergence fails under the RSI dashed green line again. Wheat does love that green dashed line!

RSI pulls back and marginally slips under the thin red horizontal line. But look right to the second purple arrow on RSI. RSI has been here before when it was working to develop a market bottom in 2017.

The rally works its way back up and we see RSI topping at the green dashed line four more times highlighted in gold squares.

Where are the reentry signals or pyramid position additions? Yes, the RSI pivots off the thin red line in the middle of the chart.

This is going to shock you. I typed the new symbol to switch the chart from Natural Gas in Figure 5.3 to Wheat. But I never made an adjustment to the horizontal lines. They are the same lines on RSI at the exact same levels in both charts. In Technical Analysis for the Trading Professional is a chapter concerning range rules for RSI. Let me give you a quick summary here so you understand how two charts can create the same levels in RSI for support or resistance.

Microsoft Corporation - MSFT (US) - 1 Day Bar Chart - USD - No Layout

Chart by Optuma

14 Period RSI

Figure 5.5
Microsoft Co. (MSFT) - Daily
Bottom - 14-period RSI

208     Trading Market Dynamics

# 14-PERIOD RSI TREND ANALYSIS RULES & GUIDANCE

We will now pause briefly in our discussion of RSI signals to focus on a unique characteristic within RSI we can use to evaluate trends. Figure 5.5 is a daily chart of Microsoft (MSFT) in a strong uptrend during 2021.

There are two solid red horizontal lines on RSI. If you had bought MSFT every time MSFT had a pullback and formed a 'W' on this horizontal level in RSI, you would have been right that the uptrend would continue.

Only a 14-period RSI will paint the following picture. When a stock or market pulls back and holds at or near the 40 RSI level, it is a correction in a bull market. After writing Technical Analysis for the Trading Professional, I had emails like this one that stated, "my stock fell to 38 and 40 doesn't work." Use your common sense! That is why I drew a narrow band in Figure 5.5 instead of a line as that is where this market defines support. If your market wants to develop bottoms within a rally with RSI at 43, it is the same thing. Your market may have a small difference from 40. Do not think the market has to follow your rules as I assure you, it will not. But read how your market and specific time horizon wants to operate and where. Mark that historical record of oscillator pivots in your chart. The bullish reversals will not be far from 40.

Bull markets move RSI in a range from approximately 40 to beyond 70. Bear markets will fail near the 68-70 horizontal level in RSI and drop through 40 to lower levels.

Therefore, the most dangerous level for a bull market is a failure near 68-70. This is being tested numerous times in Figure 5.5 but the market held near RSI 40 in each pullback. A market rarely crashes from above 70 right through 40. It usually makes a transition by testing RSI 40, then tries to bounce, then fails under 68-70. MSFT is not at the end of its rally in this chart. But if price can move the RSI only back to the nearby pivot just above 60 and then stalls, that may warn that RSi is about to fall through 40.

When a bear market is making a transition to a bull market, RSI will pull back to about the 40 level, or where your market has defined a historic  support level near RSI 40, and will then break out above 68-70.  Pullbacks will then test 40 and not fall below it in a healthy up-trend.

Figure 5.6
iShare MSCI Sweden Index Fund ETF (EWD) - 2-week bar chart.
Bottom - 14-period RSI with horizontal levels of support and
resistance marked.

# 14-PERIOD RSI TREND ANALYSIS RULES & GUIDANCE

When I wrote about this trend characteristic of RSI in Technical Analysis for the Trading Professional, people went a little overboard on the levels. Many markets will respect the 40+ in bull markets and bear markets will top near 68-70 and fall below 40. It does not mean all markets will gravitate to these exact levels. Some markets will ignore these ranges. There is no alternate. In that case just draw horizontal lines where the oscillator defines the pivot history and lean on those signals.

You absolutely must read the market you are trading to see how it wants to function with the RSI formula. This is where I diverge from Quants as they are black-box, rule based, and study how their rules perform. I believe a good trader can read what the participants are doing and should adjust if needed based on historical signal performance. For example, Figure 5.6 is a 2-week bar chart for the iShares ETF Sweden Index Fund (EWD).

The 14-period RSI is creating a substantial horizontal level of resistance near 80 because it topped at 'B'. Now the market is pulling back from the same RSI resistance level. There is a range of support near 30 to 32.5 marked with green lines. There is a red dashed line at 63.6 and a solid green line at 48.36. If that is where this ETF operates best, I'm not going to fight it. But I do know the solid green line at 48.36 is often challenged more than once. I will not trust a bottom based on the fact the RSI is on the green line now.

Why do I use 2-week charts sometimes? When I studied the RSI levels in a weekly chart the upper level for resistance had a poor history in the peaks. I cannot change the 14-period setting, so I change the time horizon for the chart. A 2-week chart produced the repeated reactions on the lows, and the upper range made more sense as well.

Now this chart is a challenge because it is the pattern we discussed earlier called a contracting triangle. The prior triangle was in MSFT in a daily time horizon. This triangle has taken years to form. One method for projecting a target is to measure the price range from 'A' to 'B', then project that measurement up from the pivot marked 'E'. In the rally developing from 'E', the current correction is most likely the fourth wave. A fifth wave up from lower levels is likely to follow, then back down to 'E'.

Chart by Optuma

While I always use a 14-period RSI when I use this oscillator, I will never use the RSI alone. In Figure 5.7 is a 2-week German Dax Index bar chart. The RSI under price is the 14-period oscillator as a black line. Added to this indicator are two moving-averages on RSI. They are a 9-period SMA (simple moving-average) as a red line, and a 45-period EMA (exponential moving-average) plotted as a blue dashed line.

Figure 5.7
German Dax - 2-week Bar Chart
Bottom - 14-period RSI (black) with 9-period simple moving average (red) and 45-period exponential moving Average (dash, blue)

The price action in the red square is a head-and-shoulders pattern. It is a directional signal warning of a change in trend.
An inverted pattern can form at price bottoms.

In Optuma, in the 'Brown' tools folder, you will find this configuration of RSI with these averages ready to be added to your chart. Here is why I add moving-averages on the oscillator.

Starting from left to right you will find a red arrow pointing down to a pivot in RSI. Critical, critical! When RSI tests the cross-over, in this case as the short period SMA crosses down through the slower or longer period EMA, it is a signal like a trampoline. The sharpest moves in the market can develop from this setup. It's not just the crossing over of the averages, it is the test of RSI using the cross-over as support or resistance that should have your undivided attention. The setup at this first red arrow shows this exact critical pattern.

Moving right we come to the classic bullish divergence setup between the RSI and price marked with blue lines. Be aware of the spread between the extremes. I see people marking divergences maybe five years apart! It might be divergence, but that signal is so weak you should wait for a better setup.

Next, the two green arrows pointing up. The RSI that slips down from the purple horizontal line holds above the cross-over as the fast SMA is about to cross up through the slower EMA. The RSI then rockets upwards and stays above the red SMA moving-average. The fact that the spread is positive is important.

The yellow circle on RSI forms bearish divergence to price, but the market will run you over as it makes another swing up to a new high. Never sell or buy based on the position of a single oscillator without either technical confirmation, or permission from a trigger signal. We will cover trigger signals later in this chapter when we look at Stochastics.

Then we have a second divergence pattern contained in the red circle after the yellow circle. Divergence again, but should we believe it this time? Yes. Why? The RSI failure is near the 70 level and the spread between the averages is narrowing.

Next, the RSI peak with the first of two long heavy red arrows pointing down. RSI failed under the dashed EMA. The SMA and EMA spread is negative. The RSI fails under the horizontal purple line. RSI used the same purple line as support earlier (between the two divergence circles). The second heavy red arrow shows RSI fails under the red SMA. RSI tracks below both averages into a bottom. The price bottom is not accompanied by a divergence warning in RSI. This is the primary weakness and problem in RSI.

Figure 5.8
S&P500 March Futures (ESH22) -
240-minute bar chart

Middle - 14-period RSI (black) with
9-period simple moving-average (red) and
45-period exponential moving-average
(blue)

Bottom - 7-period Detrend Oscillator

Chart by TradeStation

Everything we have discussed applies to shorter intraday time horizons. Figure 5.8 is a 240-minute bar chart of the S&P500 March 2022 Futures contract.

You will understand all the signals marked. There is one addition, be aware of the character of the RSI at tops and bottoms. The chart above shows the favorite pattern in RSI is to create "W" at reversal price lows and "^" at the top. Markets develop their own footprint.

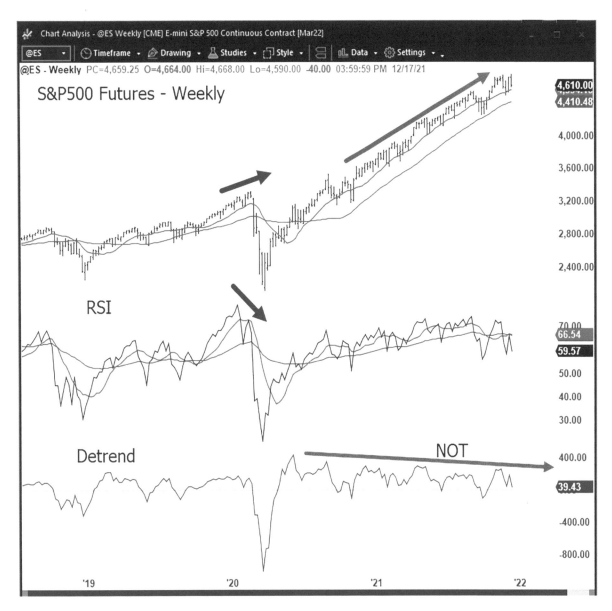

Chart Analysis - @ES Weekly [CME] E-mini S&P 500 Continuous Contract [Mar22]

@ES ▼ | ⏱ Timeframe ▼ | ✏ Drawing ▼ | ⚖ Studies ▼ | ⬚ Style ▼ | ⊟ | ⊪ Data ▼ | ⚙ Settings ▼

@ES - Weekly  PC=4,659.25  O=4,664.00  Hi=4,668.00  Lo=4,590.00  -40.00  03:59:59 PM  12/17/21

S&P500 Futures - Weekly

RSI

Detrend                                                    NOT

'19                    '20                    '21                    '22

Figure 5.9
S&P500 Futures (continuous) - weekly bar chart
Middle - 14-period RSI (black) with 9-period simple
moving-average (red)
and 45-Period exponential moving-average (blue)

Bottom - 7-period Detrend Oscillator

The S&P500 chart in Figure 5.9 is making an important point to highlight. The purple arrows are bearish divergence signals. But the red arrows are prevalent on the Internet such as LinkedIn charts, economic sites, and some online dictionaries. While the trend lines do diverge, this is not divergence for market analysis or trading. If the market is constantly running you over the entire year, how can anyone use this is an example of bearish divergence? It is not. Use patterns like those we have been discussing. A major economic certification organization used the chart pattern above to illustrate divergence. Clearly that is a poor example. The divergence failure problem of RSI will have a solution in the next oscillator.

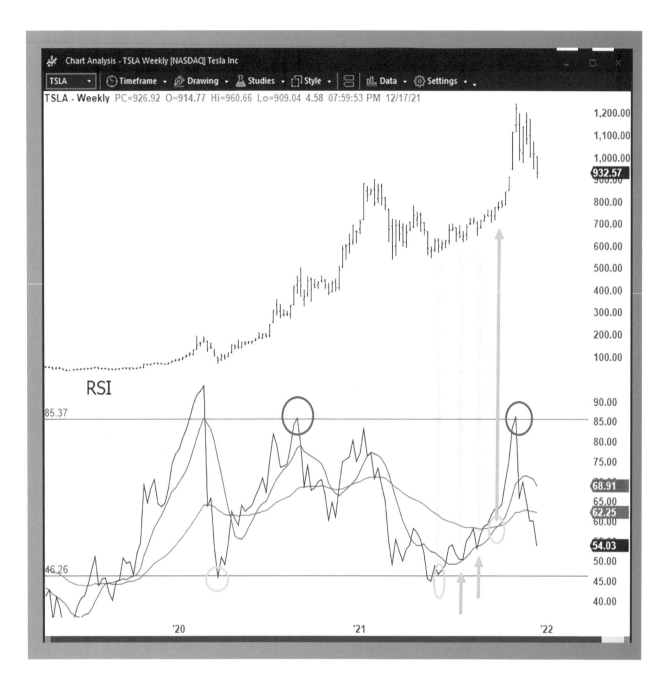

Figure 5.10

TESLA Co. (TSLA)- weekly bar chart

Bottom- 14-period RSI (black) with 9-period simple moving-
average (red) and 45-Period exponential moving-average (blue)

The last chart in our overview of the Relative Strength Index is a question. By the time you read this book the question will have been answered, but this is the current picture at the time this was written.

Is the uptrend for Tesla complete in Figure 5.10? If not, why not?

This is a weekly chart and Tesla is making a deep correction that is incomplete. However, it is then going to muster a serious bounce. How do we know this? The RSI peak in the second red circle topped near 85. Also notice that the current spread in the RSI averages is very positive. This warns that the stock still has the strength to develop a strong swing back up to give the averages time to rollover. This does not mean a new price high is assured. This is the pattern we have seen many times in various markets and time horizons. Use that information to your benefit.

Our next challenge will be to tackle the problem that RSI can fail to diverge at major trend reversals. This is a serious weakness within RSI but I have a solution for us. That will be in our next oscillator discussion.

**Figure 5.10 was captured early in the week of December 24, 2021 when the text above was written.
The insert chart below of Tesla was captured on January 21, 2022.**

The RSI discussion had already been completed, but I wanted to show you what followed in TESLA a month later.

The follow-up rally did occur back to 1200. As the rally developed the RSI could only advance to a level of 60.97. This was to the under-side of the crossing over moving-averages on the RSI. This was described earlier as the most dangerous or high-risk position for RSI to fail. It can cause prices to reverse as though hitting a trampoline. This demonstrates the reaction.

There is another high-risk formation in RSI I may not have described. Notice the 'M' pattern that RSI formed under the crossing averages. A failure from an "M" RSI formation under the crossing over averages is the most damaging as it often starts a wave 3 decline. This was described as the wave of recognition when everyone in the crowd is on the same side of the market move. Price targets in the insert chart will be covered in Chapter 6.

## Normalized + Unbound = Unbound Oscillator
# COMPOSITE INDEX: CONSTANCE BROWN

How often does RSI fail to detect a price reversal by failing to diverge from price? At right in Figure 5.11 is the NASDAQ 100 Index in a weekly chart. Compare pivots marked with arrows of like color in the two oscillators to the corresponding price action. The first arrows are red over the Composite Index and RSI. RSI failed to develop divergence before the trend reversal. Then move right to compare the oscillators with light blue arrows. The Composite develops divergence to price when RSI failed to give any warning. You have the pattern for the colored arrows in this chart. RSI fails often. Too often! I no longer use RSI, as the traits I like in RSI have been transferred into the Composite Index formula while solving many of the RSI divergence failures by modifying the formula.

The Composite Index adds a momentum comparison of the RSI oscillator creating a hybrid formula. Early in my career I would put indicators on indicators to improve the signal timing. If momentum can warn when price trends are waning, why not use momentum to know when an oscillator is losing steam? How the indicator was developed and how to use it in your own analysis and trading will be covered in depth. The Composite Index is my primary oscillator that I couple with a 7-period detrend oscillator. In my experience, I have learned it is best to use two oscillators. Many pair two oscillators, but they are both momentum formulas. I recommend selecting one oscillator from the momentum formula category that measures volatility, while the other formula should be based on price, like the detrend oscillator, to remove trend and create the unbound amplitude extremes we examined earlier.

The Composite Index also removes the percentage normalization of RSI to solve the issue all normalized oscillators have of becoming locked at the top or bottom of their ranges in strong trends.

Download from my LinkedIn posted articles. (QR-Code)
This is an extensive study - Composite Index: An evaluation of divergence signals in long-term financial markets.
Includes formula, instruction, and global equity index study.
Alternate download -
https://aeroinvest.com/COMPOSITE_INDEX.pdf
(This link is case sensitive.)

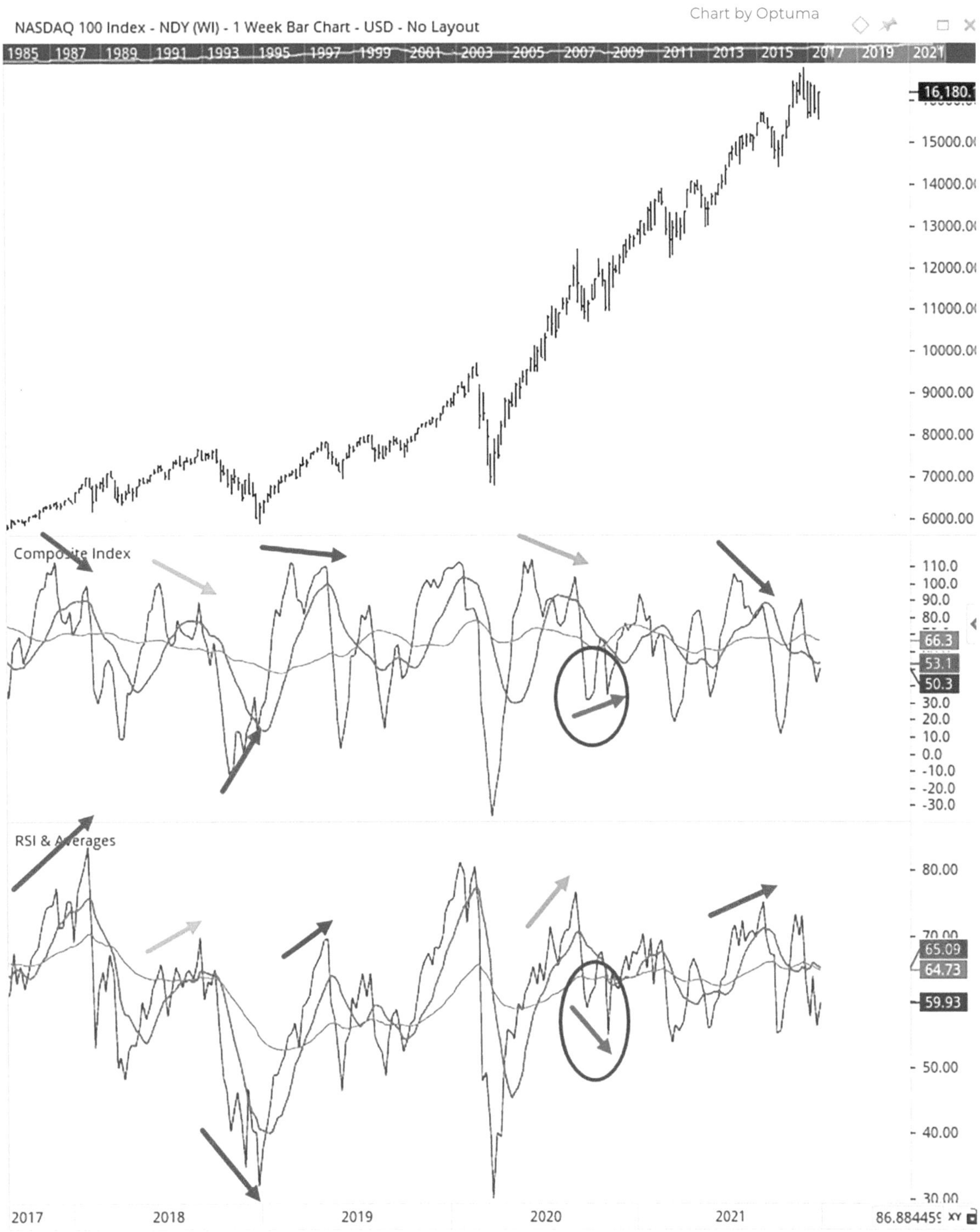

NASDAQ 100 Index - NDY (WI) - 1 Week Bar Chart - USD - No Layout

Chart by Optuma

Figure 5.11 - NASDAQ 100 (NDY)- weekly bar chart
Middle - Composite Index with two moving-averages, 13-period SMA, 33-period, SMA
Bottom- 14-period RSI (black) with 9-period simple moving-average (red)
and 45-Period exponential moving-average (green)

# COMPOSITE INDEX FORMULA

The Composite Index formula is as follows
in TradeStation EasyLanguage format:

Plot1(RSIMO9+RSI3,"Plot1");

Plot2(average((plot1),13),"Plot2");
Plot3(average((plot1),33),"Plot3");

Half of the formula is a function RSIMO9;
RSIMO9 = MOMENTUM(RSI(CLOSE,14),9)
The other half of the formula is the function;
RSI3=AVERAGE(RSI(CLOSE,3),3)

Calculate a 9-period momentum of the 14-period RSI.
Calculate a very fast 3-period RSI that is slightly smoothed with a 3-period simple moving-average. Add the two together to break the range limitations of RSI. The Composite Index is an unbound oscillator.

Add two simple moving-averages of 13 and 33-periods calculated on the Composite Index.

This will keep the character of the RSI oscillator that we liked and solve the divergence problem in RSI that we do not like. How this methodology came about and why it works as it does will be fully explained for you.

Bloomberg has been adding the oscillator by request, Optuma has it in the 'Brown' tools folder. TradeStation can be added using the EasyLanguage lines above. eSignal has the formula to help you; Metastock format is in the book *Technical Analysis for the Trading Professional 2nd Ed*. StockCharts. com lists the oscillator as an option in their online software.

**The Composite Index/Brown/**
LIBRARY OF CONGRESS - Copyright United States Copyright Office
Brown, Constance M.
Type of Work: Computer File
Registration Number / Date: TX0005244690 / 1999-05-19
Application Title: Computer index computer program code.
Title: Computer program code for the Composite Index / Constance M. Brown
Date of Creation: 1996 (First Submission Date: 1991)

On March 13, 1986, Microsoft went public at $21.00 per share. In 1990, when I worked on the 104th floor of the World Trade Center, Microsoft already had the monopoly on computer operating systems. But the operating system was not Windows and display options were fixed and limited. If you split your screen to display eight frames, the indicators looked like postage stamps and that was the maximum you could create. None of the frames could be enlarged for better viewing. The physical display limitations were the reason I went to Manny Stoller, my boss on the 105th floor, to ask how to add a missing indicator. I was very much in beginner mindset and needed to compare everything as I knew very little.

Slowly I began to select methods that spoke to me and RSI was one of the oscillators. I used to use simple moving-averages on price and that taught me how to evaluate price and averages as a tool for support and resistance. I had no price projection methods other than averages, envelops, and Manny's volatility bands.

If we add moving averages to price to define support and resistance, why not add moving-averages to RSI? In a presentation for Tim Slater at the TAG conference the interest people expressed for the idea of indicators on indicators was a major hit. I returned to New York and began to study all kinds of variations on the theme of using indicators on indicators. For years I settled into a two-frame setup shown in Figure 5.12. Price with RSI below, then on the RSI add two moving-averages with Stoller's volatility bands on RSI.

The RSI formations I found to be most useful are marked at points '1' through '5' in the stock Johnson and Johnson (JNJ). Point '1' in RSI is not a divergence signal, but the 'V' in RSI returns within the bands at the 1.5 inner band. Point '2' is the pullback on top of the short period average crossing up through the slower moving-average on RSI. Point '3' is the reverse just before the averages cross down. Point '4' is bullish divergence with the very signal described for you previously to monitor. The second 'V' fails to touch the volatility band giving a warning the selling pressure has dried up. The price rallies but fails at point '5'.

The RSI then falls back to the red line showing you this small RSI stall is always an important pivot and marks the bottom of the decline.

In 1996, when *Technical Analysis for the Trading Professional* was first released, the signals called positive and negative reversals were described. These formations are based on closing prices only and should not be used in today's markets due to current price ranges.

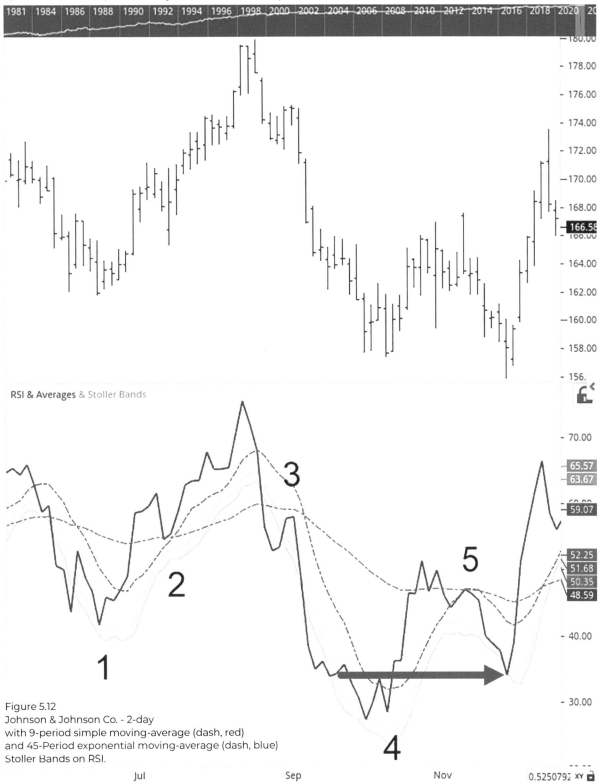

Johnson & Johnson - JNJ (US) - 2 Day Bar Chart - USD - No Layout

Chart by Optuma

RSI & Averages & Stoller Bands

Figure 5.12
Johnson & Johnson Co. - 2-day
with 9-period simple moving-average (dash, red)
and 45-Period exponential moving-average (dash, blue)
Stoller Bands on RSI.

Johnson & Johnson - JNJ (US) - 2 Day Bar Chart - USD - No Layout

Chart by Optuma

From this point forward, everything I ever learned about markets and technical analysis came out of necessity.

One day all my RSI secret setups to rule the world blew up in my face. A major trend reversal developed, and RSI gave no warning. RSI failed to warn with divergence that a major trend reversal would hit with extreme gusto. I had to come up with an answer to the problem as the cost was a very large hit and damaged my confidence. We all know that a trader that has shaky confidence will trade not to lose rather than trade to win. That mindset will bump you out of the industry.

I went to Manny Stoller. He taught me how the Momentum formula was used on price to warn when trends were waning. Maybe there could be something there in how I use indicators on indicators that could help. It was Manny who sent me off to explore, as he knew RSI had a history of failing to diverge at critical market reversals. He never taught by giving you a list to learn, he waited until you came to him and asked a question or had defined a problem. He then knew how to guide you through a process that might yield a path towards a solution.

Figure 5.13 was the first step after that conversation. I added a 10-period momentum histogram of RSI under RSI with the averages. The first thing to examine is the purple arrow and the histogram divergence that is present relative to the RSI and price. A light vertical dashed line shows the histogram is near the zero line when price shows a bottom October 11, 2021. Prices bounce up and the actual price bottom in the 2-day bar chart occurs on November 30, 2021. But notice in RSI the indicator pulls back to a blue horizontal line in the RSI frame, and the level is the same amplitude displacement as the sharp price key reversal. It is the price low in the chart and is circled in blue on October 30, 2020.

Then notice two price lows within the rally circled in green. The RSI bottoms on the same horizontal level are marked with a green arrow in the RSI frame.

The blue momentum histogram also bottoms on a horizontal level, but use the dashed vertical line to see that the histogram in the first low is earlier than the "V" in the RSI. The red horizontal line captures my interest. The problem is the histogram has too much noise.

Figure 5.13
Johnson & Johnson Co. - 2-day
14-period RSI with 9-period simple moving-average (red)
and 45-Period exponential moving-average (blue)
Bottom: 10-period Momentum of a 14-period RSI plotted as a histogram.

Johnson & Johnson - JNJ (US) - 2 Day Bar Chart - USD - No Layout

Chart by Optuma

How do we smooth anything? George Lane's Stochastics has a Fast and Slow line. Slow is just a 3-period moving-average of the 'Fast' to smooth the oscillation. I knew the answer to my momentum histogram problem was to put a simple moving-average on it to smooth the result. Then plot the moving-average, not the raw momentum calculation. I kept the display as a histogram and just gave it a new name. The Derivative Oscillator was born.

I had already discovered I needed a 9-period momentum as it improved the divergence character to solve the RSI divergence problem. But when I smoothed Momentum, and examined it as the Derivative Oscillator, it was only then that I found the horizontal levels repeated and they told their own story. They painted a picture in their history of pivots that gave a probability for the amplitude aligning on the horizontal. The real work began in hundreds of charts and time horizons. These were then tested on the battlefield in real-time. The conclusion was to stop trying to draw trend lines on oscillators and pay attention to the horizontal levels they create and what happens to prices at these oscillator support and resistance levels. That was where the real magic was happening.

I also learned that the oscillating peaks and troughs provide a probability. If price respects the oscillator reversal often on this horizontal level, then odds are high it will do so in the current or future oscillator position testing the same amplitude. If half fail and half are respected, it is about 50:50 that the current market position will respect the oscillator reversal at this horizontal position. If the market history repeatedly ignores all the oscillator pivots that develop at this recorded horizontal amplitude displacement, chances are very high that the current test will be a sucker punch as well. Do not trust it.

As I studied the oscillator to price it was clear very shallow reversals in the oscillator near the zero line were extremely important. For example, bounces up to zero that failed, would then lead to some of the largest meltdowns in price. It made sense because the bounce would be wave 2 up and the price action that followed would become wave 3 down. If you know the Elliott Wave Principle, then you will understand when I comment that second and fourth waves of the same degree would define the same horizontal level

Figure 5.14
Johnson & Johnson Co. - 2-day
14-Period RSI with 9-period simple moving-average (red)
and 45-Period exponential moving-average (blue)
Middle: 9-period Momentum on 14-period RSI
Bottom: 9-period Momentum on RSI smoothed.

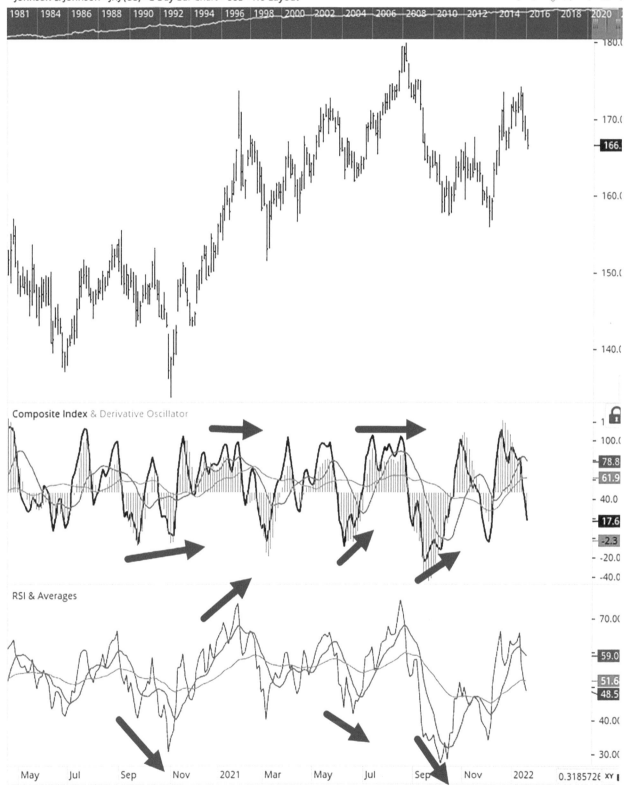

Johnson & Johnson - JNJ (US) - 2 Day Bar Chart - USD - No Layout

Chart by Optuma

near the zero line, then the larger degree second and fourth waves would reverse at the same horizontal levels with a greater amplitude away from the zero line. For example, waves (2) and (4) would reverse maybe at 50, but waves 2 of (3), and 4 of (3) would reverse nearer the zero line such as 20. Therefore, I began to use the oscillator to help define developing wave structure. This was extremely helpful in trends that extend.

However, the problem was that the Derivative Oscillator was in a separate frame. I still wanted to use the detrend oscillator and three oscillators took up too much room on the screen. I needed tall displays of price because I use geometry, Fibonacci price projections, and the Elliott Wave Principle.

Figure 5.15 was the next step. I favor oscillators displayed as lines. The Composite Index formula went through a few more changes to help accentuate the divergence pattern. When you compare the Derivative Oscillator to the Composite Index in the same frame, they are very similar, but the line oscillator plot is easier to read when horizontal levels of support and resistance form in the amplitude changes. I deleted the Derivative Oscillator and just use the Composite Index.

Figure 5.15 gives you the 14-period RSI for comparison under the Composite Index. There are many similarities because both oscillators have the 14-period RSI calculation within their formulas.

But the Composite Index is unbound, and the RSI is normalized and restricted from moving beyond a fixed range.

The biggest difference between the two oscillators is in the divergence patterns to price. This was the primary goal of doing all this work. Though it does not solve every one of the divergence problems in RSI, it does solve most of them.

RSI and the Composite Index will develop a pivot history at a specific amplitude displacement of their choosing, but they create their support and resistance levels differently. I find using the unbound range of the Composite Index of greater value so that the extremes can be recorded as a historic record. Therefore, the RSI was deleted from my screen, and I only use the Composite Index with a 7-period detrend oscillator. The Composite Index is a momentum formula. The detrend is on price. Detrend is a trading signal we will cover in Chapter 7.

Figure 5.15
Johnson & Johnson Co. - 2-day
Middle: Composite Index with moving-averages and Derivative Oscillator.
Bottom: 14_Period RSI, 9-period simple moving-average (red) and 45-Period exponential moving-average (blue)

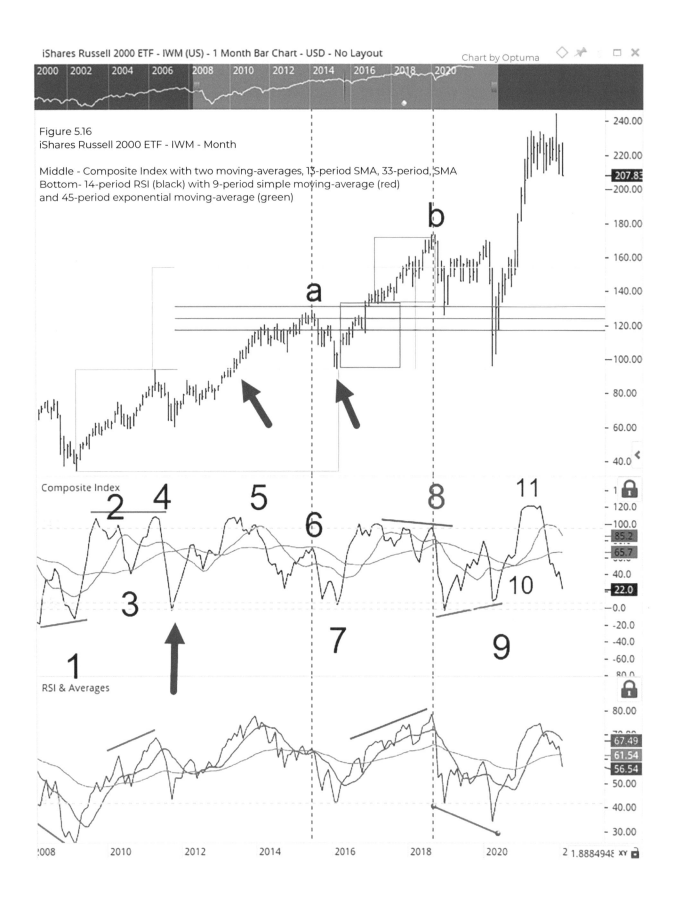

Figure 5.16
iShares Russell 2000 ETF - IWM - Month

Middle - Composite Index with two moving-averages, 13-period SMA, 33-period, SMA
Bottom- 14-period RSI (black) with 9-period simple moving-average (red)
and 45-period exponential moving-average (green)

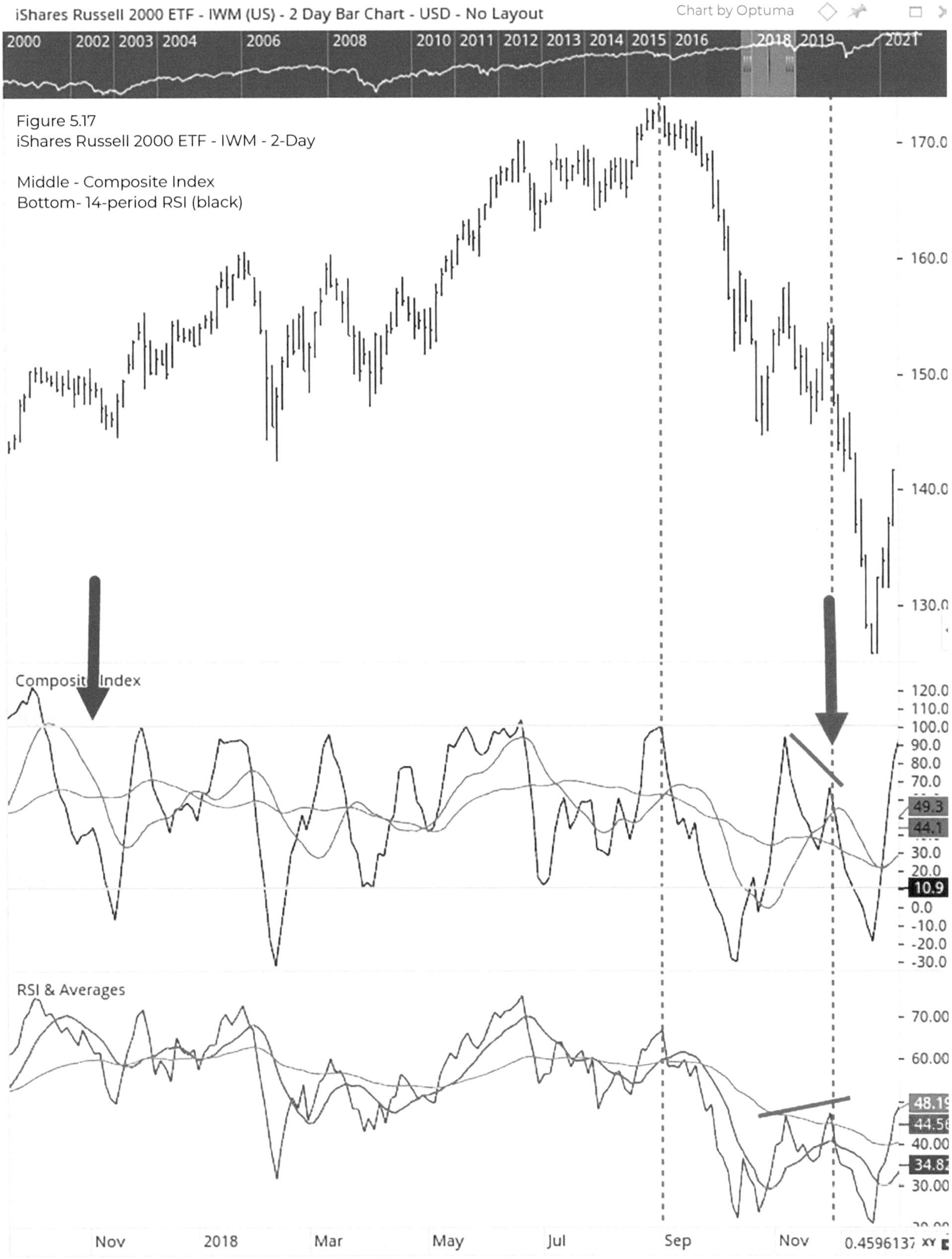
iShares Russell 2000 ETF - IWM (US) - 2 Day Bar Chart - USD - No Layout
Chart by Optuma
Figure 5.17
iShares Russell 2000 ETF - IWM - 2-Day
Middle - Composite Index
Bottom- 14-period RSI (black)
Composite Index
RSI & Averages
Nov
2018
Mar
May
Jul
Sep
Nov

The full-size view of Figure 5.16 is on the prior page when needed. The only reason this chart was selected is I realized I have not offered many ETF examples. What is important is how I will be working through the chart and point '8' will give us an opportunity to discuss using multiple time horizons.

Start with the divergence between price and the Composite Index at point '1'. It is divergence and the question is whether to buy based on the oscillator position? No. I will explain how to read the oscillator, but oscillators alone will not tell you to pull the trigger. They give the signal, and the triggers will be the confirmation. What are the triggers? Put that on the shelf until we look at George Lane's Stochastics. George explains triggers of confirmation best. You will also see that 'trigger' signals can come from two different time horizons. That too we will cover later. The point here is to resist selling or buying because a single oscillator crossed or has an extreme displacement. That is not sufficient reason to execute a trade position.

Point '2' in the Composite Index is a small 'M' divergence pattern to price and the RSI. RSI gives no warning, but notice the signal in the Composite does not ever indicate the magnitude of the decline that will follow. Oscillators alone never will give you the size of the reaction to follow. That is why you want to learn Elliott Wave patterns. That gives us the missing puzzle piece.

A lime-green dashed horizontal line is projected from '2'. Why? It is still very early in the larger rally, but '2' is a first wave up when mapping the sentiment of a crowd. Therefore, it is worth marking.

A small pullback follows, and the Composite falls to the oscillator trough at '3'. This is on the 33-period SMA. The oscillator holds the SMA and the up-trend resumes. While the RSI did not diverge, the pullback holds the 45-EMA and then the RSI swings up into a new high.

The Composite Index at peak '4' defines a double top. The double top proves to be meaningful. The ETF pulls back, and the Composite Index falls to the trough low marked by a purple arrow on the Composite Index. The low has a double horizontal green dashed line. The horizontal level was selected based on Composite Oscillator lows made earlier in the data off to the left-side of the frame. The horizontal lines have been in this chart for some time and the Composite just happened to stop here again. For this reason the pivot that develops in the RSI below the Composite is also marked with a horizontal green dashed line. If '2' is the first swing up, then the pullback is the second of five. Any oscillator marking where a third wave develops should be recorded. It is often the level of support that the oscillator will use to extend the developing trend. This becomes a reality at points '7' and '9'. But what we discussed regarding the RSI levels is also valid. The dashed line on RSI is near 40 and the range rules are demonstrated. When RSI held the 40 area, the pullback defined an entry opportunity for the resumption of the larger trend.

For years I compared both oscillators for this very reason, then removed RSI in favor of a 7-period detrend oscillator.

From the purple arrow on the Composite Index, both oscillators rally and track above their moving-averages. Only the Composite Index diverges at '5'. Now this is very important. From point '5' the Composite Index declines while price just consolidates sideways. An oscillator that declines with limited action in price is a death trap! The prior trend will resume. IWM rallies for several more months into the price high marked 'a'. The Composite swings up into point '6'. The moving-averages on the Composite Index now have a negative spread. RSI averages are crossing-over. This setup is far more bearish than '5'. The Composite Index at '6' has an unmarked pivot at this level if you scan left. It is halfway between the purple arrow on the Composite Index and point '5'.

The IWM ETF now makes a three-wave swing down where the Composite makes a double test at '7'. While the RSI does not diverge, the second RSI low is on the horizontal green dashed line. We know this level has been shown respect before. The market rallies into price high marked 'b'.
Now we need to talk about the rectangles on price. You likely need to view the full-size chart.

I am using the same method described in Figure 4.11. On price two purple arrows point to bars that we know are fourth waves. The rectangle was drawn from the price chart low to the first purple arrow. If you missed that important marker, you would wait and know to use the price low at the second purple arrow on price. They happen to be the same level. Copy/paste the rectangle and project it upwards from the top of the first box. The top of the second box was a long way up when it was drawn, so subdivide the box using the Fibonacci tool. We then have subdivided the second box into the ratios of 38.2, 50.0, and 61.8. Point 'a' fails under the 61.8 percent of the second rectangle. The market pulls back. The Composite Index falls to '7'.

The rally resumes to the price high marked 'b'. The same price swing is calculated using the blue boxes. Knowing the price target when the Composite Index defines a series of divergence oscillator peaks, clarifies the red point '8'. RSI never does define a divergence warning. Point '8' is in red because you will never form a final opinion from just a long horizon chart. Signals develop like dominoes and travel down through charts to shorter time horizon bar charts. The divergence is a warning and not the execution signal. You are missing the confirmation trigger we still need to discuss.

From the price high at 'b' the Composite falls to the horizontal green band. Price rebounds and then look closely. The Composite Index fails at the same amplitude marked at point '6'. The Composite Index falls back to the horizontal green dashed support zone at '9' with bullish divergence. The RSI fails to diverge. Point '10' is the test on the cross-over of averages. "11' warns the rally is over-heated.

Figure 5.16 and Figure 5.17 were kept together as full page side-by-side chart comparisons to help you learn how to read oscillator positions in two different time horizons. In Figure 5.12 the market was selected because point '8' in the monthly chart would be read incorrectly by many if they only used the monthly chart.

Before carving your opinion into stone, examine a shorter time horizon chart like the 2-day chart in Figure 5.17. This chart focuses on 2018 when the monthly chart developed several divergence patterns in a series of declining highs. In the 2-day chart we see that every time the Composite Index rallies to the upper horizontal green line, it develops a pullback. The pullbacks from March to July all hold the lower green support line on the Composite Index. That is the warning that the market can attempt another move up into another new high.

Figure 5.16 and Figure 5.17 were kept side-by-side because the goal is to trade when the position of the oscillators is a signal in both charts. When they are out of sync and one is at a top and one on a bottom, the market can come back and bite you! The best ratio is 4:1. Whatever your chart's time frame is on the left, use a quarter of that time horizon for the chart on your right. Why? It has to do with harmonics, and we really do not need to go down that road today in order for you to benefit from the result.

Every time the Composite rallies to the upper horizontal line, it develops a pullback. The pullbacks warn that the market can attempt another move up. How will we know the market top is finally in place?

Here are some ways to help define a market top:

1. The market realized a major price target.

2. Oscillators in multiple time-horizons are diverging from highs within their oscillator time horizons.

3. The mass crowd completed a five wave swing up (or down) in price.

4. Look under the surface of your index. For Figures 5.12 and 5.13, the leading stocks within the Russell 2000 will also define a top.

4. Global equity indexes that correlate to the Russell 2000 will give the same warnings.

5. Read the 'tape'. What does that mean? Study how the closing prices of each bar are positioned relative to prior bars once the market begins to pull away from a top.

You can pick any combination of these. But the list has a very significant omission. Cycles. We can never overlook cycle analysis.

The price projection methods are a major and critical part of everything I do. We will cover these methods in Chapter 6. Do not skip Chapter 6 as it is one of the most important chapters in this book. Chapter 6 can be followed by my book *Fibonacci Analysis* if you want more examples and further details. It is now free in PDF format throughout the Internet.

Figure 5.17 (repeat for easy reference.)
iShares Russell 2000 ETF - IWM - 2-Day

# COMPOSITE INDEX ONLINE

The Composite Index has a growing list of vendors offering the oscillator. You will now find a new menu selection called 'CMB Composite Index' in the online software at StockCharts.com. My oscillator was added to their product called StockChartsACP. This is a full featured product priced for easy entry into technical analysis.

It is also a great addition for professional level analysts. The software has stunning point-and-figure charts, and numerous sorted package offerings that make our job easier when you do not have assistants or a team of researchers for support. The Composite Index oscillator is a simple menu selection you just click to add. The size of the frame and colors are easy to change to your preference.

EquiVolume charting is a standard bar chart with volume influencing the width of each bar. The

concept was developed by Richard Arms. The concept then evolved.

The two charts in Figures 5.18 and 5.19 use the chart style called CandleVolume that was the EquiVolume idea developed further by Richard Arms. The width of the real bodies reflect volume adding value to pattern interpretation. The wider the candle, the greater the volume for that period. Thin candles develop on low volume. Few vendors offer CandleVolume charts.

Figure 5.18 easily shows you how CandleVolume charts adjust the width of each candlestick as volume increases or declines. Figure 5.19 shows you how more compressed candles will still highlight volume changes. The volume plotted under price can be removed. Add the Composite Index for further confirmation. The oscillator interpretation is not impacted by the chart style you favor to plot the price data.

## Normalized Oscillator
# STOCHASTICS: DR. GEORGE C. LANE (AND RESEARCH GROUP)

Everything you may know today about Stochastics could be incorrect. It is not your fault.

How can that be? The original instructions that explained how to use this oscillator were written *by the programmer* who developed the first software package for Tim Slater called CompuTrac. CompuTrac was founded by Tim Slater and was the greatest spark to the growth and acceptance of Technical Analysis in our history. His software was the first package to collect end-of-day data from third-party vendors and offer computer generated analytics. It was a huge break-through for us. Before CompuTrac everyone charted by hand.

CompuTrac did not wait for George Lane to write his recommendations about how his oscillator should be used. Lane felt the company was still in the evaluation and development phase and that they needed real-time environment testing. The release was premature he said. CompuTrac went ahead and wrote their interpretation of how to use the oscillator. Thereafter every vendor repeated the same misinformation that began with CompuTrac about the buy and sell of the 20/80 levels. It has become a standard but was never the interpretation George Lane taught! In fact, when a market crosses down and back up through the 80 level, George would buy the market. He said it is often the start of a move that will run another 50% to the upside. Same for the 20 level. Pass up through 20 and then cross back down 20, it becomes a strong sell signal with significantly more price action expected to follow in the downtrend. We must set this straight. Most documentation on Stochastics in our industry is incorrect.

How do I know the industry is moving down the wrong track on this? I was taught by George Lane how to use Stochastics. I returned to his trading room many times. He was a close and much respected mentor who provided guidance most of my career. I did not realize the Internet had lost so much of his original documentation. Readers of my ninth book, *Thirty-Second Jewel*, wrote to me to say they could not find a document I had referenced in the book. So many emails were sent to me that I finally began to research this problem for myself. Readers were correct. I could not find any of George's original charts and no meaningful documentation at all. It was possible I was holding the only known complete week-long course that George Lane had developed and taught. Part of the materials I had saved included all of George Lane's S&P500 trades in 5-minute bar charts for an unbroken sequence across three and half months. His signals, decision tree, execution timing, and a mountain of information about how he traded using Stochastics were all there. I copied the entire binder with my seminar notes and his trade-room charts. Then I started a personal campaign to set the record straight.

When I asked George why the industry was so off on how Stochastics should be used, he said, well, I cannot say what he actually said, but it goes like, "To heck with them, if they want to know how to use my oscillator they should come and ask me!" The problem being that the documentation he developed has been lost over time and, with his passing, only the vendor's guidance and countless authors duplicating this incorrect information about 20/80 levels remain. We need to straighten this out now.

STEP 1. The place for you to begin is to download the original course. Use this direct link:
https://aeroinvest.com/STOCHASTICS.pdf.

Important! Do not download to a mobile phone. It is a massive file, and the document is a double-spread layout. I wanted you to have the exact binder as it should be viewed. Download to your computer first and save it. The only way to view it is in full screen mode. The color surrounding the binder pages should be black. If it is gray, you are not in full screen mode. Press CTL+L to toggle full screen on/off. This is the same information we ask you to follow for the magazines I create. It means the charts and fine lines will be displayed as in the original. Otherwise, there is a distortion that an unprofessional eye would accept as the best view possible, when it is not as crisp as the original.

STEP 2. You now have a video presentation I gave for the IFTA 2021 Annual Conference discussing the George Lane course. It will give you a highlight, so you do not miss any of the important sections. It will also help you know some of the background.

Go to IFTA.org. It is part of the 2021 Conference video files.

Now you have more references to help you and together with this overview you will have a better understanding of how George Lane used Stochastics for analysis and trading.

Detrended Price Osc (Close,7,3,false,Yellow,Magenta,...

Stochastic Slow ( High , Low , Close ,27, 5 , 3 , 1 , 1,.....

STEP 1.

Take the first step. Download the original full week Lane course.  Use this direct link:

https://aeroinvest.com/STOCHASTICS.pdf.

This is a double page spread with all my opriginal lecture notes.

**Please do not download to mobile phone** as you need "full screen mode" (CTL+L) on your computer to read it like the original binder.

**LEARNING OBJECTIVES**

Learn how oscillators can be used for analysis of trend, overbought/oversold conditions, signal probability. Learn how to read volume. Develop the understanding of signal confirmation for position execution.

Figure 5.19
Facebook (FB) -weekly

Chart by TradeStation

George taught me how to read volume. Nothing is determined in his oscillator without using volume as an important relative comparison. Facebook (FB) crashed February 3rd, 2022. There were warnings long before. The double top in the weekly FB chart above shows Stochastics rolling over. That is not the sell signal. It must come when there is lower volume on divergence.

Compare the volume histogram on the second price high in Figure 5.19. Compare the first price high and the two matching volume notations below. The first price high is considered to be high volume. The second price high as a relative comparison is accompanied by lower volume. Always WAIT for the confirmation that is lower volume.

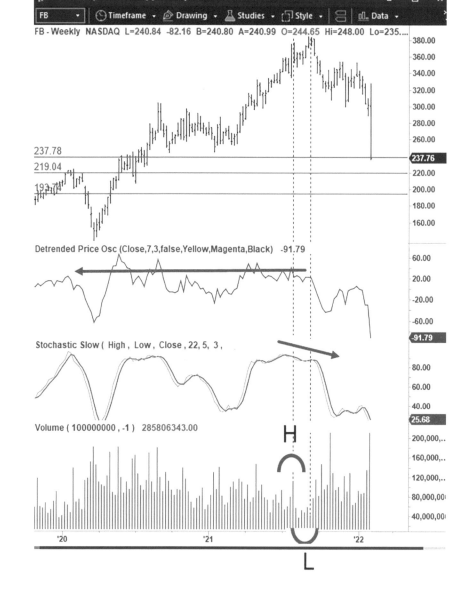

High volume does not mean it is a histogram bar on the top of the frame. It is always just a simple comparison. High volume versus lower volume may be well near the bottom of the histogram frame.

In Figure 5.20, showing the monthly chart for

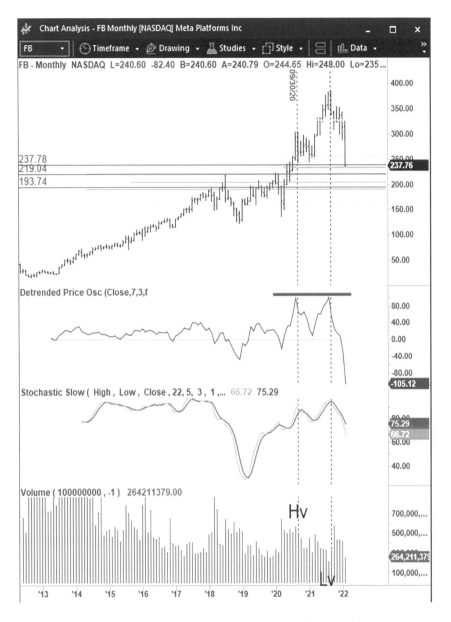

Figure 5.20
Facebook (FB) - monthly

Chart by TradeStation

Facebook, compare the vertical dashed lines.

The first key reversal in price at a peak in the detrend oscillator forms with high volume (Hv). The price high with the second detrend oscillator peak forms with lower volume relative to the volume September 30, 2020.

The detrend oscillator shows a clear double top, but we do not have any divergence in the monthly chart in the Stochastic oscillator.

Signals are like dominoes and progress through charts in descending time horizons. A signal in a monthly chart, in this case a double top confirmed by lower volume in Figure 5.20, is then seen in the weekly chart where Stochastics displays bearish divergence, and the signal is when the divergence is confirmed by lower volume.

**Always wait for the confirmation of lower volume**. It is rare the monthly signal will be confirmed in a weekly chart at the same time. Normally you will see the monthly chart setup first, then time passes and the weekly chart setups, then daily. When indicators do not align complex price patterns, or extensions, develop until the different time horizons do align their signals.

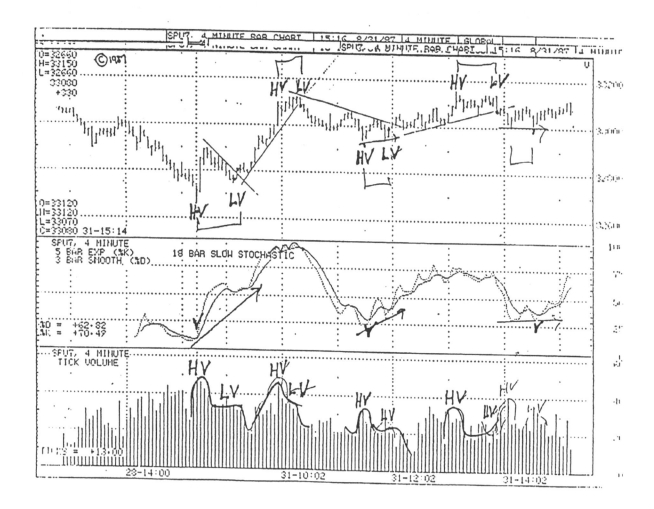

Figure 5.21
S&P500 September 1987 Futures - 4-minute bar chart
Charts by George Lane

Figure 5.21 is a George Lane chart from his trading room. If you study it closely you will see his weighting and decision tree is heavily leaning on volume. Therefore we began with a discussion of Hv and Lv comparisons. It is the way confirmation is obtained, but it is not the trade trigger signal. We still have much to discuss.

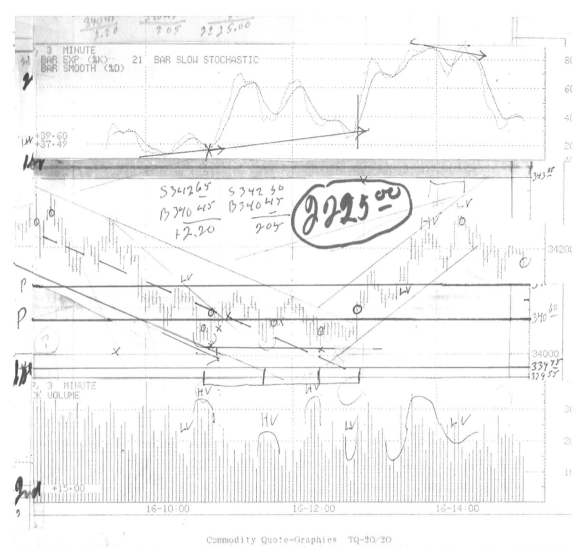

Figure 5.22
George Lane original chart.
S&P500 September 1987 Futures - 3-minute bar chart.
Slow Stochastic over price, Volume under price.

Figure 5.22 is a chart from George Lane's trading room. We have covered volume and you understand oscillator divergence. To understand the colored horizontal bands you should download the Lane course I put online. They are called price pivot points, and this is not my method of creating support and resistance levels. My method we will cover in Chapter 6.

What we need to discuss next is George Lane's trigger signals. On price in Figure 5.22 you will see George marked some price bar closes with small circles. These are trigger signals. Places of execution. You must be able to see and understand these as they are critical for any trader.

## Normalized Oscillator

# STOCHASTICS: GEORGE LANE'S 'CPR' TRIGGER SIGNALS

George Lane called his trigger signals 'CPRs'. This was the acronym for *Closing Price Reversal of Trend Signals*. When you are new you will think this is just a list of directional signals. They are far more important. They are the final shoe to drop giving you permission to risk your capital.

There are ten CPRs. CPRs are ALWAYS accompanied by low volume. The diagonal line is a trend line. You are looking at the close relative to the trend line and current price relative to the close of the prior bar. Study the double bottom patterns. C1 is strongest, B1 is strong, and A1 is the weakest pattern.

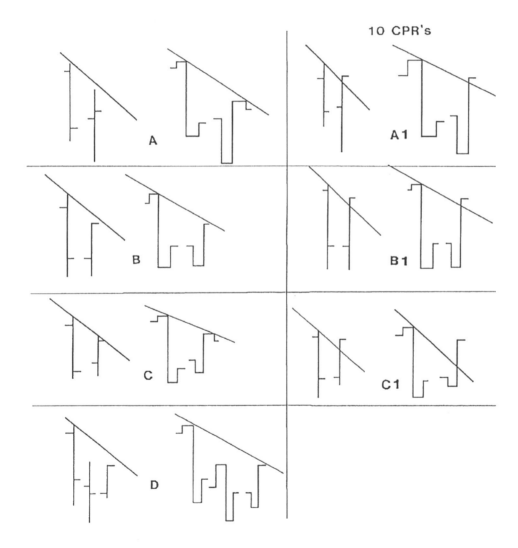

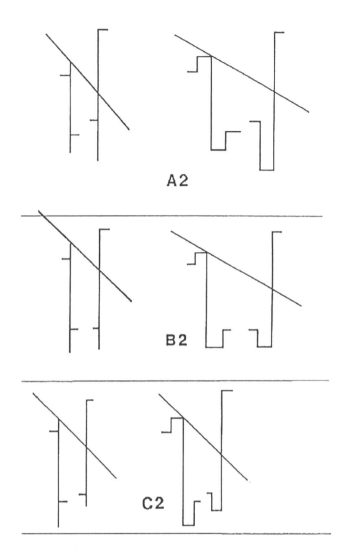

A2

B2

C2

Of the ten patterns 'A' is the weakest and 'C2' above would be the strongest trend reversal signal.

In all signals you want to be aware of whether the current bar can exceed the high of the previous bar or not. A2, B2, and C2 show the three different double bottom patterns from weakest to strongest. Then, in the three CPRs above, the current price exceeds the high of the bar behind it. These last three CPRs are the strongest trend reversal signals. Clearly all ten signals also apply to bear markets but will be inverted. These drawings are George Lane's.

Now we are ready to learn how to set up Stochastic periods correctly, understand the formula, and understand George's method of oscillator position interpretation.

TRIGGER SIGNALS FOR TRADERS

Learn the execution price bar formations that George Lane used for short-horizon trading.

# Normalized Oscillator

# STOCHASTICS: CORRECT PERIOD SETUP

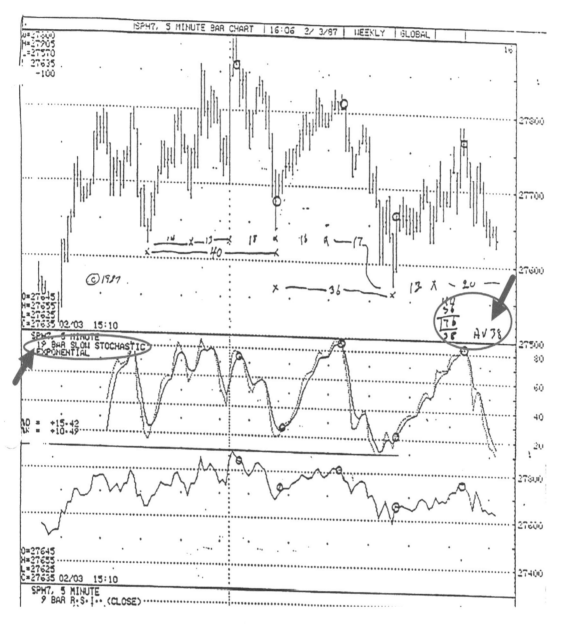

Figure 5.23
Chart from George Lane's week seminar showing the
correct period to use. It is one-half the cycle length.

2. Determine the Cycles in the charts you select, using the tools available in Computrac. Pick the optimum Cycle for you, one offering the greatest potential profits commiserate with the greatest risk you can afford moneywise and psycologically.

3. Use a periodicity (number of bars) that is 50% of the Cycle you choose to trade.

Stochastics is not a mechanical "black box" system, nor is it a simple crossover system. If you try to use the process that way, you're very likely to get hurt. There is a certain amount of study, interpretation and flexibility of mind necessary to use Stochastics successfully. However, in combination with conventional charting techniques and common sense, it beats anything else I know!

The text above is copied directly from George Lane's manual you are going to download. Right?

Lane instructs us to use one-half the cycle length. Generally, we use a cycle tool now on our charts and take half that cycle period, rather than averaging cycles as he shows at left by manually counting the bars. But this is good to know when you must analyze some very odd price action for the first time. You will find I have a need to do this manual method in Chapter 7 when I run into an issue with a Treasury yield chart.

Dominant cycles vary in different time horizons within the same market. Do not assume the same cycle in a 60-minute or shorter intraday chart will be the same in a weekly or monthly chart. Once you find the correct period for that time horizon, it does not change.

**What is the Stochastic formula?**

%K = ((C-L14)/H14-L14))x100.

That's it. 'C' is the most recent closing price. 'L14' is the lowest price traded within the last 14 price bars. 'H14' is the highest price within the 14 prior bars. The result is then normalized to be a percentage. %K is known as the Fast Stochastic. Then a moving-average is added as the signal line.

%D is a 3-period moving-average of %K. Then a moving-average of %D is calculated. If you plot this average and %D, it is known as the Slow Stochastic oscillator. Read the manual to learn why and where George used 6 periods in the formula and not most vendors' default setting of 5.

## Normalized Oscillator
# STOCHASTICS: INTERPRETATION

The sequence of the information being shared is in the same order George Lane used in his courses. He did not start with the Stochastic oscillator.

Many people know he said to look for three divergences. But what many people misunderstand is how he counted divergence.
The chart below is one he used in a presentation. There are many that look similar. It shows that the count starts from the first peak and the first divergence is not counted.

Figure 5.24
George Lane chart showing his method of counting to '3',
though he described it as the third divergence. There are
actually 2 divergences and three peaks.

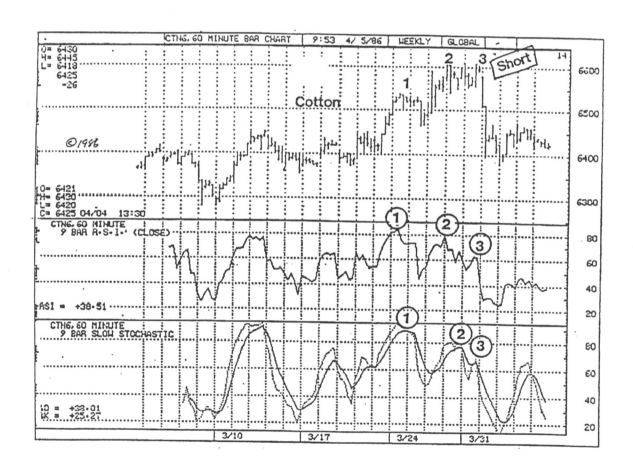

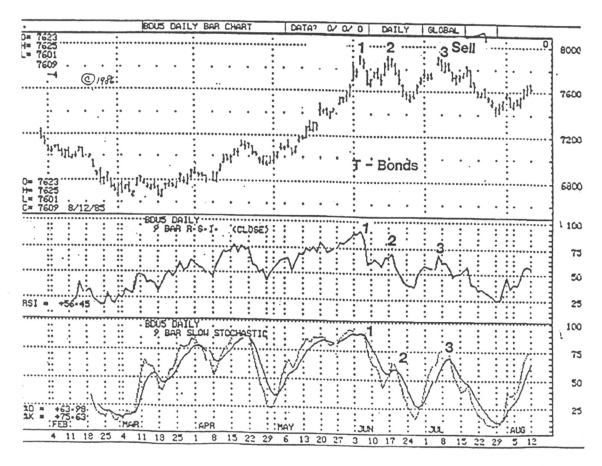

Figure 5.25
George Lane chart showing divergence is not always in
Stochastic but in alternate oscillators.

It is also important to know that Lane used more than Stochastics. He used a 9-period RSI, and then began to use my Composite Index due to the divergence problem in RSI. It is for this reason he endorsed the formula in the foreword of my book *'Technical Analysis for the Trading Professional'*.

Over the years I really do believe the most important oscillator is the 7-period detrend to be used with your preferred oscillator formula.

You will find that in his course material he explains that it does not matter if divergence develops in %D or the moving-average signal line.

Always know and refer to a chart of the next larger degree complete with Stochastics. This will contain the next larger Cycle than the one you are trading. Keep the big picture in mind.

With this chart, you can anticipate the type and speed of the next change in trend. When in doubt, trade in the direction of the longer-term Stochastic.

Keeping monthly, weekly and daily Stochastics on 20+ commodities was a tedious, time-consuming job. Now -- thanks to CompuTrac-- - it's easy!

I find that keeping Stochastics with another oscillator, such as R.S.I., Demand Index or Demand Aggregate, or Commodity Channel Index --- or any of the 18+ assorted indicators available in CompuTrac --- is very helpful.

However, in my opinion, the best is Volume --- tick, or real. We feel so strongly about Volume that we teach it in every one of our courses.

Figure 5.26
George Lane 'gems' in the course binder you will be downloading.

The most important text is below. It never tells us to sell 80 or buy 20. Stop doing that! In fact, crossing back through 75 and 25 Stochastic levels are likely only 50% of the developing price swing. It makes sense because then you hit the third wave in trending markets. If you sell 80 or buy 20 you will be crushed. There are many examples in George's trade room charts showing that his decision tree was very different. All part of the download package. From here I will ask you to study his material in depth.

The link is free ... aeroinvest.com/STOCHASTICS.pdf

At this point I have reached my goal of giving you preparatory guide to his material and highlighting some of the things you absolutely should not miss. It is best you see his interpretations from his own charts and words. My notes are included. Be sure to use '6' so the 'knee' patterns do not cross %D. You will see which setting that references in my notes in the package.

In a market returning to the major trend: the short-term trend is up, the intermediate trend is up and the long-term trend is up. When %K reaches the 75% overbought level, the commodity is frequently only halfway to its price High.

So, your plan of action is as follows:

    A. Plan on taking profits (or moving a stop-loss up close) when the stock or commodity has moved up to a price that is twice the price it had at the 75% level, its 100% price objective; or

    B. Take profits when %K falls below 60%; or

    C. Take profits when %K crosses below %D.

Figure 5.27
George Lane never told us to use the 80/20 levels to sell or buy..

## Unbound Oscillator
# MACD: MOVING-AVERAGE CONVERGENCE DIVERGENCE
# GERALD APPEL

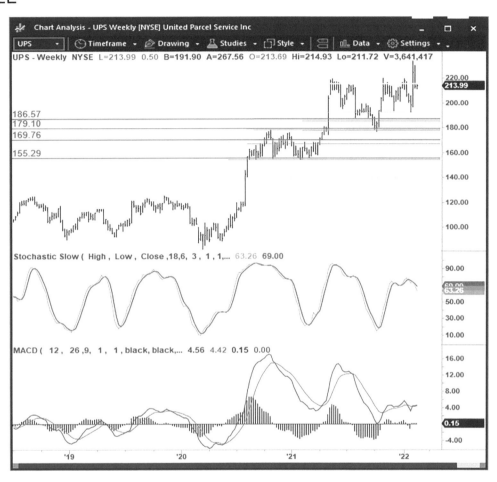

Figure 5.28
United Parcel Post UPS -
weekly with Stochastic (18,
6, 3) and MACD (12, 26, 9)

Chart by TradeStation

The United Postal Service (UPS) weekly chart shows a common setup by those who favor MACD. Please visit en.wikipedia.org/wiki/MACD to obtain an excellent and detailed description of this oscillator. You are plotting the spread of two moving-averages. It has a timing lag I do not care for because of the spread periods used for the two moving-averages. It is used by longer-horizon investors and funds. Gerald Appel used two MACD setups, one setup as above to enter a position, and one with shorter periods for position exits to minimize the lag problem. MACD is often paired with Stochastics.

As I do not trade using this oscillator; please reference the Wikipedia article for those interested.

# 6

PRECISE KNOWLEDGE OF PRICE
SUPPORT/RESISTANCE LEVELS

# CHAPTER SIX

# Price Confluence Zones

## ENTRY/EXIT LEVELS, POSITION SIZE, AND RISK MANAGEMENT.

If you learn nothing else from this book, let it be the contents of this chapter. Had I named the chapter Fibonacci, many would skip on by thinking they already know it. So many I have taught started off with the perception that they do not need this. HA! Then they become the very people who struggle the most because they discover all they knew was theory while they did not understand real-time application.

What is the difference? To begin, you will do all you can NOT to select the high and drop down to the swing low on the bottom of your chart. That is the theory. You learn that a selected range is subdivided by the ratios 38.2, 0.50, and 68.1.  Never use 25% or 75%. We will create multiple ranges and hit these subdivisions using just the three. Then you should know you can add, subtract, multiply, or divide any Fibonacci ratio and the result will be another Fibonacci ratio. So only use three.

# DISNEY (DIS)- AN INTRODUCTION

Figure 6.1
Disney Co. (DIS) weekly

Fibonacci confluence
zones of major support.
7-period detrend oscillator
below.

Chart by TradeStation

This will be the abridged notes version for what is in my book *Fibonacci Analysis*. Lots of illegal free downloads online for you to select. The people who love it see it working every day in their trading. The people who hate this book cannot handle something different and will fight it. They like envelopes and trend lines. Useless for defining price targets. Know this... of all the methods I know, this is the one above all else that has allowed me to have a career and longevity in the markets. Period.

Markets expand and contract. Study swings that follow after the middle of a large trending move relative to the swings that began the trend. The last half may accelerate and expand in successive swing lengths. The momentum after the strongest middle thrust might contract causing the swings to contract and shorten relative to the earliest swings to set up the move. This is the normal market action. So how the heck is just tapping the price high and extreme low ever going to give you the correct price targets? In expanding markets your target will be too low and the market will reverse above your calculation. In markets that begin to contract your target will be broken and the reversal will then develop and pass right through your simple target. You will think Fibonacci retracements do not work. They do. But not if you only know theory.  Yes, a selected range should be divided into the ratios 38.2, 0.50, and 61.8. That's it, not  25.0 and 75.0 which most vendors add as defaults. But the difference is knowing how to apply these subdivisions, so you reveal how the market is using them, not how your textbook defined the basic principles.

Every Fibonacci ratio that you add, subtract, multiply, or divide together will give another Fibonacci ratio as the result. Since we use multiple selected price ranges, we will calculate any other ratio that could be important. Simple. Stop clicking the high and the extreme low and think you have Fibonacci analysis in the bag.

Here's how it really works. You are going to avoid the market highs, and especially key reversals like they are the Covid virus! You will be looking for strong bars and gaps in this method. For support you want to start the range you select as LOW as you can on the top of a price bar. Why? That way you will be able to create several confluence zones of major support. I know... what is confluence? That is where two DIFFERENT Fibonacci ratios overlap one another or cluster very close together. If we call the start 0% and the end of your selected range 100%, change these line colors. I use soft gray. Confluence is not a Fibonacci ratio that lands on 0 or 100% defining the range limits. It has to be at least two ratios.

Big problem. Many vendors have it wrong. The first place you tap should be 0% and you should end with 100%. Vendors may mark the start as 100%. That's wrong. Just turn the label off so it doesn't mess with you because the subdivided ratio labels will be backwards as well. Does not matter because the lines fall at the same place within the subdivided range. You are good.

The Disney chart at left begins with ALL ranges selected from the pivot marked with a red arrow. Yes, that just fried many people who only know the theory. Get over it. Pick the top of a strong bar as low as you can. The very next and last bar drops hard to a Fibonacci confluence support zone.

This is important to understand. You are creating a grid and not a forecast. I did not forecast a drop to that horizontal band in the chart; my oscillators and Elliott Wave interpretation told me the decline is not over. Therefore, I know where it should move to next when it does break. It gives no indication of 'when'. However, it does tell me it will be fast and sharp. How? When there is nothing to interfere with the move between the horizontal bands, I know it has little resistance and just falls fast to the next one.

There is a single Fibonacci ratio above the support band that Disney landed on. View single Fibonacci ratios as minor support. You need the cluster, or what we call the confluence zone, to define major support. If your indicators tell you to look for more to the downside, then it is also a target and not just a grid line of support.

Before I show you how I created these horizontal bands of major support, let's fast forward in time to see what happens next. First extend all your lines to the right so they meet with the y-axis. That way the new data coming into the chart has lines beneath.

You are looking at a real-time working chart I prepared for my clients. At the time I told them the Disney target was 128.80. There is a horizontal line running through one of the confluence zones marking the price at 128.81. It is on the lower floor of that confluence band. Normally I mark the top of the band, but I wanted to know in this case where the low occurred that would mark a failure that would lead to the next lower band at 121. Disney stopped right on the 128 support zone. Big problem for Disney though. The bounce now at 154.25 is an Elliott Wave fourth wave rally. It is corrective. A simple swing projection points to 121. The 128 level will fail. That is when you take a new look at it and the general indexes.

How did I know this was the target and not the band above it? There is a red arrow marked '1'; trace the swing up and you will find the small gap above it. Markets fill gaps. I had calculated the Fibonacci confluence zones of support to find out if the decline would fall short of the gap or run drop a little beneath it. The confluence zone formed just under the gap. I did not tell clients all the reasons. I just said the target was 128.80, a bounce, that should then lead to the 121 Fibonacci support zone.

Notice the oscillator position into the price support zone at 128. Price pushes the oscillator to the same amplitude displacement or pivot behind the oscillator low. Just trace backwards along the green arrow marked on the oscillator. We sure found the right math grid this stock is working within to develop future swings. Price action on the target zones is a confirmation we have the right ranges. Long horizon or intraday charts work the same.
     Ready to learn how it is done? Good. Let's do it.

Figure 6.2
Disney Co. (DIS) - weekly, Chart by TradeStation

Fibonacci confluence zones of major support.
7-period detrend oscillator below.

The three red arrows mark the end of the selected Fibonacci
ranges. The subdivisions then create the band clusters under
the stock marking major support.

# S&P500 FUTURES (ESH22)- RESISTANCE

Figure 6.3

S&P500 March 2022
Futures (ESH22)
20-minute bar chart

Middle - Composite
Index
Bottom - Detrend
Oscillator

Chart by TradeStation

We are going to screen capture a series of charts in real-time. In the y-axis the price in a black oval is the current price. That is true for all TradeStation charts which have a black chart title in the book. I am starting with a 20-minute chart of ESH22. The futures market has advanced off the low from the previous day. It is as you see it in Figure 6.3. This is how I first saw the chart. First question is to understand is whether the market consolidation is under major or minor resistance? Then we need to know if the market moves up, where is it going to move to next?

Most will tap the low and high, the gray lines, and subdivide the range. Market is at the 50% line. Rare, but we will go with this. How will you know if it is minor or major resistance? You cannot not. Where is the next target? The 61.8% retracement level marked on the chart near 4500? No. It does not work that way.

Figure 6.4

S&P500 March 2022
Futures (ESH22)
20-minute bar chart

Middle - Composite
Index
Bottom -  Detrend
Oscillator

Chart by TradeStation

Start the range you select for calculating resistance from the low of a price bar. Select a LONG price bar. We will avoid key reversals whenever possible. Learn to look at internal action and NOT just the start of a swing. Huge problem for beginners to only look at the start and end of a swing.

Figure 6.4 is the first range I select. The bottom is the start and the end of the range is a price high just UNDER the key reversal. The market Is under the 61.8% retracement. It is only a single Fibonacci ratio and is therefore only minor resistance. This does not tell us where the market will move up to next if resistance is broken.

It is important to see that 61.8% in Figure 6.4 is slightly lower than the 50% level in Figure 6.3.
The next steps willtell us whether the market is under major or minor resistance. It will also tell us where the next target will be if the current highs are broken.

The second Fibonacci range begins from the same

Figure 6.5
S&P500 March 2022
Futures (ESH22)
20-minute bar chart

Middle - Composite
Index
Bottom - Detrend
Oscillator

Chart by TradeStation

low as the start of the first. Always use the same low when calculating resistance. Then end the new range on a long bar. We will also use gaps but there are none in the chart. As I draw the cursor up, I am looking for a strong bar that starts the confluence pattern, this is when two DIFFERENT Fibonacci ratios cluster next to one another or very close together.

Add a third Fibonacci range. When we created two ranges, the confluence zone confirmed that S&P500 was under and respecting major resistance. I need a third range to identify exactly where the next target will be if nearby resistance

ESH22 - 20 min  PC=4,394.00  O=4,393.50  Hi=4,468.00  Lo=4,381.75  49.00  12:00:40 PM  02/15...

Figure 6.6
S&P500 March 2022
Futures (ESH22)
20-minute bar chart

Middle - Composite Index
Bottom - Detrend
Oscillator
Chart by TradeStation

is exceeded. The purple arrow points to the 38.2% retracement making the nearby highs serious major resistance.

This is likely a fourth wave corrective rally. Corrections make three wave swings in price. There are three Fibonacci ratios that are clustered together. The ESH22 might fail with a third test.

I want to know resistance zones higher than just the next one. I need a series of resistance price zones. What if the market suddenly launched upwards? I need to be prepared before that may happen.

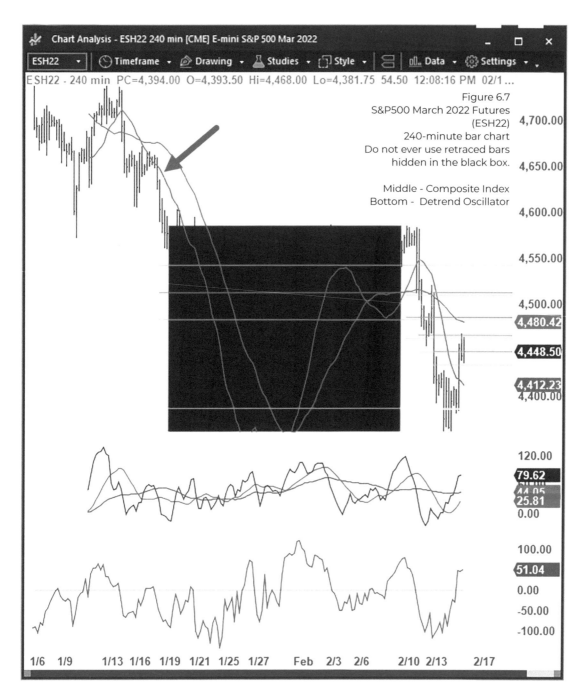

Figure 6.7
S&P500 March 2022 Futures
(ESH22)
240-minute bar chart
Do not ever use retraced bars
hidden in the black box.

Middle - Composite Index
Bottom - Detrend Oscillator

I change my time-horizon to 240-minutes. I need to see the data in a higher time frame. Select another range. Start from the same price low on the bottom of a bar and select a higher strong bar. Red arrow shows where I end. You CANNOT use any bars that have been retraced. Therefore, I am hiding the swing down in a black opaque box. The ending of each range must be higher than the last.

We have very well-defined Fibonacci confluence zones that define resistance in the 240-minute chart above. The first red arrow at the top shows you the bar I selected for the end of the third range. If you went to the high the Fibonacci ratios, you would just create lines of noise. I need tight clusters.

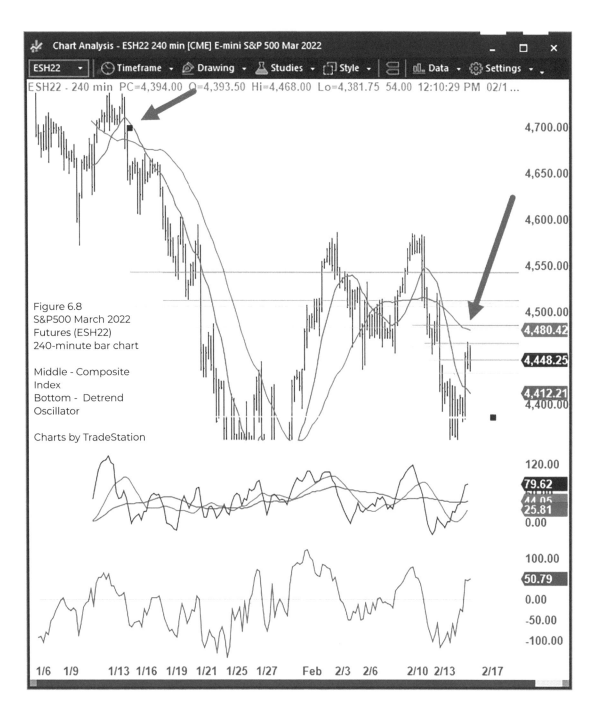

Figure 6.8
S&P500 March 2022
Futures (ESH22)
240-minute bar chart

Middle - Composite
Index
Bottom - Detrend
Oscillator

Charts by TradeStation

The second red arrow shows you the blue 312-periods SMA intersecting the Fibonacci confluence zone. MAJOR resistance! The shortcut is the blue average marking a Gann target as well. That is why I use averages of 9, 13, 33.

While we wait for the market to make its next move, I start making a geometric calculation in the 60-minute chart for NQH22. The two charts showing 240-minutes S&P500 futures and 60-minute NASDAQ futures are now glued together on my screen. Notice the time horizon ratio of 4:1. Will one breakout first ahead of the other?

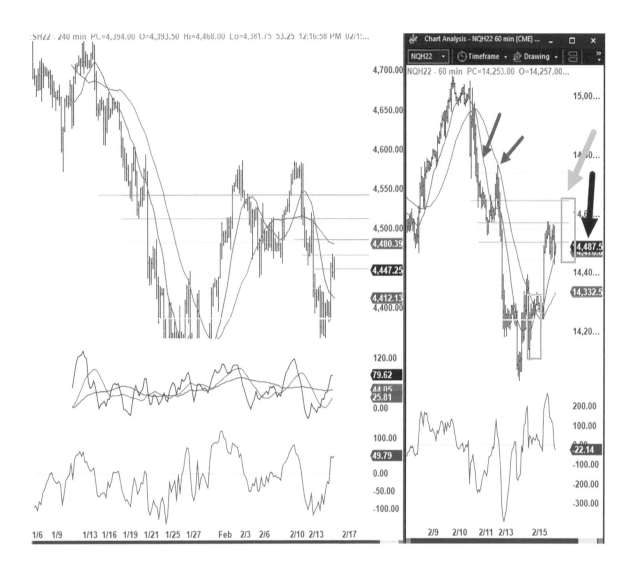

The lower yellow rectangle measures a small swing. Copy/paste the same rectangle and project it up from the bottom of the current consolidation. The top of the yellow rectangle aligns with the next Fibonacci confluence zone. The same zone is in the 240-minute chart where the blue SMA intersects the same area.

Now we have a geometric swing confirming the same Fibonacci calculations. That area is a high confidence target. But the market must break through nearby resistance. These are all just grids and not a forecast that it will happen. That must come from the oscillators.

The detrend oscillator made a new momentum high in the 60-minute chart. That means the market has enough strength to move the oscillator to the lower peak behind the new momentum high. That could be enough to pop through nearby resistance. We are still waiting.

The S&P500 ESH22 futures contract pops up into the next resistance zone at 4485. That's my target to sell into. I am selling into the target and not the pullback after. That's just my style after years of doing this. Market stops dead at the line, but NASDAQ tries to break through. You need to scan the chart on the next page. The key here is that the NASDAQ could not close above the 14,644

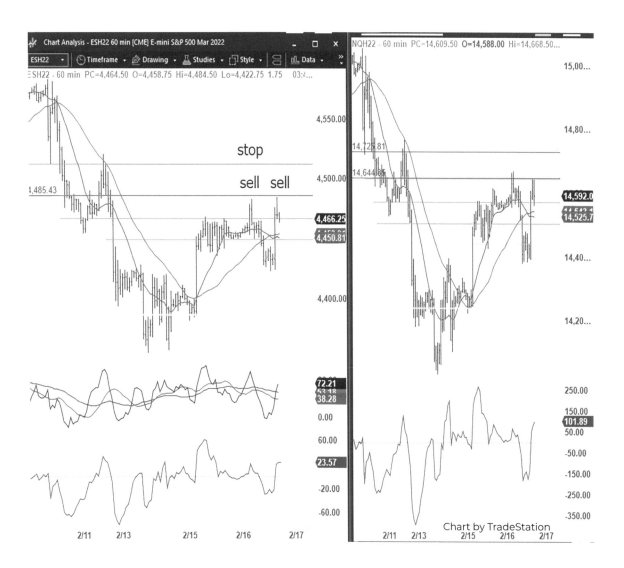

resistance zone. It fails immediately.

I sold ESH22 into 4485. Where is the stop? This is important, it is over the next confluence zone. So be careful when creating the zone to understand the true width. You do not want a stop anywhere in the zone. It must be outside the zone. If I had sold NASDAQ the stop would be over 14,725.

The ESH22 S&P500 contract bounces a second time into the 4485 resistance zone. NASDAQ cannot break above. I sell again. Then I increase the quantity of my stop, but the price level remains the same.

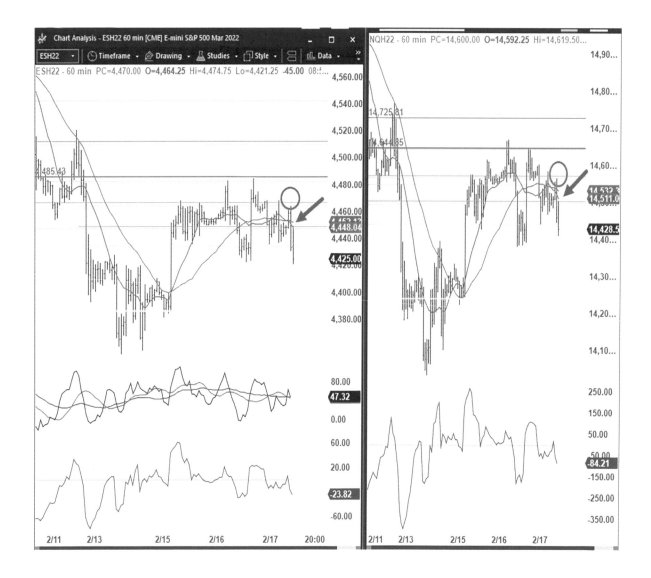

Both charts are 60-minutes for the S&P500 March 2022 contract and NASDAQ March 2022 contract. The markets both break down. The rebounds test the lower resistance zone where the first few charts in this series began.

My stop is still just over 1485. I am going to move it down now to just above the lower resistance zone at 4466. Move the stop using a cancel/replace at 4471. I hate using stops on exact even numbers.

Figure 6.11
S&P500 March 2022 Futures (ESH22)
60-minute bar chart

Middle - Composite Index
Bottom - Detrend Oscillator

NASDAQ March 2022 Futures [ESH22]
60-minutes
Bottom - 7-period detrend

Chart by TradeStation

Figure 6.12
NASDAQ March 2022
Futures (ESH22)
60-minute bar chart

Middle - Composite Index
Bottom -  Detrend
Oscillator

Charts by TradeStation

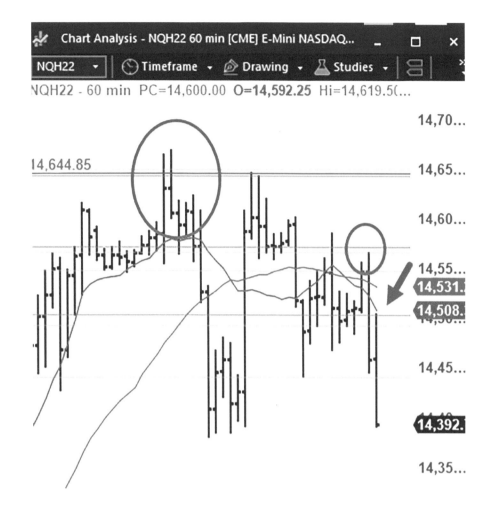

The chart above was captured so you could more easily study the key reversal in the first red circle. The closing prices in both bars are below 14,644.  When the market tests resistance a second time, it drops dead right at the zone.

The second red arrow shows you how the market tests the lower resistance band and declines. The last bar fails under the red SMA and a wider resistance confluence zone. It is therefore weaker, but no less important.  NASDAQ March 2022 contract is now trading at 14,392.

ESH22 - 60 min  PC=4,470.00  **O=4,464.25**  Hi=4,474.75  Lo=4,413.50  **-55.75**  08:5...

Chart by TradeStation

Figure 6.13
S&P500 March 2022
Futures (ESH22)
60-minute bar chart

Middle - Composite
Index
Bottom - Detrend
Oscillator

S&P500 futures are now trading 4414. The red moving-average is at 4447 and it bisects the confluence resistance zone. It is the lowest confluence zone in the chart above.

Move the stop down. Cancel/replace with a new level at 4451.

Figure 6.14
S&P500 March 2022
Futures (ESH22)
60-minute bar chart

Middle - Composite
Index
Bottom - Detrend
Oscillator

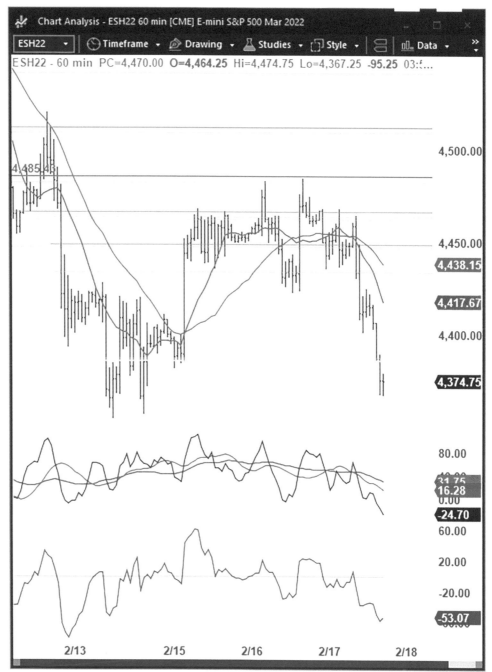

Chart by TradeStation

The trading session closes at 4374 in the March 2022 S&P500 futures and 14,164 in the March 2022 NASDAQ futures contract. Where is support? This is something I would have done last night or much earlier before today's session. But this new data could mean a revision is ahead.

# S&P500 FUTURES (ESH22)- SUPPORT

Figure 6.15
S&P500 March 2022 Futures (ESH22) - weekly
Middle - Composite Index, Bottom - Detrend Oscillator

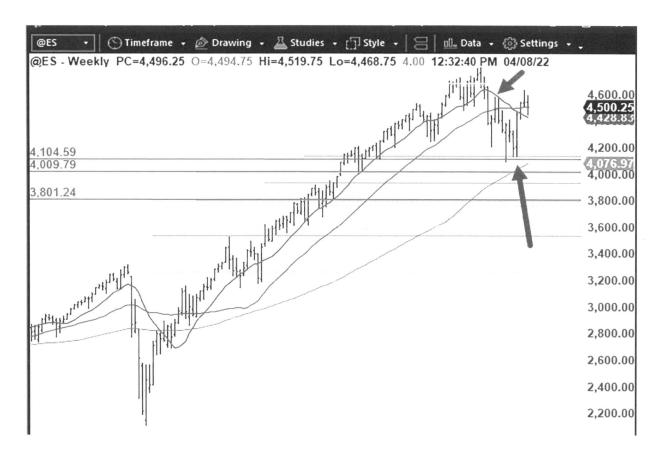

@ES - Weekly  PC=4,496.25  O=4,494.75  Hi=4,519.75  Lo=4,468.75  4.00  12:32:40 PM  04/08/22

Figure 6.16
S&P500 June 2022 Futures
(ESM22) - weekly

Charts by TradeStation

To learn more about
Fibonacci support/
resistance levels please
read 'Fibonacci Analysis' by
Constance Brown. There
are numerous free PDFs on
the Internet.

The chart at left is the weekly chart for the S&P500 March futures contract with the support Fibonacci confluence zones. They zones were calculated in February, 2022. This is a continuous futures contract and the differential of the new contract basis to the old is subtracted from the entire historical dataset when the front contract rolls over. It is best to remove all Fibonacci ranges and recreate the confluence zones. There is often no change except for the basis differential between the back and front months. The front month is June, 2022 in Figure 6.16. It was the chart prepared for the rollover from March to June. The 4104 major support zone in Figure 6.16 is the same target zone as the 4094 zone in Figure 6.15. The market fell to the next zone at 4094 in Figure 6.15, or 4104 in Figure 6.16. The double test of this zone confirmed the calculations started from the correct price level. Confirmation is our best teacher.

All the support ranges begin from the same bar marked with multiple gray lines near the chart high. What happens when the market retraces through the bar that is being used to start the ranges? Delete all Fibonacci ranges and start over (see Figure 6.7 about retracments). If you bought near 4104, where would the stop go? Below 4009 in Figure 6.16. Keep in mind that the win:loss ratio should be 3:1 or greater.

# RISK MANAGEMENT

Figures 6.17
Left-side of a spreedsheet for risk and position leverage analysis. The left side is the dollar value for a number of shares to tick movement.

| | A | B | C | D | E | F | G | H | I | J | K | L | M | N |
|---|---|---|---|---|---|---|---|---|---|---|---|---|---|---|
| 1 | | | stock | | | | | | | | | | | % c |
| 2 | | tick(.10) | | 25 | 50 | 75 | 100 | 200 | 300 | 400 | 500 | 600 | 700 | |
| 3 | 0.50 | 0.50 | | 13 | 25 | 38 | 50 | 100 | 150 | 200 | 250 | 300 | 350 | 0.50 |
| 4 | 1.00 | 1.00 | | 25 | 50 | 75 | 100 | 200 | 300 | 400 | 500 | 600 | 700 | 1.00 |
| 5 | 1.50 | 1.50 | | 38 | 75 | 113 | 150 | 300 | 450 | 600 | 750 | 900 | 1050 | 1.50 |
| 6 | 1.80 | 1.80 | | 45 | 90 | 135 | 180 | 360 | 540 | 720 | 900 | 1080 | 1260 | 1.80 |
| 7 | 2.00 | 2.00 | | 50 | 100 | 150 | 200 | 400 | 600 | 800 | 1000 | 1200 | 1400 | 2.00 |
| 8 | 2.50 | 2.50 | | 63 | 125 | 188 | 250 | 500 | 750 | 1000 | 1250 | 1500 | 1750 | 2.50 |
| 9 | 3.00 | 3.00 | | 75 | 150 | 225 | 300 | 600 | 900 | 1200 | 1500 | 1800 | 2100 | 3.00 |
| 10 | 3.50 | 3.50 | | 88 | 175 | 263 | 350 | 700 | 1050 | 1400 | 1750 | 2100 | 2450 | 3.50 |
| 11 | 4.00 | 4.00 | | 100 | 200 | 300 | 400 | 800 | 1200 | 1600 | 2000 | 2400 | 2800 | 4.00 |
| 12 | 4.50 | 4.50 | | 113 | 225 | 338 | 450 | 900 | 1350 | 1800 | 2250 | 2700 | 3150 | 4.50 |
| 13 | 5.00 | 5.00 | | 125 | 250 | 375 | 500 | 1000 | 1500 | 2000 | 2500 | 3000 | 3500 | 5.00 |
| 14 | 5.50 | 5.50 | | 138 | 275 | 413 | 550 | 1100 | 1650 | 2200 | 2750 | 3300 | 3850 | 5.50 |
| 15 | 6.00 | 6.00 | | 150 | 300 | 450 | 600 | 1200 | 1800 | 2400 | 3000 | 3600 | 4200 | 6.00 |
| 16 | 7.00 | 7.00 | | 175 | 350 | 525 | 700 | 1400 | 2100 | 2800 | 3500 | 4200 | 4900 | 7.00 |
| 17 | 7.50 | 7.50 | | 188 | 375 | 563 | 750 | 1500 | 2250 | 3000 | 3750 | 4500 | 5250 | 7.50 |
| 18 | 8.00 | 8.00 | | 200 | 400 | 600 | 800 | 1600 | 2400 | 3200 | 4000 | 4800 | 5600 | 8.00 |
| 19 | 8.50 | 8.50 | | 213 | 425 | 638 | 850 | 1700 | 2550 | 3400 | 4250 | 5100 | 5950 | 8.50 |
| 20 | 9.00 | 9.00 | | 225 | 450 | 675 | 900 | 1800 | 2700 | 3600 | 4500 | 5400 | 6300 | 9.00 |
| 21 | 9.50 | 9.50 | | 238 | 475 | 713 | 950 | 1900 | 2850 | 3800 | 4750 | 5700 | 6650 | 9.50 |
| 22 | 10.00 | 10.00 | | 250 | 500 | 750 | 1000 | 2000 | 3000 | 4000 | 5000 | 6000 | 7000 | 10.00 |
| 23 | 11.00 | 11.00 | | 275 | 550 | 825 | 1100 | 2200 | 3300 | 4400 | 5500 | 6600 | 7700 | 11.00 |
| 24 | 12.00 | 12.00 | | 300 | 600 | 900 | 1200 | 2400 | 3600 | 4800 | 6000 | 7200 | 8400 | 12.00 |
| 25 | 13.00 | 13.00 | | 325 | 650 | 975 | 1300 | 2600 | 3900 | 5200 | 6500 | 7800 | 9100 | 13.00 |
| 26 | 14.00 | 14.00 | | 350 | 700 | 1050 | 1400 | 2800 | 4200 | 5600 | 7000 | 8400 | 9800 | 14.00 |
| 27 | 15.00 | 15.00 | | 375 | 750 | 1125 | 1500 | 3000 | 4500 | 6000 | 7500 | 9000 | 10500 | 15.00 |
| 28 | | | | | | | | | | | | | | |
| 29 | | | | | | | | | | | | | | |

This spreadsheet for various futures markets and stock trading ranges is etched into my soul. It was so important when I was a fund manager, that I only allowed new investors in every quarter. A depositor coming in with 40 million would upset my intuitive tables and required manual references for a week or two until they were memorized again.

The table tells us the leverage and size of a position that is correct for the size of a portfolio. Positions that back into a confluence zone make a huge difference! The spread between zones defines the risk and stop placement.

On the right in cell O2 in red is the stock portfolio size for this explanation. It assumes you have an account of $50,000. When you win or have a loss, this must be updated. When you have a large portfolio the amount is change with larger changes or monthly.

Figures 6.18
Right-side of the same spreedsheet for risk and position leverage analysis. The right-side is the % of account change based on position size and market movement.
Example... cell **P3 =E3/$O$2** where $O$2 is the account dollar value.

| M | N | O | P | Q | R | S | T | U | V | W |
|---|---|---|---|---|---|---|---|---|---|---|
| | | % of Acct | | ALLOCATIONS | | | | | | |
| 700 | | 50000 | 50 | 75 | 100 | 200 | 300 | 400 | 500 | 6( |
| 350 | 0.50 | 0.03% | 0.05% | 0.08% | 0.10% | 0.20% | 0.30% | 0.40% | 0.50% | 0.6( |
| 700 | 1.00 | 0.05% | 0.10% | 0.15% | 0.20% | 0.40% | 0.60% | 0.80% | 1.00% | 1.2( |
| 1050 | 1.50 | 0.08% | 0.15% | 0.23% | 0.30% | 0.60% | 0.90% | 1.20% | 1.50% | 1.8( |
| 1260 | 1.80 | 0.09% | 0.18% | 0.27% | 0.36% | 0.72% | 1.08% | 1.44% | 1.80% | 2.1( |
| 1400 | 2.00 | 0.10% | 0.20% | 0.30% | 0.40% | 0.80% | 1.20% | 1.60% | 2.00% | 2.4( |
| 1750 | 2.50 | 0.13% | 0.25% | 0.38% | 0.50% | 1.00% | 1.50% | 2.00 | 2.50% | 3.0( |
| 2100 | 3.00 | 0.15% | 0.30% | 0.45% | 0.60% | 1.20% | 1.80% | 2.40% | 3.00% | 3.6( |
| 2450 | 3.50 | 0.18% | 0.35% | 0.53% | 0.70% | 1.40% | 2.10% | 2.80% | 3.50% | 4.2( |
| 2800 | 4.00 | 0.20% | 0.40% | 0.60% | 0.80% | 1.60% | 2.40% | 3.20% | 4.00% | 4.8( |
| 3150 | 4.50 | 0.23% | 0.45% | 0.68% | 0.90% | 1.80% | 2.70% | 3.60% | 4.50% | 5.4( |
| 3500 | 5.00 | 0.25% | 0.50% | 0.75% | 1.00% | 2.00% | 3.00% | 4.00% | 5.00% | 6.0( |
| 3850 | 5.50 | 0.28% | 0.55% | 0.83% | 1.10% | 2.20% | 3.30% | 4.40% | 5.50% | 6.6( |
| 4200 | 6.00 | 0.30% | 0.60% | 0.90% | 1.20% | 2.40% | 3.60% | 4.80% | 6.00% | 7.2( |
| 4900 | 7.00 | 0.35% | 0.70% | 1.05% | 1.40% | 2.80% | 4.20% | 5.60% | 7.00% | 8.4( |
| 5250 | 7.50 | 0.38% | 0.75% | 1.13% | 1.50% | 3.00% | 4.50% | 6.00% | 7.50% | 9.0( |
| 5600 | 8.00 | 0.40% | 0.80% | 1.20% | 1.60% | 3.20% | 4.80% | 6.40% | 8.00% | 9.6( |
| 5950 | 8.50 | 0.43% | 0.85% | 1.28% | 1.70% | 3.40% | 5.10% | 6.80% | 8.50% | 10.2( |
| 6300 | 9.00 | 0.45% | 0.90% | 1.35% | 1.80% | 3.60% | 5.40% | 7.20% | 9.00% | 10.8( |
| 6650 | 9.50 | 0.48% | 0.95% | 1.43% | 1.90% | 3.80% | 5.70% | 7.60% | 9.50% | 11.4( |
| 7000 | 10.00 | 0.50% | 1.00% | 1.50% | 2.00% | 4.00% | 6.00% | 8.00% | 10.00% | 12.0( |
| 7700 | 11.00 | 0.55% | 1.10% | 1.65% | 2.20% | 4.40% | 6.60% | 8.80% | 11.00% | 13.2( |
| 8400 | 12.00 | 0.60% | 1.20% | 1.80% | 2.40% | 4.80% | 7.20% | 9.60% | 12.00% | 14.4( |
| 9100 | 13.00 | 0.65% | 1.30% | 1.95% | 2.00% | 5.20% | 7.80% | 10.40% | 13.00% | 15.6( |
| 9800 | 14.00 | 0.70% | 1.40% | 2.?% | 2.80% | 5.60% | 8.40% | 11.20% | 14.00% | 16.8( |
| 10500 | 15.00 | 0.75% | 1.50% | 2.2?% | 3.00% | .00% | 9.00% | 12.00% | 15.00% | 18.0( |

Here is how it works. The confluence zones we have been creating defines the entry/exit levels and where to place stops. Therefore, the spread between zones, or two zones away for longer horizon investors, determines the position size allowed. If you only want to risk 3% per idea and the stock gives you a 15 dollar spread shown in cell A27, then the maximum number of stocks you can buy or short, would be 100 shares for a $50,000 account size.

If cell A9 is correct because your stop is only 3 dollars from your entry level, then you can buy 500 hundred shares based on the result in cell V9 that shows 3% risk. I'll admit I am not this conservative.

To enter a trade you must expect at least 3-times in return that you risk. Therefore, the first postion with 100 shares must have a target at least 45 dollars higher or lower. The trade with 500 shares must have a target 9 dollars higher or lower.

LEARNING OBJECTIVES

How to create your own spreadsheet to evaluate risk, determine position size, and evaluate win/loss ratios.

# 7

## A TRADER'S DIARY: THE THOUGHTS, SIGNALS, AND EXECUTION IN REAL-TIME

# CHAPTER SEVEN

# Trading Dynamics

## THE PROCESS, SELECTION, EXECUTION, AND MANAGING THE TRADE

**N**ASDAQ. January 2022. The start of a new year. All the prior discussions we have shared might be brought into action. *This is live.* One full month recording the daily process, trades, decision tree, execution levels, and thinking during each day. This is a real-time trader's diary log.

We know the markets to couple with the NASDAQ for correlation purposes: Nikkei 225, and then the technology stocks Amazon, Google, Microsoft, and Apple. Add Facebook and these five are 40% of the NASADAQ.

January 2022 is a time when people are concerned about rising Oil prices and rising U.S. 10-Year Treasury Note Yields. Bitcoin has been falling. When Bitcoin falls the NASDAQ can be weak. This is likely due to panic contagion for a group that trades both.

The world is watching the political tensions build as Russia and the Ukraine align tanks and lethal arsenals along their border. Uncertainty everywhere except in the NASDAQ. This is a correction unfolding and we will track the progression. It has to be recorded live or I will forget what I was thinking, and the intraday data may roll off the chart. I am a short horizon trader. Any method you see me use can be applied to longer horizons. Current price is always in black ovals on the y-axis.

# JANUARY 4 (TUESDAY), 2022

Amazon (AMZN) - weekly
Microsoft (MSFT) - daily

Charts by TradeStation

January 4, 2022. The year opens with the DJIA producing a weak rally, but MSFT is breaking down. The weekly chart for Amazon shows the stock is creating a similar setup as MSFT. Both stocks have very large swings marked a-b-c. Amazon made a double top. We are headed for trouble. I love trouble. The stochastics oscillator on the weekly Amazon coincides with the top marked 'c' on price. MSFT has Stochastics rolling over in the daily time horizon. The large a-b-c price swings are bearish coiling patterns in both stocks in two different time frames.

# JANUARY 5 (WEDNESDAY), 2022

Jan 5 . AAPL makes a hard break.

Fibonacci confluence targets of support are calculated and a target of 169.60 is considered the minimum.

Notice the Composite Index fails under the moving-averages after defining an "M" pattern.

The detrend oscillator peak failed at an amplitude that marked the market high in September of 2021.

January 5th. The DJIA is advancing. The index prints 36,832 in the March DJIA futures contract. Be patient. The conflict between indexes is cause to review all the DJIA stocks.

# JANUARY 5 (WEDNESDAY), 2022

Jan 5 continued. The cross comparison is Amazon in a weekly time horizon against Google in a daily chart. Google is breaking down hard today. The swing marked 'A' at a price bottom, and 'B' tops in both stocks are known patterns. Both stocks should fall back to the price low at 'A'. It is an Elliott Wave Expanded Flat pattern. The oscillators cannot bottom in current positions.

What if I am wrong? Then the two stocks must develop corrective triangles. This is where triangles normally develop. The problem here is the hard break in Google. This is not the character you see develop within triangles. They are hard-fought battles between buyers and sellers. This looks like buyers have tossed in the white towel of surrender. AMZN oscillators can support a minor drop and retracement. However, the problem here is Google is leading AMZN in a similar pattern.

**Chart Analysis - DIS Daily [NYSE] Disney (Walt) Co**

DIS - Daily NYSE L=155.32 -0.41 B=155.04 A=155.65 O=156.52 Hi='...

Detrended Price Osc (Close,7,3,false,Yellow,Magenta,Black) 1.59

Chart by TradeStation

I have been watching the DJIA stock Disney (DIS) for many weeks. The larger decline is incomplete. Today's close is below the last two prior bars. A George Lane trigger signal. The detrend is making a double top.

The amplitude displacements have similar levels in both the first and third swings up. The red arrows will guide your eye to these critical price positions. I think wave 'a' and 'c' are complete because the amplitude in both swings is the same.

A crowd developing a corrective pattern will form a sequence of three swings. It is a more complex subject how to count these swings, but Disney just made the simplest, called a zigzag correction from the chart low.

Done. Disney has not retraced back to the gap that formed in the last big swing down. Disney is preparing to run towards the old price lows near 129, a DJIA warning.

# JANUARY 6 (THURSDAY), 2022

@TY - Monthly  PC=128'17.0  O=128'20.0  Hi=128'23.0  Lo=128'19.0  0'05.5  07:35:52 PM  01/0...

Chart by TradeStation

One of the problems upsetting equities is the rapid rise in inflation and interest rates. The U.S. 10Yr T-Note futures should drop further towards 127. This is where a Fibonacci confluence zone marks major support, not much support under the current position at 128'22 in this monthly chart. So the cause for concern should not change for stocks.

Perfect place to sell NASDAQ with a stop ABOVE the higher Fibonacci confluence zone at 15,990. The problem is I do not feel well, issues from post-Covid complications. Do not trade when you are sick. I have to let this one go. It should make a new low and come back up. I have to sit this dance out. Hate when that happens... but we all know the feeling!

# JANUARY 7 (FRIDAY), 2022

Light, Sweet Crude Oil Futures - CLSpot (NYMEX) - 2 Week Bar Chart - USD - No Layout

Chart by Optuma

Composite Index

Crude Oil in the 2-week chart shows the minor pullback to $78.25. This is enough to trigger a rally in stocks. Rising Oil prices is the other factor making stocks around the world get worried. In this 2-week chart the pullback in Crude Oil is developing from an angle called a Gann fan angle. Please do not think your software offers Gann angles if you cannot lock the aspect ratio of your screen and set the angles to the same ratio. Chart above is set at 0.65. Do not understand? Many people are with you. If you do not use specified aspect ratios you will be creating speedlines, not Gann angles. Oil should run towards 87. Bearish for stocks.

# JANUARY 10 (MONDAY), 2022 AFTER MARKET CLOSE

Both the NASDAQ and DJIA declined today, but the market looks like the drop may be a 5th wave down in the move from the top. Several indicators warn a bounce could develop. The problem is clearest in stocks. Too many stocks look like they can produce a rally up. Could be a mistake on my part.

To help my conflict I need to look to markets outside of the USA. European markets need to be reviewed and the French CAC is one of the major indexes I was leaning on last quarter.

I have not looked for several weeks. Surprised to find the French CAC 40 is pulling back from the swing projection made in this 2-month chart a year ago. There is also a time cycle target over the bar. Just know there is a cycle beat the market is respecting in this chart. A bigger cycle is coming in June.

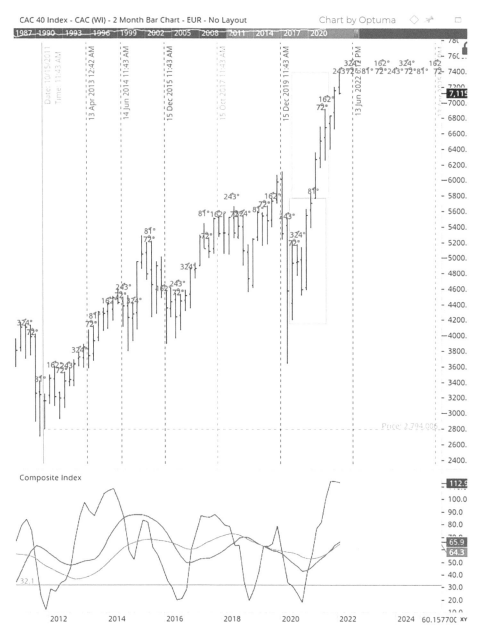

The two rectangles together mark the interim target, though not the final top for the entire swing. Seeing this pullback from this target means we need to study shorter time horizons than a 2-month chart., and then examine other European charts. Are they in a similar position, which would warn that this could become a more notable decline? It cannot happen in just a single market.

# JANUARY 10 (MONDAY), 2022

The French CAC 40 3-week chart. I will explain the vertical dashed lines later. The market is not near one currently. What I pick up is that the CAC 40 has formed a key reversal top and closed under an ascending angle. A key reversal was followed by a consolidation before breaking down under the same angle in 2018. Look for the label 6 Sep 2018. It is the same angle. Do we have a repeating pattern about to form?

# JANUARY 10 (MONDAY), 2022

Spain's IBEX 35 weekly is interesting because it is lagging other markets. It is currently under a key angle on a time cycle that this market has been respecting through its history. The rally was off the Fibonacci confluence zone four weeks ago. This is a noted high-risk position for this European index to fail. The Composite Index has returned to the same amplitude displacement as a prior pivot that start the hard swing down in 2021. We could be developing a high-risk setup in European markets.

# JANUARY 10 (MONDAY), 2022

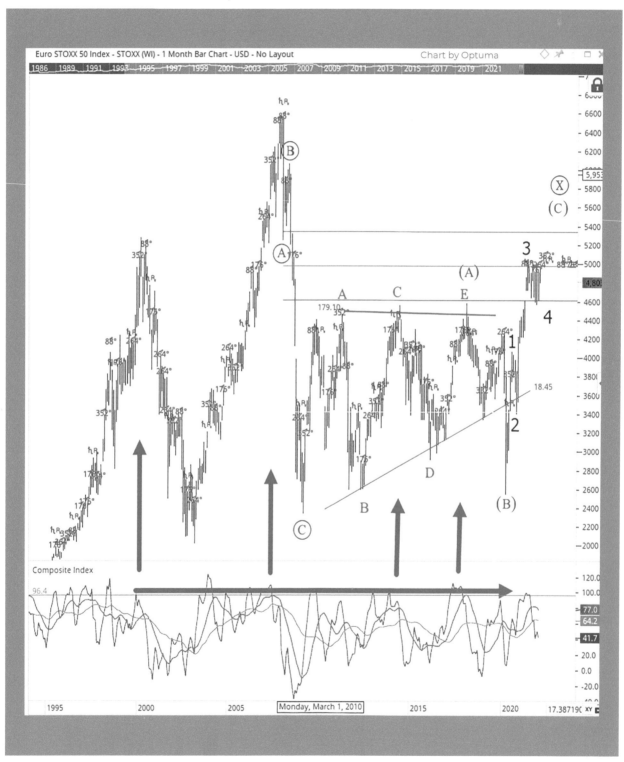

# JANUARY 10 (MONDAY), 2022

I once worked for Elliott Wave International and covered S&P500 for the institutional side of the firm. It is difficult for to turn the Wave Principle off. This chart is very advanced containing Elliott Wave structure and Gann time cycles. Here is what it means.

The chart for the Euro STOXX 50 Index in a monthly bar chart shows what I am thinking. It shows I believe that the index is producing a large degree five wave swing up from the low marked (B). that is corrective. The message is that this corrective swing up will lead to a major decline.

The 50% Fibonacci line is an ideal place for a fourth wave correction to occur within (C). The rally started from the (B) price low. The range of the Fibonacci subdivision started from the bottom of wave 2 up to the market high. One subdivided range will only mark minor levels of price resistance.

The Euro STOXX 50 Index has been stuck under this 50% Fibonacci ratio for several months now. That is concerning. A drop to the 38.2 ratio near 4600 would be very common and has done so several times. The second wave down that fell towards 3400 was brief and sharp in the advance from (B). The guideline of alternation suggests that this fourth wave developing now should be time-consuming and complex in character because wave 2 was so sharp and quick to develop. That seems to be the case unfolding now that wave 4 is complex. But the message and interpretation is the rally unfolding is corrective. The consolidation developing is at risk of becoming a distribution top. But even a single pop up toward 5400 has th same outcome ... a decline back to the March 2020 price lows. We will see this warning in other markets if this is the correct outlook.

The Composite Index has pulled back from the red over-bought horizontal line with a history marked on the oscillator. This consolidation developing now started from a similar amplitude displacement that caused trouble for the rally. Waves 1 and 3 had similar amplitude displacements. That is rare. This indicates that the rally does not have the conventional strength one would expect into the top of a third wave. The amplitude should have been able to break out into a new higher range than this history has developed over 10 years. (See the red upwards pointing arrows that start from the same amplitude levels.) I see nothing here to challenge this market wave interpretation at this time.

# JANUARY 10 (MONDAY), 2022

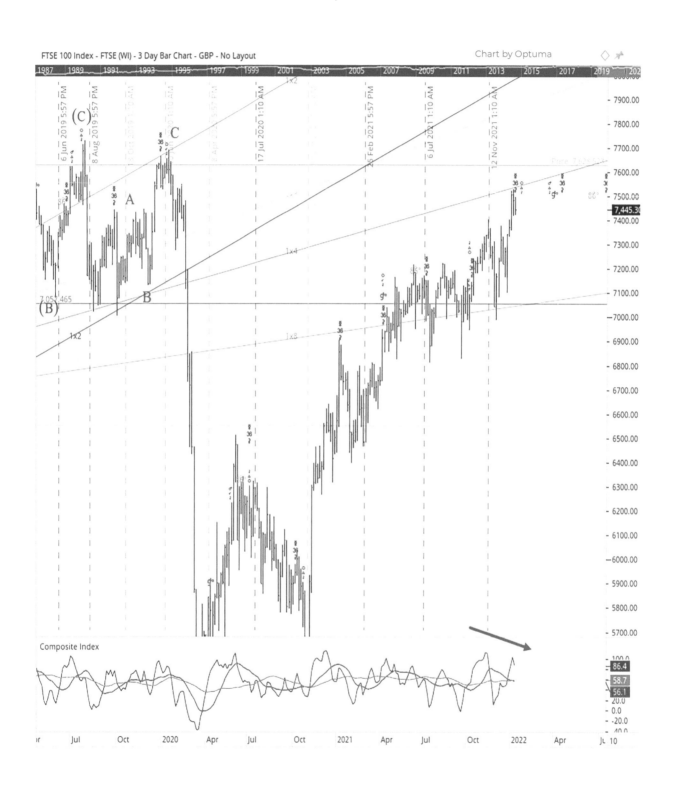

# JANUARY 10 (MONDAY), 2022

I am preparing these European charts tonight for clients. The FTSE 100 Index in a 3-day bar chart is at left. What we have is a Gann angle, but what you need to see is the red angle which the FTSE 100 is currently under. It was used as support in a major reversal in 2019. In 2019 the market then rallied into the price high marked 'C'. That then developed the waterfall decline as the pandemic took hold. These angles have an important history and FTSE is under one currently.

We are still not at one of the vertical dashed cycle lines. I'll explain them another time when one becomes relevant within the chart.

There is a red cycle notation over the current market. It means the FTSE 100 has arrived at a target viewed as a confluence target in price and time. Price is under the trend line and cycle beat. That's a problem. While the larger rally is incomplete, the market is vulnerable to a larger setback. The European markets continue to paint a picture that is a cohesive warning for the current uptrend.

The Composite Index is diverging. Also take notice of the spread of the moving-averages on the Composite Index. They have come together and the shorter (red) is at risk of crossing down. Maybe the Composite just pulls back to the moving averages as they flatline. That would be a normal setup for the market to then launch a new leg up. The market rally is not over, but other European charts suggest FTSE 100 will need to build a lower support level from which to launch a move that can break above the angle defining resistance. FTSE 100 is a tough market. If I needed a higher level of confidence, I would switch to FTSE 350. It is an index composition issue. But I do not need more to develop an opinion about Europe equities.

This is all very helpful regarding the NASDAQ and DJIA. There is a clearer picture coming into focus. If Europe experiences a pullback, then my market could also see a larger correction. That's all I wanted to know.

# JANUARY 11 (TUESDAY), 2022

Yesterday's Monday decline in the NASDAQ, S&P500, and DJIA, was a fifth wave swing down. Today was spent retracing the Monday decline.

The Fibonacci resistance zone just above 16,000 is the first area where major resistance forms. Several stocks by market close have incomplete rallies. There is not much news to report.

# JANUARY 12 AND 13 (WEDNESDAY/THURSDAY), 2022

Wednesday the NASDAQ has opened up and the session open presses right into the Fibonacci confluence target zone.

Sold NASDAQ a little after 11 AM (EST). The chart is Chicago time an hour behind. I am a seller into the immediate pullback reaction from the 16,023 Fibonacci confluence zone. The rally into the zone is a zigzag corrective pattern that I know. The average market order fill was 15,932. MSFT is rolling over.

A GTC stop (Good-until-Canceled) is entered at 16,162. This is ABOVE the next confluence zone at 16,133. A price low at 16,139, marked wave 'i' in the decline (which is wave i of 3), is just above the second resistance zone. The market should not retrace back into that pivot low at 16,139.

Expectations are for a decline back to the price low marked '3' that was made on Monday. The win:loss ratio must be at least 3:1. That criterion is in place between the price levels of my entry/target/stop levels. I usually enter market orders against the crowd into confluence zones like this position. This time I paused long enough to see the market respect the Fibonacci target.

Thursday the NASDAQ pops up early in the session but not to the old high. It then starts to decline through the rest of the session, closing in the last hour with a hard break into the close. Hold the position.

# JANUARY 14 (FRIDAY), 2022

Nuts. Friday is going to be complex. The media has a tone of panic because a major winter storm will hit the eastern USA. It is expected to become what meteorologist call a 'Bombogenesis'. It is a rapid intensification of a cyclonic low and the pressure drops at least 24 millibars in 24 hours. It is called by us commoners a weather bomb and is serious stuff. The bull's-eye is New York City up to Boston. The prime financial center of the USA is about to be shut down. Is the NASDAQ advancing because people want to get home early to prepare? MSFT does not have a completed decline in place. Tesla last week made a major key reversal. I decide to hold.

# JANUARY 16 (SUNDAY), 2022

Late Sunday Night:

Barometric pressure is plummeting as a meteorological bomb forms directly over my location. I am under the birth of this monster. We experience major winter storms maybe once every ten years. Oh goody, tonight's the night. The Asheville/Tryon area is my home. Still short the NASDAQ from January 12 and now we risk no power or Internet the coming week. While I have a Generac power backup for the building, if the town goes black, we will have no Internet. What to do? Sigh. Stay put. I hold.

Monday, January 17 is a national holiday, and the exchanges are closed. Just as well as we are trapped, and the storm is still with us until Monday afternoon.

By Tuesday on January 18, there is too much stress. I decide to cover the position near the early lows at right. Fill 15,289. Market order. All my position offsets are market orders. It does cross my mind that I just covered on the bottom of a first wave before a weak bounce leads to a total meltdown. But Internet service is flickering on/off/on/off, and the distractions force me to the sidelines. Without a position on I can think and breathe again. With the long weekend, it was mentally tough to stay short through the storm.

Now the hard part... how to get back in with a low-risk entry in a market that could begin a waterfall decline? Be patient for the setup. Wait for the trigger. Go shovel snow! The decision was made to step away. Do it!

The setup always comes, but it is so hard to be patient for it. The secret is to use two intraday time horizons 4:1 and wait for both charts to develop confirming signals. Do not rush.

# JANUARY 18 (TUESDAY), 2022

Start the process from the beginning again. Oil is looking toppy in the daily chart, but it should go next to $86.70. We know that will upset stocks.

# JANUARY 18 (TUESDAY), MARKET CLOSE - 2022

The 10-Year U.S. Treasury Notes have realized the target in the monthly data. Now that we have arrived, we can see that the 127'08 support zone is an incomplete decline. Next target is 125'02 and 122'23. A negative for stocks.

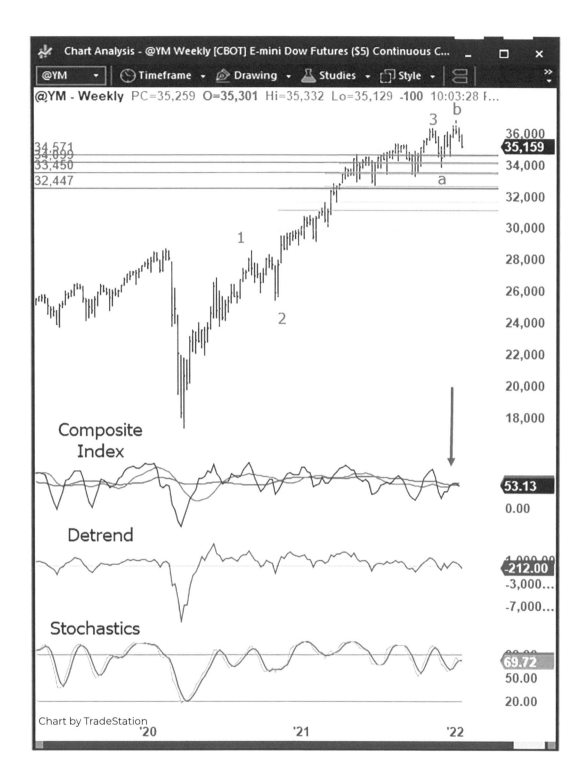

Weekly DJIA March Futures still have a long way down to go down because of the 'a'-'b' swing into the high. It should break major support at 34,571 because the DJIA should target 33,450. If this is a corrective pattern it would be an *expanded flat*. The 122'23 T-Note level is a bigger problem for the NASDAQ

# JANUARY 18 (TUESDAY, LATE EVENING), 2022

Late evening after the day session, Globex opens weak.

I rarely trade Globex sessions unless I am in trouble. I do not want to work that hard anymore.

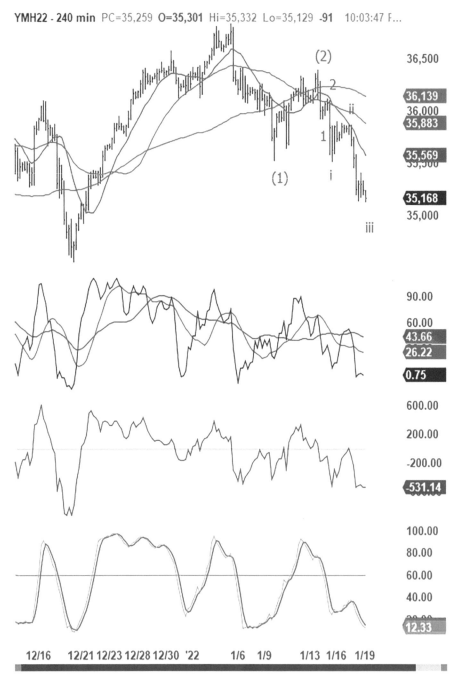

YMH22 - 240 min  PC=35,259  O=35,301  Hi=35,332  Lo=35,129  -91  10:03:47 F...

Chart by TradeStation

YMH22 - 15 min  PC=35,259  O=35,301  Hi=35,332  Lo=35,129  -92  10:0...

35,900

35,800

35,700

35,600

35,500

35,396

35,300

35,262
35,237

35,200

35,167

80.00

38.54

20.00

-8.50

50.00

-95.71

80.00

50.00

13.30

1/16    1/17   05:00  10:00      1/18   05:00  10:00  15:00      1/19

Chart by TradeStation

The internal structure at right in the 15-minute chart suggests the next low may end wave 3 down. That would mean the DJIA would retrace back to the moving-average near 35,396 in this chart.

The same level is also opposite the pivot high marked 'iv'. Fourth waves love to cluster together. The gap is another reason to bounce toward 35,396 in the DJIA.

Nothing I can do about it tonight at current levels. Still flat and it is getting to me. Patience. So hard but you cannot force it.

We could make a swing projection from this 15-minute data. Draw a rectangle from the top of "iv" to the 35,900 area. Copy/paste the rectangle starting the lower rectangle on the price pivot marked 'iv' and let it swing down. Good rough estimate. Fibonacci confluence zones are far more accurate.

# JANUARY 19 (WEDNESDAY), 2022

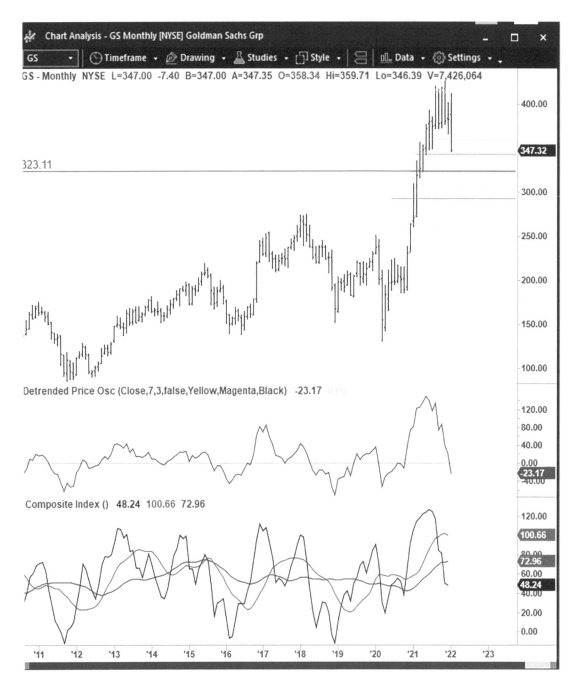

Pre-market open, Goldman Sachs (GS) makes a hard break missing earnings. It is on major support in a monthly chart on market open. Amazon is on minor support in the weekly chart.

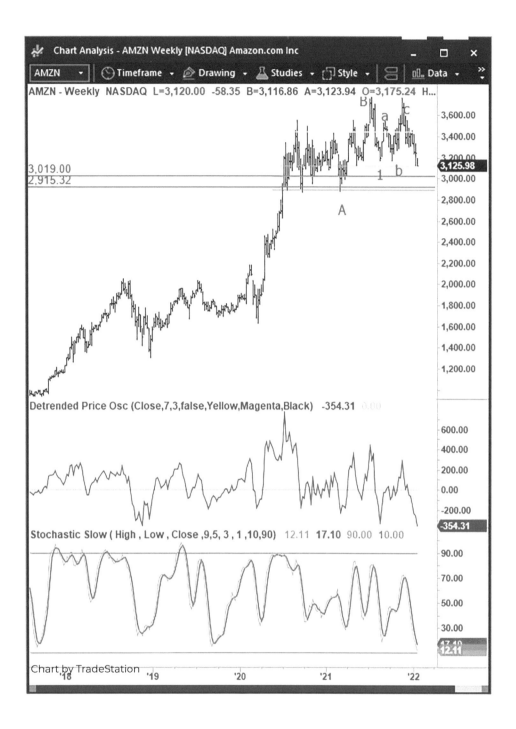

AMZN will target 3019 where major support resides. Neither stock shows a complete decline. GS should fall to 323. The downside will accelerate because the spread between the two major support zones has no interim minor support levels. I do not chase. There is no setup to sell NASDAQ. Sigh.  Now it is killing me to be on the side. Patience, Brown! Yes, I talk to myself and to my computer screen.

Some will sell as the market breaks beneath the previous bar's low. I need a better setup than that to know where to place stops.

# JANUARY 19 (WEDNESDAY), 2022

Because of the break in GS, we need to look over other banking/investment stocks. We understand the impact of the banking sector on global indexes. (See page 61 where we studied Equity Indexes around the world.)

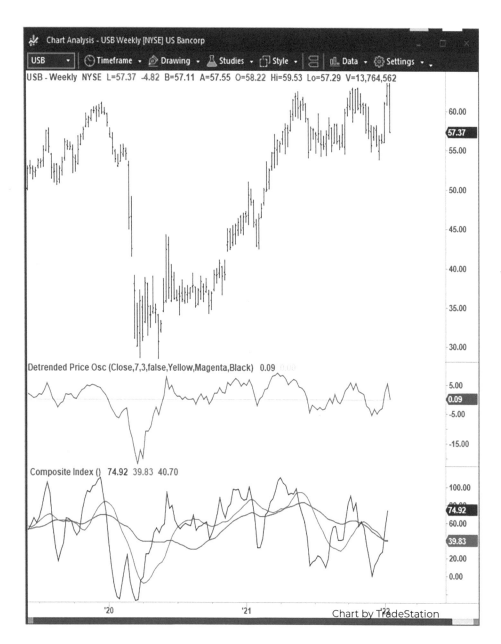

USB broke hard today. This move down in the weekly chart is the price range from just today. Bank of America is lagging the decline. They must follow regardless of earnings soon to be released. Earnings trigger moves before the regular day session opens. Often the ideal execution setup is at 3 AM in Globex. I hate earnings season. I am still flat.

The banks hold the morning lows in intraday time horizons and trigger a very weak bounce up. It has my attention.

# JANUARY 19 (WEDNESDAY) AND 20TH (THURSDAY), 2022

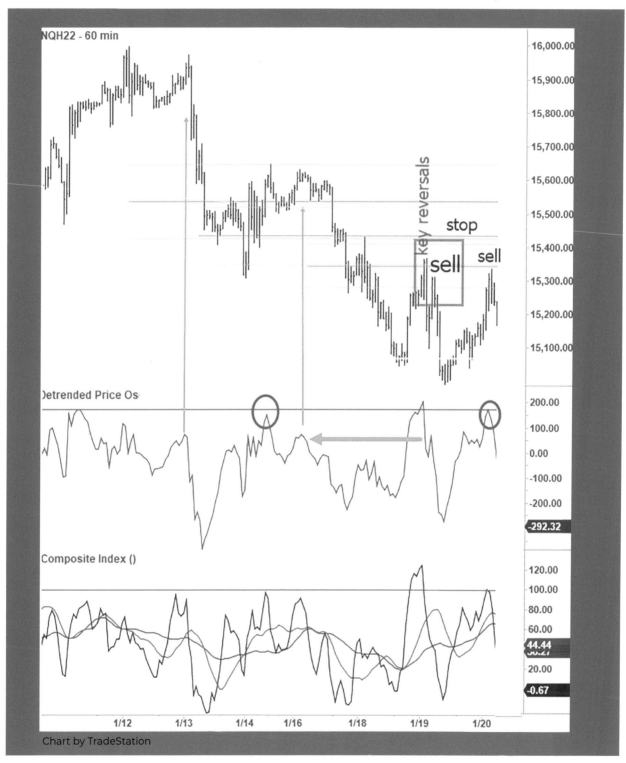

Chart by TradeStation

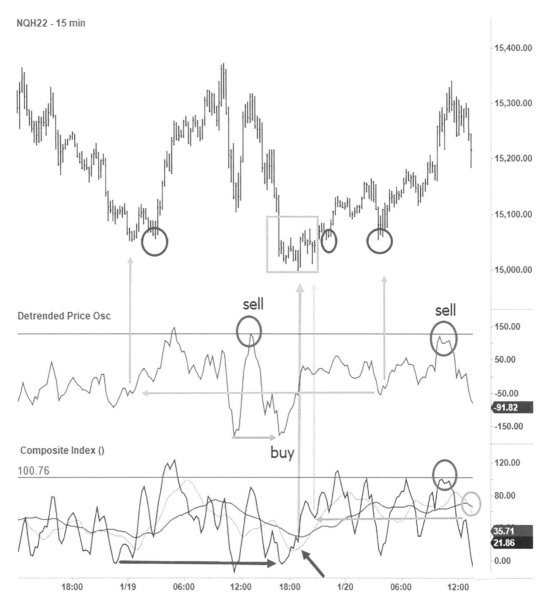

NQH22 - 15 min

Detrended Price Osc

sell    sell

buy

Composite Index ()

100.76

**There it is!** The afternoon of the 19th. The 60-minute chart marks the entry signal with the YELLOW arrow. The sell signal is the second lower peak where the same amplitude topped the market on the 16th. Back-to-back key reversals in price. The sell signal fails to test resistance creating the second key reversal. Study the two charts with a time ratio of 4:1. The 60-minute chart at the start of the yellow arrow (page left) ... wait for it... then the signal in the 15-minute detrend at the first red circle is the safer place to sell. The 4:1 time ratio has saved me so many times from selling early and helps to avoid the kick-back that often develops. It happens this time too. Scale in? No. We know what is coming and have a chance to position for it. Market order. 100% leverage. Stops? Entered just as fast. GTC over the higher Fibonacci zone in the 60-minute time horizon.

As the break down unfolds, the detrend and Composite Index trigger buy signals. I buy 30% back. Risky to take anything off the table? I have been caught before, but that's my style and what I do. Some will strongly disagree.

# JANUARY 20 (THURSDAY), 2022

On Thursday I do get my bounce up and a second setup to sell. The charts are on the prior page. Do I sell 30%? No. Market just handed me a second entry gift and *it is coiling*. The break could be bigger than expected. Sell 70%. Now short 140%. I increase the size of the GTC stop. This is rare. I treat pyramid additions as their own individual trades with their own resistance targets for stop placement. Do not average futures. In this scenario we are back where I started. Therefore, the stops are the same for both tranches.

Suddenly, whoosh. NASDAQ falls like it is a hot knife cutting through soft butter. This is no fifth wave. The sentiment does not fit. Panic just started so we sold futures into the second wave up in an extending wave (3) decline. Now that is Elliott and I cannot turn it off. What the sentiment of the crowd is thinking is clear. It is also not over. We will do nothing... except change the labels on the 60-minute NASDAQ chart below. HOLD.

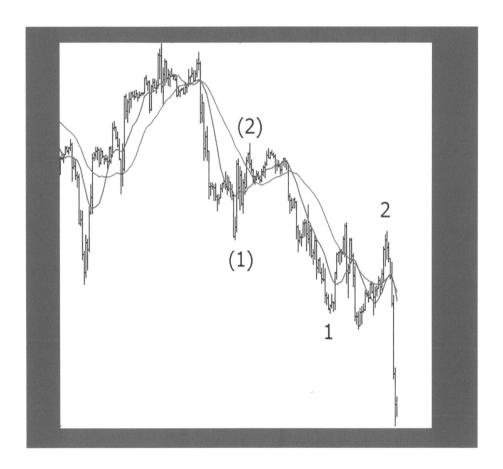

# JANUARY 20 (THURSDAY), 2022 (MARKET CLOSE)

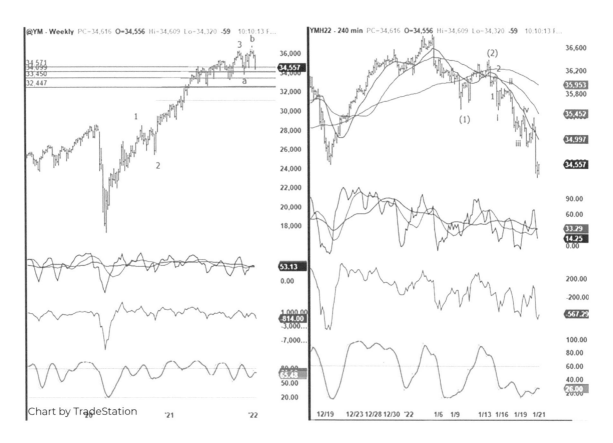

Chart by TradeStation

The DJIA futures close on major support in the weekly chart. All the key support levels were prepared long ago. Next target is 33,450. That is 1100 DJIA points lower. Now this is when it gets interesting. If there is a trigger, or the crowd for some reason loses their collective mind by morning, these Fibonacci confluence zones mark where the gap will occur as the point of recognition in the middle of a third wave decline.

Notice that the 240-minute DJIA March 2022 contract (above) has the stochastics oscillator near a bottom. Ignore it! That is the start of the problem that normalized oscillators trapped in a fixed range will develop. You cannot use a normalized oscillator in this situation. The Composite Index, being a hybrid oscillator, is still giving good signals, but if we open gap down tomorrow, only use the detrend oscillator. Then drop the time horizon of the two charts. Keep the 4:1 time ratio comparison. But go shorter in your time display to see detail signals. We'll see what comes.

# JANUARY 20 (THURSDAY), 2022 (MARKET CLOSE)

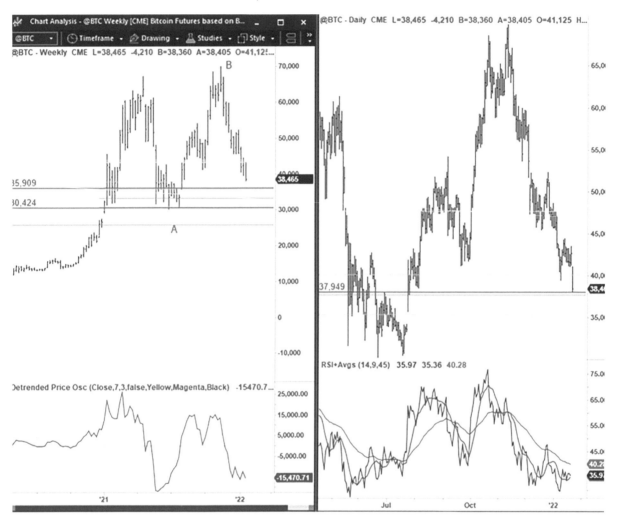

We need to do some prep analysis before tomorrow's session. The NASDAQ selloff is being fueled by the carnage in Bitcoin. Bitcoin fell to the support zone at 37,949. Now that is the top of the zone and the close at 38,468 has not broken it. Can it bounce up? More likely support under the market calculated in the weekly chart is the better target. Then Bitcoin can catch a pause. Why? Not only is this major support, but track left along the heavy horizontal line. The line bisects the place where a gap occurred. It is not just any gap, that was a break-away gap that started the entire swing up into 'B'. A very important technical area for Bitcoin. Break through that gap and the Bitcoin crowd will sell any NASDAQ stock they hold. Individuals will exit the crowd mindset for personal survival. The pattern developing will ultimately push Bitcoin back to 30,000. NASDAQ market contagon will be the result.

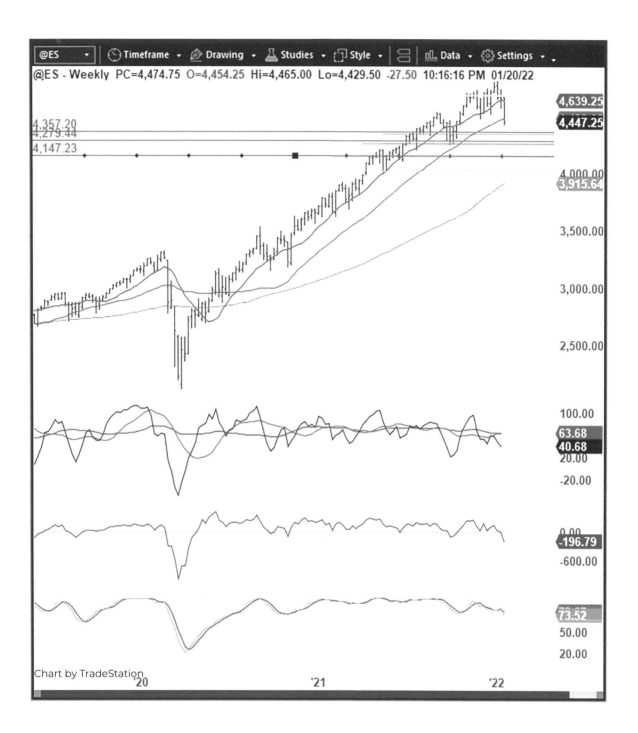

@ES - Weekly PC=4,474.75 O=4,454.25 Hi=4,465.00 Lo=4,429.50 -27.50 10:16:16 PM 01/20/22

In the weekly S&P500 futures chart the market has closed on minor support. It is a single Fibonacci level. We need confluence for major support and that is under the market at 4357. Notice the market tonight is below the blue moving-average on price. That was the 33-period moving-average (SMA). A drop through support at 4357, 4279, could target 4147 in the weekly chart.

# JANUARY 21 (FRIDAY), 2022

No gap down, but it was ugly all the same today for anyone long.

Quick check of the monthly chart. I have traded intraday declines using calculated support/resistance levels within monthly charts. Those are extremely big declines. Fibonacci confluence zones in longer horizon time charts work extremely well in extreme markets. The key is to have all the calculations in place on the chart before the waterfall breakdown hits.

The monthly NASDAQ chart shows 14,426 is the current price. The chart suggests NASDAQ must fall to 14,225 for any real support to be found. Is this target accurate? Do you see an error in this chart? Look closely at the start of each Fibonacci range. Each range begins from the same bar, but the chart shows the calculations are using bar highs that developed BEFORE the actual price top. The calculations were made in October 2021. I have new calculations already in my weekly chart. Next major support target is at 13,700 NQH22 March basis. When the weekend work is done this chart

and everything will be recalculated or checked.

It is Friday and we are closing the week on the lows at 14,411. When that happens ignore every technical signal before you. The detrend oscillator shows divergence. False. No confirmation. Wave structure within the decline is an incomplete pattern. The key is the position of the close. A market that closes on the price low for the entire week is in trouble. We hold short. Only action taken the last 30-minutes was to lower the stop to above the blue moving-average in the 60-minute NASDAQ chart.

The stop was moved down to 14,815. Why? I calculated resistance from the next major target at 13,700. Pretend the market already reached the target and then calculate the new resistance levels. The 14,809 average is in a major Fibonacci confluence zone. The last pivot high will be important. It is all mathematics. Each pivot has a relationship to another pivot in the move. Find them. Understand their relationships and how they are connected.

# JANUARY 22 (SATURDAY), 2022

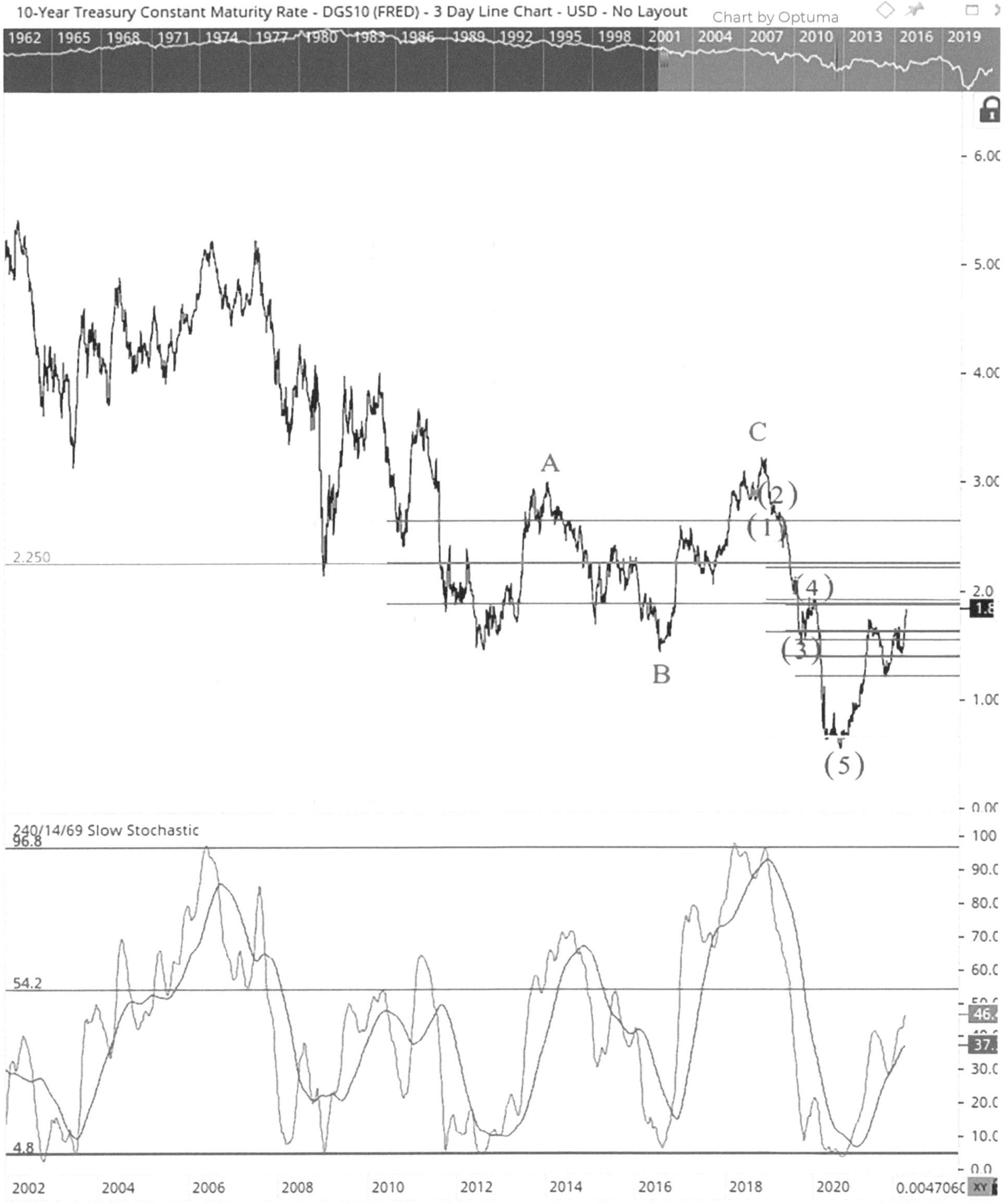

Scanning charts over the weekend. Starting with the U.S. 10-Yr Treasury Constant Maturity Rates. It is one of the issues unnerving equities.

Under resistance, but the target is 2.25. Nearby resistance is nearly back to the pivot marked (4). That is a problem for my bearish happiness. When I add oscillators, I run into a problem. This chart is an ultra-compressed 3-day line chart. The Composite and RSI both use fixed periods for their own reasons.

Solution: use Stochastics. Determine a cycle and use half that cycle to setup the Stochastics period. The result is correct, and the procedure requires no modification. The chart at left has inputs of 240/14/69. I will guess you have never seen values like that before. Now look at the signal performance. It has solved the problem and stochastics shows it is not topping. The problem in the Composite Index relative to the Stochastics solution is shown below. Same problem if we used RSI as I only use 14-periods. Glad this came up as I forgot to mention the stochastics oscillator can be used to solve market analysis issues with unique situations. We just happened to step on an example today.

# JANUARY 22 (SATURDAY), 2022

TECH

## Bitcoin falls another 8% as cryptocurrencies extend steep losses

PUBLISHED SAT, JAN 22 2022·3:36 PM EST

Late Saturday afternoon I turn to my favorite financial news apps to read any articles that may be of interest. Wow! Bitcoin falls another 8%. Really? I did not even know Bitcoin traded on a Saturday! Well, learn something new every day.

My chart cannot update, but based on the articles, Bitcoin is now said to be on major support near 33,014. OK, that is cool. We know the next target is 30,690. Do study closely how the Fibonacci confluence zones were created. The lower you can start the Fibonacci range of subdivisions, the more confluence target zones you can create under the current market. This is only a grid. It does not imply we will trade down to the lowest target zone. We always use the indicators to tell us. Monday is going to be interesting.

Now that we have this new puzzle piece, we need to see what impact it may have in other markets. There is a lot more work ahead of us because of this news. It means all the long horizon charts must be checked to ensure the monthly views have support calculated ahead of Sunday night's open.

Next, keep a broader window of time. We need to start thinking about what evidence is developing that this swing down will be retraced when the dust settles. We must be thinking about both the current and future swing ahead that will follow. What am I going to buy? I know my answer now.

Bitcoin / US Dollar - XBTUSD (FX) - 3 Day Bar Chart - USD - No Layout

Chart by Optuma

Bitcoin / US Dollar - XBTUSD (FX) - 3 Day - USD

33,014.201

30,690.313

29,828.741

26,775.486  26,643.282

22,860.659

Composite Index

# JANUARY 22 (SATURDAY), 2022

When I opened my 2-month Nikkei 225 chart, all I saw were the rectangles in the chart. I'll walk you through the steps I then applied.

I subdivided the range using Fibonacci from the top of the highest rectangle down to the strong bar I believe is the strongest move within a third wave rally. What I found was that the current Nikkei price high developed on the 38.2 retracement ratio. That's a good thing. It means the upper target is still valid and a future consideration.

Next, create the Fibonacci confluence zones. The chart at right shows the second range selected. Start from the top of the rectangle and end the range on a strong bar that ends on a lower bar than the ending of the first range. I do this very quickly because I know the strong bars are the markers to use. Skip the others as they will be noise. We know the price target. It is 25,980.

The oscillator positions are studied next. The Composite Index has no horizontal oscillator peaks or lows that align on this same horizontal amplitude displacement.

The Composite is on its moving-average, but I am not seeing anything to get concerned about. The market is under a major Fibonacci confluence zone and hugging just under the zone at 27,522.

The 7-period detrend oscillator has pulled away from the over-bought condition and closed at -625. This amplitude does not have a strong repeating pattern to match price reversals. There is one, but the oscillator setup is nothing like the start of the rally that began from near 8000 in 2012.

We know that new amplitude extremes do not end rallies. All I see is confirmation that the decline is in the context of an incomplete larger uptrend. Moving on.

# JANUARY 22 (SATURDAY), 2022

What I desperately need is Time. The dashed vertical lines mark a Gann cycle technique.

December 19, 2011, marks the starting bar placement. The next bar is counted as '1' on forward. The vertical lines mark the square counts. Simply the square of 3 equals the 9th bar. The square of 4 equals the 12th bar. The square of 5 equals the 25th bar, and so on. Often the first couple in the series are not of much interest. But once you count the square of 5, or the 25th bar, you want to pay attention. You can see Feb 18, 2016, and December 19, 2017, were important cycle beats. The next one is August 18, 2022. That will not help us much now from a 2-month chart.

The cycle of greatest impact is the 361st bar or square of 19. That ends the cycle series and is often a major swing.

We want to apply this method in a shorter time horizon.

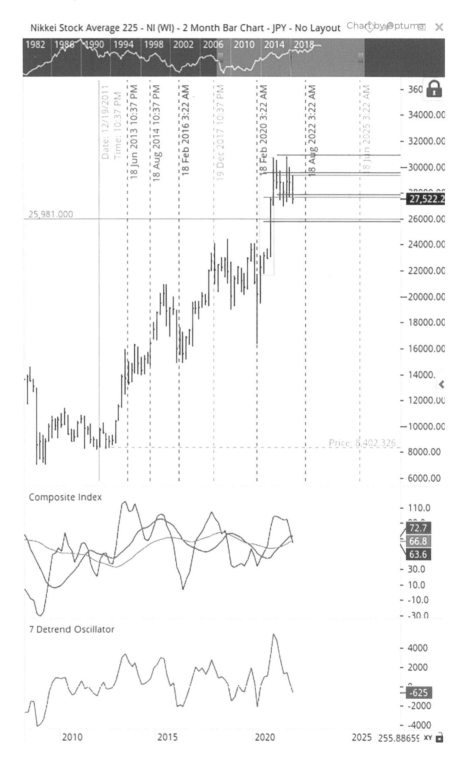

Nikkei Stock Average 225 - NI (WI) - 2 Month Bar Chart - JPY - No Layout

Nikkei Stock Average 225 - NI (WI) - 2 Week Bar Chart - JPY - No Layout

The cycle series is calculated in the 2-week chart. The starting point needs more explaining than this book can address. (Gann is in *The Thirty-Second Jewel* but only for advanced please. You need oscillators well established first.)

The information we need is knowing that May 30 is the next beat. But one single cycle alone does not cut it. You have to discover where a cluster of cycles will congregate. I am not going to do that work now. We do not need it. We know the time cluster of interest nearterm is Jan 30 to Feb 10 +/- a week. Do not assume it is a bottom. Keep reading oscillators.

The last step is to mark the horizontal Fibonacci confluence support zones in the chart. These charts are now ready. Where is the Nikkei 225 going? At least to 26,613. The move down is incomplete.

# JANUARY 22 (SATURDAY), 2022

Light, Sweet Crude Oil Futures - CLSpot (NYMEX) - 3 Week Bar Chart - USD - No Layout

Chart by Optuma

Composite Index

We looked at rates in the big picture, we still need to refresh our opinion regarding the Crude Oil market.

Wether you knew Gann analysis or not, it would not matter, as I had shared with you how to let the market guide you to detect important angles. This happens to be a Gann Fan using a fixed ratio of 0.52. That value is located on the bottom right corner of the chart. The small locks on the y-axis mean everything will stay true to this x-axis/z-axis scale proportion.

All you need to see is the red descending angled line just over the 3-week Crude Oil prices. The angle could have been detected if you knew to truncate key reversals and connect the highs in 2013 and 2014. Oil is not at this angled line just yet, but many will not know it is approaching and has a relationship to the major tops in 2013 and 2014. I'll say about $90-92 is the next price range. An angle has a time element involved to bisect the actual price target. We have a way of using geometry to make the calculations, but I'll spare you that long dialogue as we do not have the time. Oil is under the red angled line. All we need to know is that it can rally.

You can see the square of 15 cycle beat falls on December 15, 2021. That is one bar off the actual launch of this swing up. There is a cluster of cycle notations into the near future. They suggest the Oil market can rally into March. Will it be a fifth wave rally up? What makes it difficult is knowing the 3-month, 3-week, and 3-day charts do not have the same allignment. All we need to know is the two longest time charts have an upward bias for a couple more months.

I did project price targets on the horizontal axis and the time target warns Crude Oil may break above the higher descending Gann Angle. What do I use when this happens? Fibonacci confluence zones of resistance. There are targets near 96 and 100, which would impact other markets.

Once we defined the Fibonacci cluster zones of support or resistance, we can then draw horizontal lines through the confluence zones, and then delete the Fibonacci. How they were created is no longer needed if you want to clean up the display.

# JANUARY 22 (SATURDAY), 2022

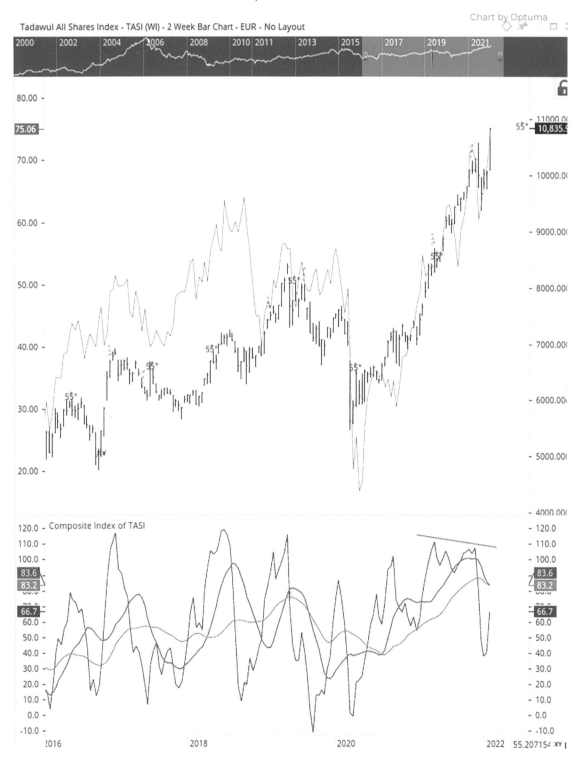

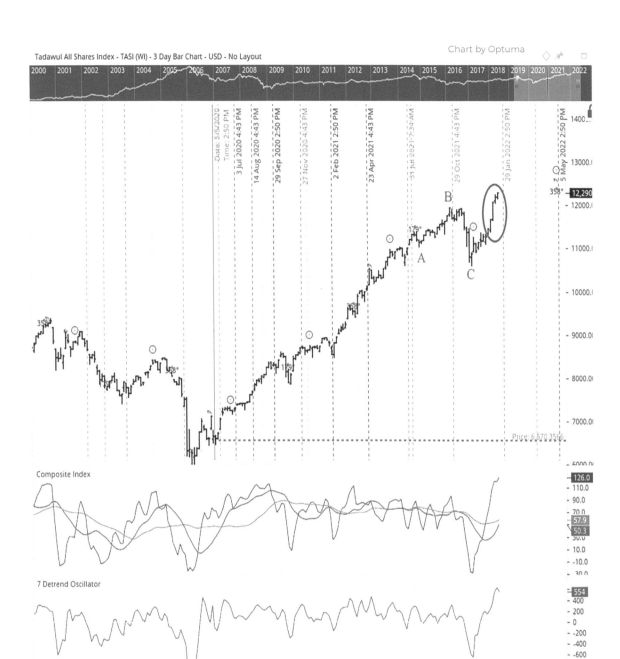

Tadawul All Shares Index - TASI (WI) - 3 Day Bar Chart - USD - No Layout

Chart by Optuma

The Saudi TASI is compared with Crude Oil in a 2-week chart. Notice how the Composite Index is moving up towards the intersection of the two averages in the overlay chart? Knowing there is more to the upside in TASI is all I need. Adds depth to the view that Crude Oil must advance. That will upset stocks. The Saudi 3-day chart shows a third wave in the red circle. The advance is incomplete.

# JANUARY 22 (SATURDAY), 2022

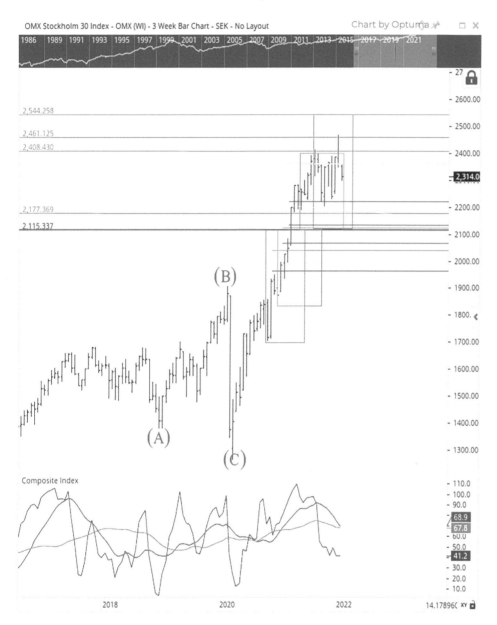

The 3-week chart of the Stockholm OMX 30 Index has been a secret weapon when it exceeded the price high marked (B). Both the OMX and French CAC have been the cleanest chart patterns in Europe. The chart shows target projections and support. That is a very ugly key reversal directional signal into the market high. The decline developing is the fourth wave within the rally that began from the low marked (C) in March 2020. The OMX midpoint is at 2115. The uptrend is in force and will continue...provided the midline is not broken before 2544 is realized.

Chart by Optuma

13,062.101
12,799.812
12,537.522

12,355.5

B

1

(3)

5

2

3

A

4

C

Composite Index

68.8
64.4
59.8

35.8

2018    2020    2022    46.308160 ×

The 2-week chart of the Swiss Market shows a key reversal top. The Composite Index is currently a huge warning. The Composite formed a '^' under the point where the two moving averages (SMA) are crossing over and down. I am sure I mentioned before that this can be the most damaging setup in any time horizon. The formation is in a 2-week chart making this a very nasty bearish signal.

Two Fibonacci confluence zones are below the market. I do not care what the price is for either. When SSMI arrives, I will need to recalculate as these targets were calculated from the top of the rectangle.

# JANUARY 23 (SUNDAY), 2022

Sunday morning coffee, time to study the technology stocks.

Apple (AAPL) in a monthly chart looks like a completed five wave advance from the bottom of the screen to the top. I know the consolidation in the middle marked 'iv' was a contracting triangle. Break 156 and the stock will fall back to the apex of the triangle. Stay above 156 and AAPL could muster one extension up... but only one. Either way the decline for now is incomplete and the next level of support is 160.56 in the weekly chart at right. What is very telling is the Fibonacci support gap under 160. Nothing until 156.55. That usually warns of a fast market condition. These three charts are all on the same screen displayed together.

Based on the wave count offered in AMZN's weekly chart, AMZN will target 2718. That support zone has a significant number of Fibonacci ratios all overlapping one another. That could stop Amazon and be the level to test several times as other markets decline. Certainly need to see indicators once at 2718.

As far as developing a guide for the NASDAQ, these stocks support further loses. But the profile is incomplete as we also need MSFT and GOOG.

AAPL - Monthly NASDAQ

156.55

162.41

Detrended Price Osc

Composite Index ()

Chart by TradeStation

**IFTA**

**Where Market Technicians from Around the World**
**Speak the Same Language**

See more of Malaysian Association of Technical Analysts - MATA on Facebook

Log In  or  Create new account

https://www.facebook.com/malaysianchartist/

**About**

👍 12,686 people like this

✓ 13,450 people follow this

🌐 http://malaysianchartist.com/

✉ mata.secretariat@gmail.com

Nonprofit Organization

# JANUARY 23 (SUNDAY), 2022

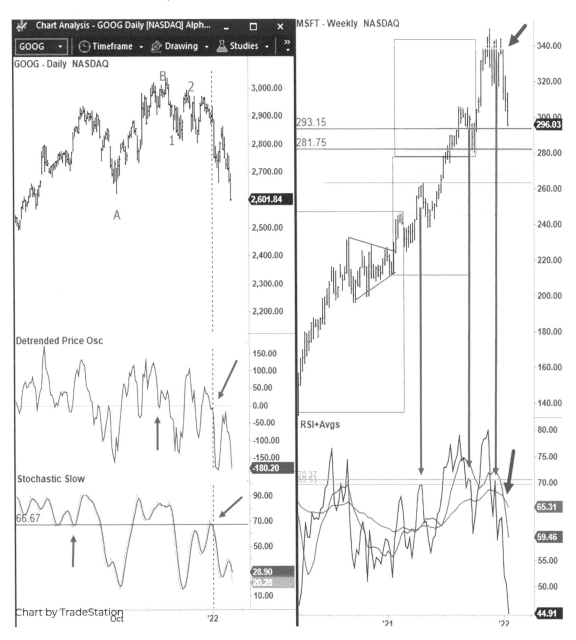

Google shows an incomplete decline. The detrend is trying to develop a 'W' pattern in the oscillator. I need to add the Fibonacci confluence zones to this chart. Stochastics does not show any reason to buy.

MSFT is on major support. It will break to 281.75. Major funds may want to step in near the next target zone to buy there. We will see.

# JANUARY 23 (SUNDAY), 2022

NQ - Weekly

start

16,00..

13,654.66

12,950.16

12,413.58

11,440.20

14,004.

12,00..

10,00..

8,000.0

65.24
41.68
18.88
0.00

1,500.0

500.00

-86.18
-500.00

-1,500.

20          '21          '22

At left is the data for the NASDAQ June 2022 contract. I like to develop support calculations for both the active and nearby forward contracts.

When the market shows respect to these support or resistance levels in weekly and monthly charts, it creates an understanding of how the trend is building new targets from prior important price levels. These same starting points and confluence target zones I use for Gann tools like a Gann Fan or cycle projection.

The weekly March Nasdaq contract is at right.It shows the Fibonacci ranges all start from just off the highs. With the new price bar created this week, I will recalculate the start of the ranges to the price high of the current bar. Why? It is the strongest price bar now within the entire decline off the high. Strong bars and gaps are always the most valuable anchors.The lower start also allows confluence zones to form in a series under 13,512 as well.

The two yellow arrows in the June contract at left mark the same horizontal level. This where the Fibonacci ranges all start after a revision. The former calculations are at left starting from near the high. With the hard break this week the new strong bar high is where all the indexes should begin the range selection to define support. The longer horizon levels are now refined and we have support Fibonacci confluence zones of support below 13,654 now.

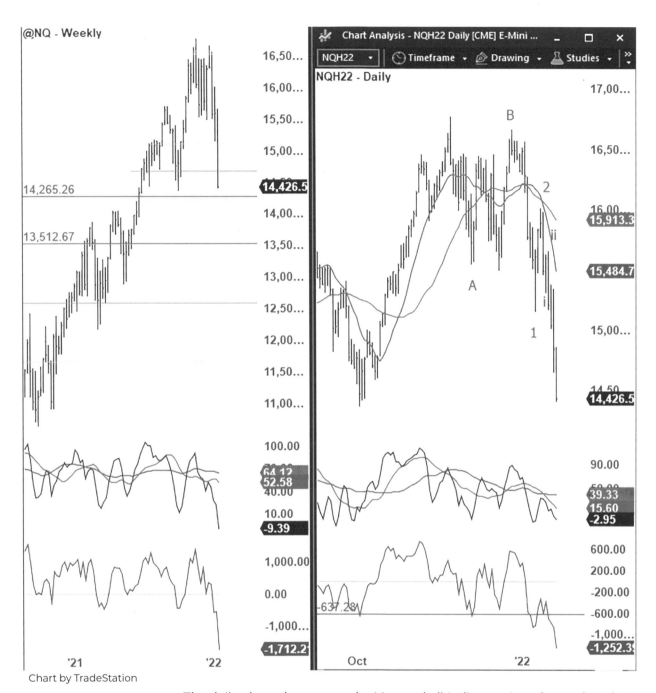

Chart by TradeStation

The daily chart shows you why I ignored all indicators into the market close on Friday. The market sentiment to the downside is clearly incomplete. The decline is defining wave 3 and we know this is where most people will be on the same side of the market for different reasons. Closing the week on the price low for the week means a gap down open could develop. Gaps down often start from just under the nearby Fibonacci confluence zone. The 14,265 level is only the top of the confluence zone. It would open a little lower under the floor of the zone.

# JANUARY 23 (SUNDAY), 2022

One last chart. The chart at right is the Russell 2000 ETF IWM. I like to look at a few charts and stocks in a different charting styles. My brain gets tired of always looking at the same bar charts repeatedly. I do not use candles because they require a much wider x-axis spread and that messes with my Elliott Wave interpretations. But I do look on the weekend at CandleVolume charts that give a quick measure of crowd sentiment by volume width of a Candlestick. (See StockSharts.com APC Version). The majority of the time I need fairly compressed data because I am always looking at wave structure and historical references in the amplitude of oscillators. So a quick view of a point-and-figure chart, or an equivolume chart, or a Gann swing chart is my alternate quick check display preference. Gann swing charts have similarities to point-and-figure. Not many people use equivolume charts.

The IWM chart simply confirms that the decline is not complete. The more important information is to know the midpoint of the rally. It is at 184. If at anytime 184 is broken in the mid-cap index of stocks, we could then return to 142. Therefore knowing the mid-point of the strongest price move up is very informative about the trend in the bigger picture.

Neither of my vendors have point-and-figure charts with this clarity.   I use StockCharts.com for these displays online.

It has taken all weekend, but we are ready for tomorrow.

# IWM iShares Russell 2000 ETF NYSE

21-Jan-2022, 16:00 ET, daily, O: 199.76, H: 203.02, L: 196.99, C: 196.99, V: 85820624, Chg: -3.76 (-1.87%)

**P&F Pattern** Double Bottom Breakdown on 18-Jan-2022

Scaling: Traditional [Reversal: 3]

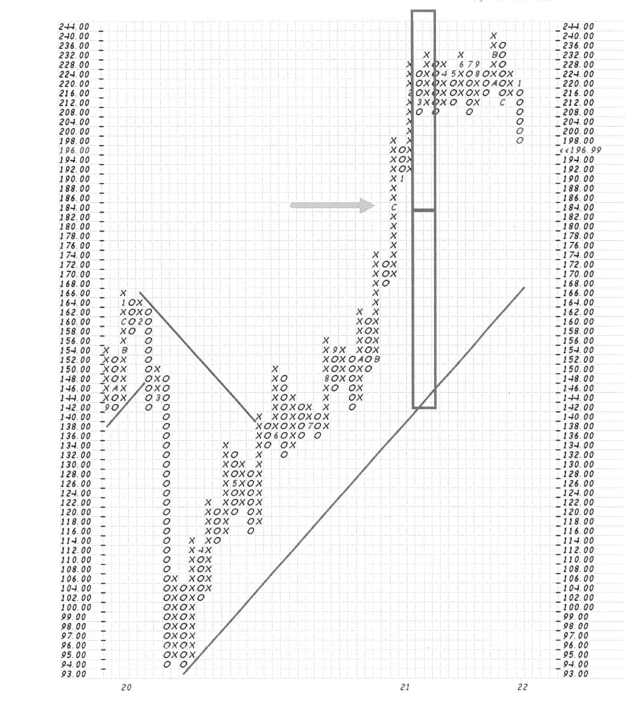

(c) StockCharts.com

# JANUARY 24 (MONDAY), 2022 - 10:30 AM (EST)

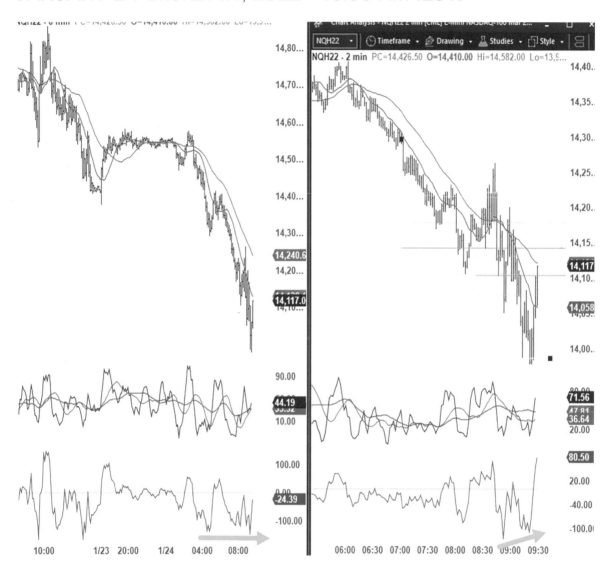

The diary page titles will be in EST, or New York City time, though the screen/chart display is in Chicago time an hour earlier. I know, it messes me up too. So 9:30 in the chart is 10:30 in New York City already.

Ever since the open the NASDAQ has chopped buyers and sellers establishing positions. I am using an 8-minute to 2-minute bar chart to read the action. The pop up near the open was to the 8-minute blue 33-period SMA on price. Most of the action is under the red 33-period moving average. There is a pop up developing right now. The move up comes from the detrend oscillators showing an aligned agreement.

# JANUARY 24 (MONDAY), 2022 - 10:38 AM (EST)

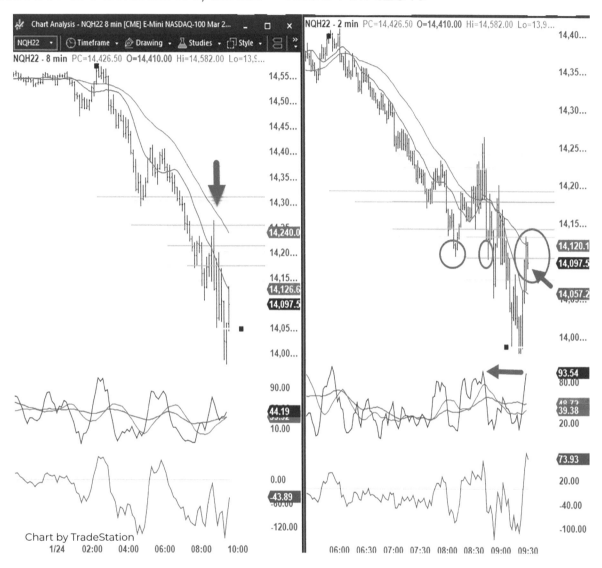

Chart by TradeStation

I need to add resistance levels to the 8-minute chart. The resistance levels in the 2-minute chart are just an early gauge, the 8-minute price action produces very distinct Fibonacci confluence zones. These are important. The resistance zone that the blue moving-average on price is on in the 8-minute chart is the … "you-are-in-deep-trouble" line in the sand. The 2-minute chart shows a very small reaction to minor resistance near the blue SMA. Small but important, as it is under two pivots in red circles. The Composite Index is approaching the same amplitude in the 2-minute chart as the market open. The 8-minute Composite shows averages crossing up. Check MSFT, SP500, and DJIA!

# JANUARY 24 (MONDAY), 2022 - 11:22 AM

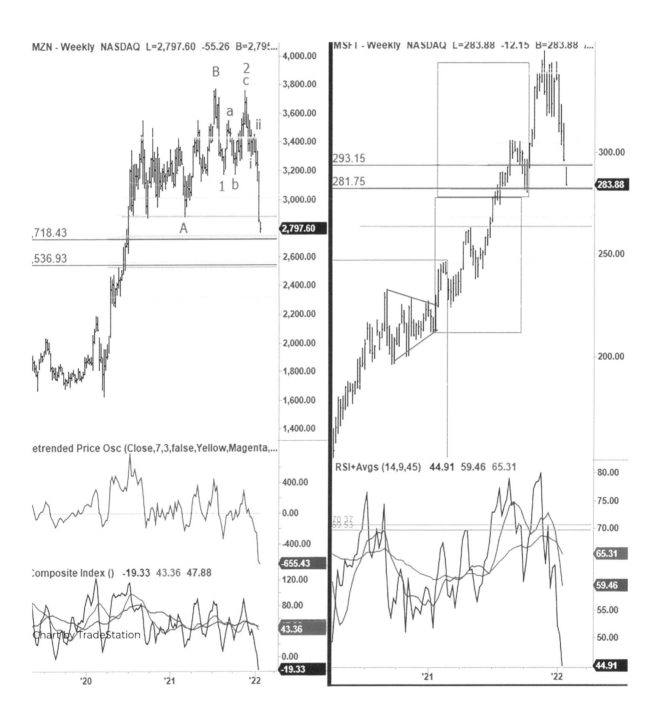

I am watching MSFT and AMZN all the time in 15-minute charts. MSFT is my primary lead indicator. It has broken down and is trading to major support in the weekly chart at 281. What is really telling is MSFT is near major support and the shorter 60-minute MSFT chart is incomplete. (Sorry, forgot to copy it. It comes later near 3:05 PM). Same gap being referenced now. There is a gap just under this support zone. MSFT can stall here, but it must break and move towards the lower gap because the oscillators are not set up to define a bottom. That is a big problem for the market. MSFT at 280 is a level Funds would view as a buying opportunity. It has to do with the arc that connects the price lows throughout the rally in the weekly chart. You can see 280 does not do any real damage to this long-term trend. A break will push MSFT to the next confluence zone near 277 and damage the parabolic rally. That would set the NASDAQ off to another leg down. MSFT at 277 however could be very tempting. We'll see what the index says.

Now this is important. A 14-period RSI is under the MSFT weekly prices. The RSI has a steep decline, but has fallen to the 44.91 amplitude level. Don't forget bull markets rn the RSI well above 70 and then declines near 40 will be corrections within a bull market. These are the range rules in action in this longer horizon chart. The bottom is not in place, and this is not an RSI formation that supports a bottom here. But after such a steep decline, to target the range rule guidelines is important. It is a corrective decline within the larger uptrend.

AMZN is not on support in the weekly chart. The bottom of the support zone is at 2718. AMZN is trading 2797.

I check the S&P500, DJIA, and a few DJIA stocks. Close, but all are missing a swing down in their 60-minute charts.

The NASDAQ chop is mentally doing a number to me, but all the evidence is pointing to another leg down. We know the target levels. HOLD.

# JANUARY 24 (MONDAY), 2022  11:49 AM

Finally, the break comes. NASDAQ shows the current price in black on the y-axis. The index is trading 13,854. The market is in the Fibonacci support zone.

Elliott Wave Principle suggests this move down in the daily chart is wave iii of 3. That tells me to be very careful here because the chop from hell this morning could be a really ugly contracting triangle and this fast thrust down is the fifth wave decline to end wave iii. I know, no fair using methods we have not covered, but I'll use everything I can to protect this profit in my account.

Do you see the divergence forming in the Composite Index in the daily NQ chart? I am taking 40% off my position with a market order. For now, I'll keep 100% leverage. Stops? No change. Many will disagree.

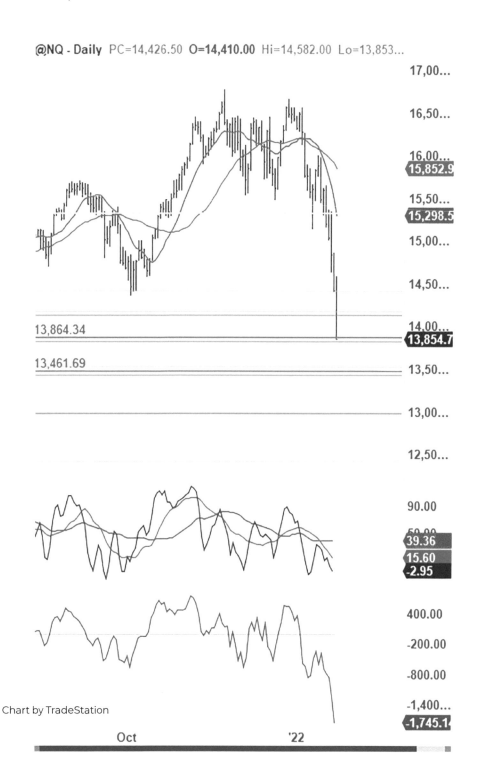

@NQ - Daily  PC=14,426.50  O=14,410.00  Hi=14,582.00  Lo=13,853...

Chart by TradeStation

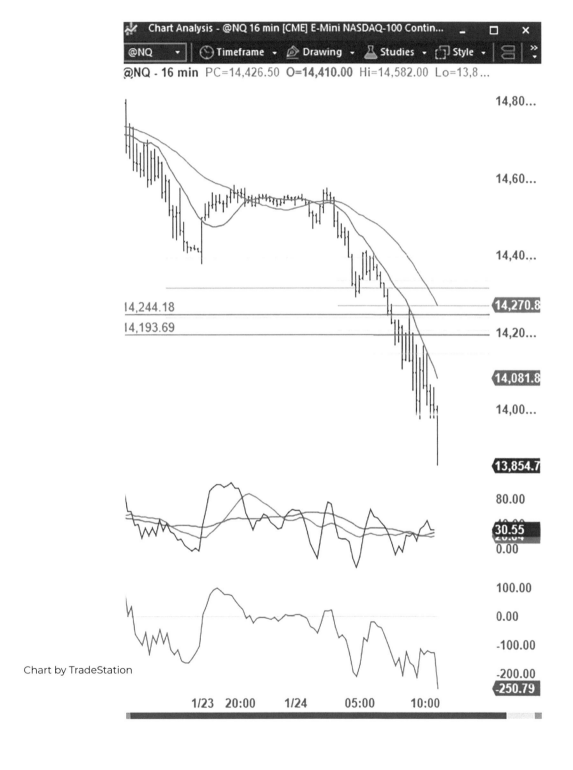

Chart by TradeStation

**IFTA** Where Market Technicians from Around the World
Speak the Same Language

association française
des analystes techniques

Homepage    Afate ▾    Technical analysis    Resources ▾    Members Area    Forum    Contact

AFATE's missions: 1. Promote technical analysis.

## ASSOCIATION FRANÇAISE DES ANALYSTES TECHNIQUES

**Promouvoir l'analyse technique**

**Contribuer à l'émergence de critères de qualité**

**Proposer des ateliers et conférences de qualité, dans le respect des standards internationaux dans ce domaine**

**Création : en 1990**

https://www.afate.com

# JANUARY 24 (MONDAY), 2022 - 12:32 AM (EST)

On a separate computer I have open an online charting service called StockCharts.com. Excellent platform for those learning technical analysis and offered for a low monthly subscription. I find it of value for their lists and for features my high-end software is missing like equivolume chart displays.

Here the NASDAQ 100 Index in a 5-minute chart is an equivolume display. The price range of each bar gives the volume indicated by the width of the bar. The volume is drying up rapidly as the market approaches the 13,991 low. Very, very dangerous signal the market is becoming exhausted to the downside. The 11:32 am time in the chart is Chicago time. Already 12:32 New York time. The oscillator on the bottom is a 7-period detrend.

MSFT is trading 276 with the major support target zone of 277. I decide to buy 1000 shares of the stock I have been eyeing during the decline. The market order has a $3 slippage cost. I always fear hedge funds. The stampede has not started. I have to be in front of them and take the risk before they wake up.

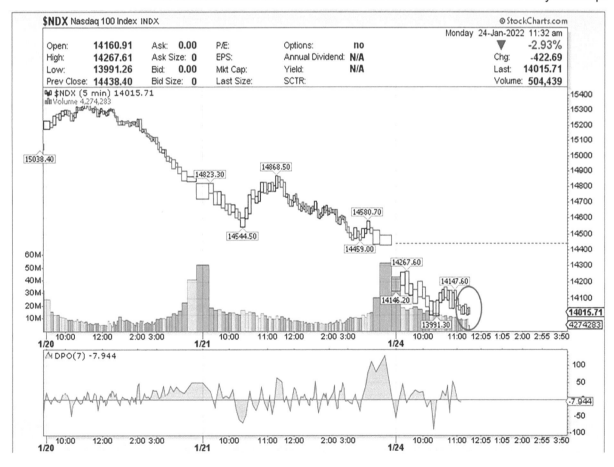

# JANUARY 24 (MONDAY), 2022 - 1:38 PM

The 16-minute vs 4-minute NASDAQ charts have buy confirmation signals in the detrend oscillator. They are circled in green. This is why the 4:1 time ratio is used. As volume diminishes into the low I bought a stock. The distraction may have been a serious mistake. I have already unwound 40% of my NASDAQ position, but my thinking that a retest of the low may prove now to be a big mistake.

Stocks are in a different account and display screen setup. By the time I turn back to the NASDAQ screen it is trading 13,874. I need the new resistance levels FAST.

The 13,980 level is where the market kept testing the morning lows. Break above these morning lows and not covering on the lows is a confirmed error of judgment.

MSFT is moving up. We have been leaning on this stock throughout the decline. It is forcing me to cover 50% at the market.

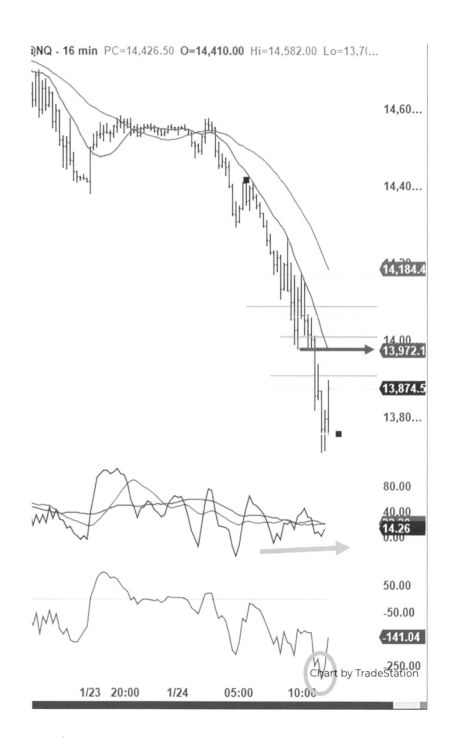

Still short 50%. Third wave declines are very difficult. Suddenly price can break hard and extend in a merciless decline against the oversold oscillators. The problem is the detrend oscillator in the 4-minute chart. It has bounced back up to the same early morning amplitude high before the market opened. In a waterfall event that is all the warning the market will give you. The bounce develops on weak volume. Then the bigger meltdown develops. But the key is volume. It is picking up. Holding my last 50% short was the wrong move.

The bottom oscillator in the 4-minute chart is my Composite Index. It should be able to pull back in the 4-minute chart to test the point where the two moving-averages are crossing up over. Resistance is at 13,927 where the 33-period SMA (blue) is mapped.

The next resistance is where the upwards pointing red arrows are located.

# JANUARY 24 (MONDAY), 2022 - 2:17 PM

Market order. Buy. I am covering the last 50% short in NASDAQ futures based on two major factors.

You can see in the 60-minute chart the NASDAQ ran to the second level of resistance that aligned with the red SMA. The 60-minute chart is my long horizon chart. The 13-period SMA in the 60-minute chart becomes a wall of resistance. The pullback that follows is to the red SMA in the 15-minute chart. This creates a key reversal bar we call a directional signal. These charts are side-by-side on my screen with a daily chart off screen to the left.

The three green arrows mark **a bullish head-n-shoulders pattern**. A second directional signal. I do not need another 2 by 4 across the head. Get out. Confirmation. The bullish head-n-shoulders is developing as volume is shrinking fast in the equivolume chart. Screams GET OUT! Bank it.

Chart by TradeStation

**Chart Analysis - NQH22 15 min [CME] E-Mini NASDAQ-100 Mar ...**

NQH22  |  Timeframe  |  Drawing  |  Studies  |  Style

NQH22 - 15 min  PC=14,426.50  O=14,410.00  Hi=14,582.00  Lo=13....

15,20

15,00

14,80

14,60

14,40

14,20

**14,09**

**13,98**

13,80

**79.33**
**59.83**
**38.62**

0.00

200.0
**126.7**
50.00

-100.0

-250.0

15:00    1/21  05:00  10:00    1/23    1/24  05:00  10:00  15:00

Chart by TradeStation

Notice the third green arrow on the right shoulder moves price to where the market broke down early this morning after the gut- wrenching stall.

Short squeeze coming. We declined all last week. Everyone who sold this morning is about to go deep in the red. The 60-minute chart has resistance near 14,454 at the moment. Simple equality swing.

In the 15-minute chart is a green horizontal arrow on the detrend oscillator. Notice the second shoulder of the head-n-shoulders price pattern is pushing the detrend oscillator to the TOP of the oscillator peaks that developed during the decline. Track the horizontal green arrow across to the current detrend position. Another warning the market has likely found a bottom.

MSFT starts to accelerate up. Hedge Funds are the buyers making the strong reversal in the stock.

# JANUARY 24 (MONDAY), 2022 - 3:00 PM

I check the DJIA weekly chart. It shows price is at 33,533 and it is resting on top of the confluence zone. The horizontal line reads 33,450; price currently is 33,533.

These support zones were calculated using the top of the bar to the immediate right of the price high. (Top red arrow.) Fibonacci confluence zones are exceedingly exact. But we recalculated the support zones in the NASDAQ and now the DJIA contract shows the ranges started still off the high. This is important. Notice in the red circle on price that the current weekly bar slipped through the support zone at 33,450. The slip under the zone is the same distance as the differential between the two bar highs marked with red arrows. The second lower arrow also marks the start of the longest bar in the decline. Strongest bars should always be

Chart by TradeStation

favored over any other we used earlier in the move. Revise these calculations tonight. Bring the start of the Fibonacci ranges down to the lower second red arrow.

With everything going on I forgot to log the exact time of this screen capture in the daily chart for the NASDAQ. But I wanted to show you I did check the daily chart and saw it was at the major support zone at 13,702. These support calculations were prepared over the weekend as part of the preparations for today. We are due for a corrective consolidation or sharp zigzag rally. Fourth waves can chop you to death.

Wave 'ii' up was fast, sharp, and brief. The guideline of alternation between a second and fourth wave warns us that this coming fourth wave could be ugly and take no prisoners by becoming range bound and time consuming. I plan to just watch from the sidelines and do nothing. I do not like giving gains back by stepping in too early. Hard lesson to learn, but after a big win do not get gready.The trader gods will take it away in my experience. Plus, I do not want to work that hard anymore. I'm good and in no hurry.

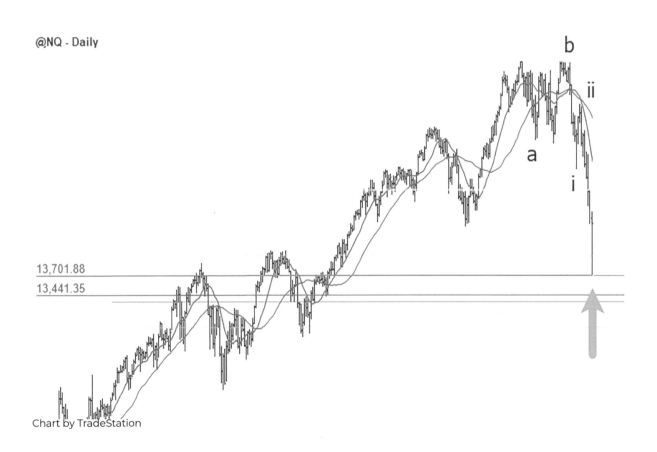

# JANUARY 24 (MONDAY), 2022 - 3:05 PM

Chart by TradeStation

MSFT - 120 min  NASDAQ  L=289.38  -6.65  B=289.36  A=:...

287.84

277.53

Detrended Price Osc (Close,7,3,false,Yellow,Magenta,Bla...

RSI+Avgs (14,9,45)  28.29  37.07  37.77

12/20    12/27    '22   1/5  1/7  1/11    1/18    1/24

Chart by TradeStation

MSFT has broken back up through the prior 287 support zone. This is still the primary market I am leaning on to trade NASDAQ.

MSFT bottomed first before the NASDAQ. The drop toward 277 in MSFT was accompanied by extreme diminishing volume in the equivolume and CandleVolume 5-minute charts. I was watching MSFT like a hawk. Now the 120-minute MSFT chart shows a formidable key reversal off the low on the screen. It should be able to fill the gap because major Fibonacci resistance is at the top of the gap. But that will be the level of high risk for a reversal. We should go back to work then.

# JANUARY 24 (MONDAY), 2022 - 3:26 PM

As I am flat in the NASDAQ now the pressure is off. The 240-minute S&P500 futures contract is trading 4337. It should target 4420, but it must break above 4379 resistance first. The previous fourth wave marked 'iv' is aligned with the red 13-period SMA on price. Maybe not today, but it should be able to realize a test of that average.

NASDAQ a few minutes later. That is an impressive short squeeze unfolding. Funds are pouring into MSFT now. NASDAQ is back to 14,308, but the session is not over.

# JANUARY 24 (MONDAY), 2022 - 3:32 PM

NASDAQ shows no indication of failing under the nearby resistance zone. It should be able to go higher into the close. The 14,441 level in the 33-period SMA (blue) is the next target. Adding more Fibonacci ranges (not in this chart), and found 14,440 is the next confluence target zone.

# JANUARY 24 (MONDAY), 2022 - 3:54 PM

Chart by TradeStation

NQH22 - 15 min  PC=14,426.50  O=14,410.00  Hi=14,582.00  Lo=13,...

Chart by TradeStation

Nice. NASDAQ March 2022 futures are soon to close. The circled pivot in the 15-minute chart will be interesting. Can the market close higher than this price swing low? No.

The detrend oscillator on close shows a "M" pattern. The 60-minute chart moved towards the 33-period SMA and Fibonacci confluence resistance zone. The pivot low circled in the 15-minute chart is the bottom of wave 'iii'. The 14,442 area is the previous fourth wave, always an ideal target.

Here is what we know. The market has started the first swing up within wave 4. The strong move up catching so many late sellers will likely take some time to digest ttoday. Do not chase a day like this thinking you can catch what you missed or can see a repeat. My primary rule is this; markets move in a manner that will catch the majority off guard. Stay away tomorrow and take time to mentally re-balance. I need to review global markets for clients and then plan the next move.

# JANUARY 24 (MONDAY), 2022 - 4:16 PM

MARKETS

## Stocks mount stunning comeback on Monday with Dow closing in the green after earlier 1,000-point loss

**BREAKING**    day with Dow closing in the green after earlier 1,000-point loss

Stocks mount stunning comeback on Monday with Dow closing in the green after earlier

The Dow Jones Industrial Average closed up 101 points, or 0.3%, at 34,366.67, gaining for the first day in seven. The S&P 500 finished higher by 0.3% at 4,410.50. The Nasdaq Composite gained 0.6% at 13,855.13. The Russell 2000 index of small-cap shares closed up as well.

The Nasdaq Composite Index turned positive after being down as much as 4.9% earlier in the session. The Dow Jones Industrial rallied after being down 1,115 points at one point. The S&P 500 closed in the green after briefly hitting a correction earlier in the session, falling more than 10% from its Jan. 3 record close.

MARKETS

## Nasdaq turns positive after being down 4.9% earlier as market mounts big reversal Monday

**Gone for Pizza and Beer.**

**Off for the night.**

# JANUARY 25 (TUESDAY), 2022

@NQ - Weekly  PC=14,426.50  O=**14,410.00**  Hi=14,582.00  Lo=13,7...

Chart by TradeStation

The wins yesterday cover a lot of bills for many months. I am very tired. I need a break and know to do nothing today. We know the market is in a fourth wave position and often chops a day or two. The people who think they can repeat yesterday will likely be chopped up.

Take the day off. Time to put the trader's hat aside and start the analysis work again. I hope you see there are two different mindsets in this process. One is the planner mindset that uses many different analytic methods. There is no immediate pressure, and we can evaluate global markets and use approaches that may take considerable thought and preparation. I liken this part of the process to being the strategic General.

The other mindset is the Warrior mindset. Simplified and very effective methods used without distraction. You may favor other methods. But have few and know them intimately. Do not entirely ignore longer horizon charts when you have to drop down the very short horizon time periods to see the details develop within a move. We always need to keep a perspective of daily and weekly charts during the session. Monthly and weekly when it is a very big move unfolding.

The process I need to follow requires a mental health day. Walk away from success. I want to go for a hike and play with my dog. Then I'll look at the screens as an analyst and make a review across many markets, adjust long horizon targets based on the new price pivots if needed. Take some time just to think and slow the pace down.

In the morning I look at a couple charts in longer horizon. The chart at left of the weekly NASDAQ 100 shows major support held yesterday in this time frame. Both the Composite Index and Detrend Oscillator are at new extreme lows. The oscillators must advance and then drop to a higher low in the process of finding a final bottom if this is going to be a normal progression. Next major support under 13,771 in the NASDAQ is at 13,286.

It is January 25. Interesting. We did some cycles work together that may become a factor in this decline. Figure 2.4 in the Cycles chapter was an annualized study for the DJIA. The 'hot zone' in that study determined that price corrections that develop in January may reverse near February 10th. View the cycle as an inflection point in time. Figure 2.4 showed the computer recorded a black band denoting a 'hot-zone' around February 10. Not a specific day. I need to do a lot of cycle work today. I need to know the density of the cycles clustering and dates. I know the market needs to burn time in a fourth wave. Will that mean a cycle inversion into the February 10th window? We have a day or two to just look things over, mentally regroup, and re-balance. That cycle means homework is needed.

# JANUARY 25 (TUESDAY), 2022

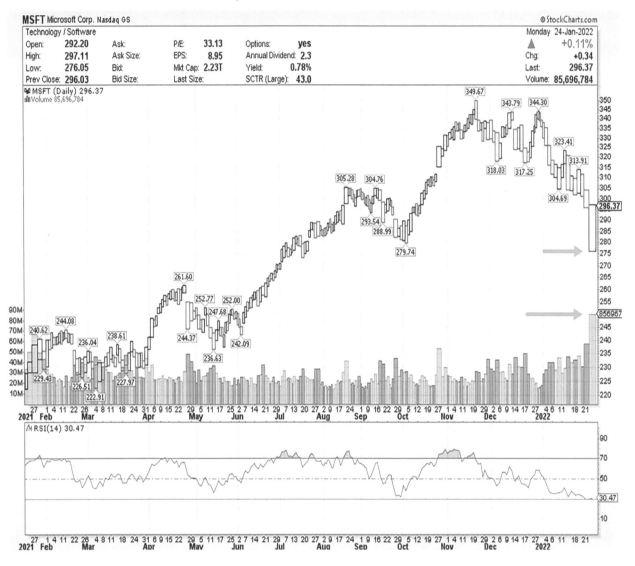

Before the market open the daily MSFT data is plotted as an equivolume chart. The more volume, the wider the rectangle that defines the price range bar. MSFT volume in yesterday's bar was huge! Greater than anything we have seen in years and that includes March 2020. What does that mean? Capitulation. George Lane taught us to wait for the retracement that develops on lower volume after capitulation or for the decline to a new low that is on lower volume.

I return after the market close. The 60-minute chart for the DJIA March futures contract shows the market did chop folks apart much of the day. What indicators warned this would happen? Just experience and the deep memorable tire-tracks etched down my back.

There is a key reversal top under the Fibonacci confluence resistance zone. The Composite Index is diverging. Likely a drop coming but the market needs more time. A complex correction is expected because the cycle dates are too far away. Patience. It is so very hard to do. Wait.

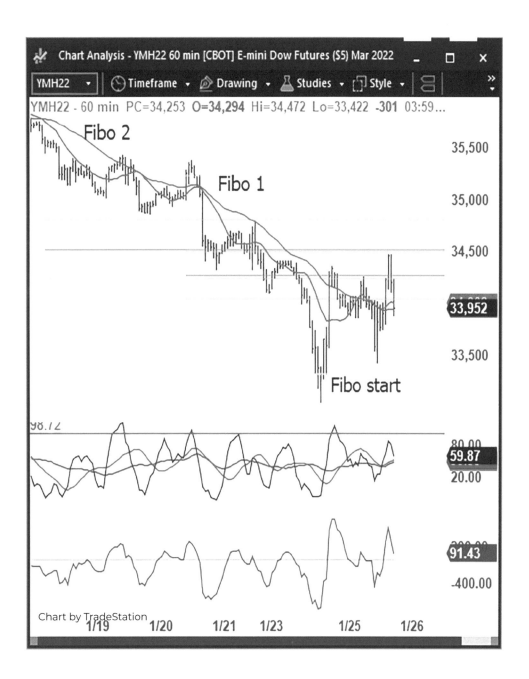

# JANUARY 26 (WEDNESDAY), 2022

MSFT reported earnings after the close yesterday. The report was very positive, but the after-market trading action pushed MSFT down 5%. That was a huge red flag for the larger market, though the corrective rally is incomplete as it needs more time.

Pre-market open on Wednesday, MSFT is up nearly $18 on the open and MSFT slams into major resistance with a huge gap up shown at left. It is trying

to define a break-away gap up. But we know the NASDAQ does not have a bottom yet and there will likely be another swing down. MSFT will not be able to hold this gain above the gap. Right from the open it begins to slide down from a 308.50 high. The stock I bought was MSFT, and that became a time conflict for me still holding 50% short NASDAQ.

I used a market order for MSFT's long position. The fill was just under 280, though the slippage was nearly $3 bucks. I did not place a stop under MSFT. I was not using margin. If wrong I felt MSFT had to return to 305 eventually, but it did launch up along with the indexes. I knew MSFT reported earnings Tuesday night. Can you ever recall a report that MSFT was wildly off expectations? Crazy oversold and the general market needed to buy time to correct upwards in a fourth wave swing. As you know I covered the NASDAQ futures Monday because of the simple bullish head-n-shoulders pattern. Sometimes simple is best. Was buying MSFT a gamble? Maybe. But I'd like to think of it as an educated guess supported by the indicator positions and MSFT falling to major support. Then when MSFT stock fell 5% last night with the release of their positive earnings report, my only thought was: "That's nuts, it will be back".

So why cover it now with a market order right at the open? I learned years ago when a stock gives you a lottery ticket gift with a gap like this, TAKE IT! We expect the NASDAQ decline to be incomplete. Amazon is incomplete. Google is incomplete. I would like to see the indexes and other tech stocks agree that the carnage decline is nearer to the end for a longer horizon position. Do you see that the longest bars within declining swings are getting longer with each market break? This market decline is far from over. The crowd sentiment is beginning to shift as individuals break away in pain. We have not seen crowd capitulation.

Time to get back to work.

# JANUARY 26 (WEDNESDAY), 2022

Chart by TradeStation

It is only now that I see MSFT in a 60-minute view had an amplitude peak at the same displacement before in the 7-period detrend oscillator. I was not analyzing anything when I wanted to cover on the open price gap. But I also see the spike up this morning aligns with two prior lows creating this angle drawn on the price. The question will be if this is an angle MSFT has respected previously.

The answer is yes. The repeating angle shows the actions of a crowd are defining geometric relationships. This was discussed back in Figure 4.8. What does that angle above the open mean now? If MSFT can break above resistance and the diagonal angle, MSFT could advance to 315 and we would have to review all the indexes.

# JANUARY 26 (WEDNESDAY) 11:42 AM, 2022

The NASDAQ 100 futures in a 60-minute chart is missing one swing up to complete the correction. Notice how the spread of the moving-averages is positive and a tight consolidation is forming on the red average.

I cannot turn-off the use of the Elliott Wave Principle patterns. A pattern called a zigzag would mean the last move up is required and the Fibonacci confluence zone of resistance at 14,628 would be the target. It is the first level above the current market position that defines the Fibonacci confluence zone. Scan the 14,628 horizontal level. A pivot low near the same level developed last Thursday on January 20. It defined the pop up into the blue descending moving average before the hard break down.
That is a significant level. I still have my eye on MSFT with the NASDAQ, but we need to monitor what else is brewing in other markets.

March E-Mini S&P 500 is under a key average on price, the 33-period average, but resistance is at 4461. I start to look at several markets and stocks. Everything is going to sleep on me! Nothing is moving.

# JANUARY 26 (WEDNESDAY), 2022

What am I missing here?

Stupid me. I do this a lot because I hyper-focus on charts. I turn on Bloomberg TV, grab a coffee. Sigh. In 37-minutes U.S. Federal Reserve Chairman Jerome Powell is expected to signal it is ready to raise interest rates. The Fed holds a two-day meeting and then on Wednesday afternoon the central bank issues a statement. That statement is today and to be announced in a matter of minutes. It explains why my charts all went to sleep and nothing is moving. People are waiting.

"Fed-Day". Ugh. That is a special day. I try to avoid markets when the Federal Reserve Chair is speaking. Over the many years of doing this my greatest losses have come on Fed-Days. Why? The Fed makes a statement, and the market makes a big swing in one direction, only to change its mind immediately and reverse in the other direction! Oh, did that hurt? I am sorry. I meant to react in this other direction. But if the market is still unsure, as the couch analysts dissect the Fed statement, they can run you over again with a repeat wash-n-rinse cycle. No thank you. You can count me out. But what if NASDAQ pops up into the target? I do not care. I will let it go this time and wait for a new setup.

As I look over charts, I am thinking Oil is a bigger risk than rates. We know the Fed will raise rates. It is a question of timing. Will they hike rates in a surprise move today or in March? Then the question will be whether they will raise rates 25 or 50-basis points? (See why we covered this in Chapter One?) A 50 basis point hike might hit technology stocks very hard.

The charts show Crude Oil is in an incomplete rally and heading towards $90. A move triggered by fears of Putin moving into Ukraine? Maybe European energy problems becoming more severe? Who knows, but the Oil chart is a warning and $90 is only a short-horizon target.

Time to be a spectator.

The announcement comes. The Federal Reserve will hike rates in March. That is exactly what everyone expected. What is the market doing?

Tempting. Very, very tempting. NASDAQ pops up right to the underside of the Fibonacci confluence zone at 14,628. The years of discipline kicks in. Don't do it! Walk away. I do. Return after the market closes.

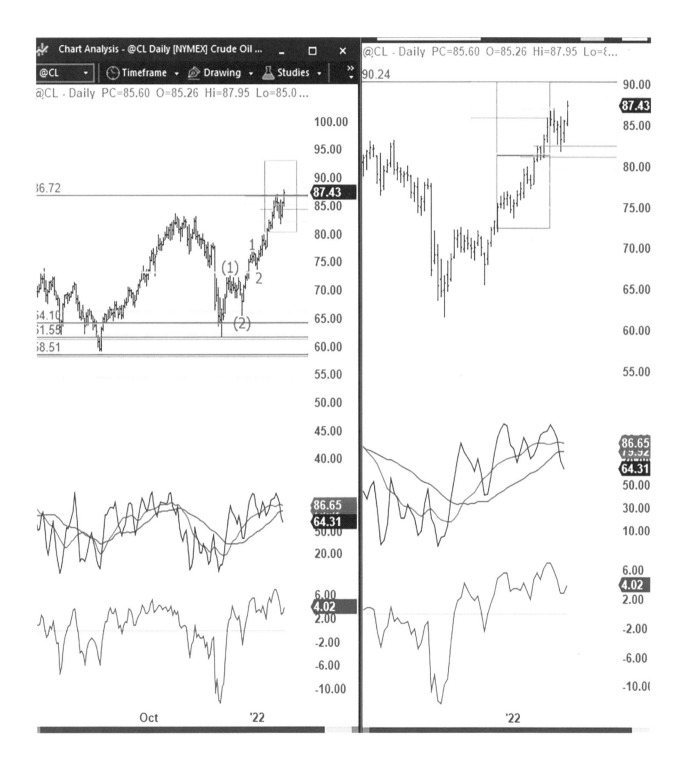

# JANUARY 26 (WEDNESDAY), 2:03 PM, 2022

The NASDAQ pop into resistance at 14,628 was the ideal place to sell. MSFT never challenged the morning high again. But something is off. As I scan many stocks they are stalling. Several are just back-n-fill price action. I need to step back to look at the longer horizon charts.

The 7-period detrend oscillator on the DJIA is important now based on the discussion we had for Figures 4.13 to 4.19.

# JANUARY 26 (WEDNESDAY), 2022 MARKETS CLOSED

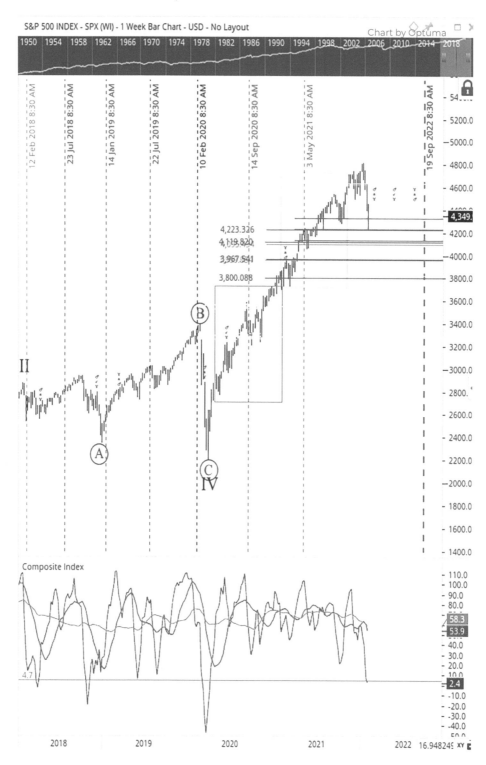

The weekly S&P500 is where to begin. It is on major support. I believe the March 2020 low ended a very large degree fourth wave. Sorry, I cannot turn wave structure off. Once you know the Elliott Wave Principle you just cannot turn it off. A large degree fourth wave into the March 2020 low means this entire rally is a fifth wave. It is not complete, but we must be very selective about the next move up. The current pullback will look small when the move up from March 2020 is done. What methods will work best? The 7-period detrend oscillator with two side-by-side time horizons in a ratio of 4:1 will keep us on the right side of a crazy large decline.

You will find two light green rectangles in the S&P500 weekly chart. The data below the bottom rectangle into the wave IV low is not in a box. That is the missing piece the market will copy and add to current highs. Just a proportional reference and not a final price target. We have other methods that will be more accurate. We will set those up when we end this correction.

I labeled the March 2020 low wave 'IV'. Those who know Elliott will know that that is an exceedingly high degree reference for a very long horizon trend. Not here. I am just trying to make it easy to read. Read it as a fourth wave working a fifth up now from the March 2020 low.

The cycle beats in the current chart are the square bar counts. You can see that the cycle cannot forecast the magnitude of the reaction when the market respects the cycle. The heavy red dashed line for the week of September 19 is the most important in the series because it is the square of 19 or the 361st bar from where the series began. That does not impact us today.

# JANUARY 26 (WEDNESDAY), 2022 MARKETS CLOSED

This oscillator should look very familiar to you. It is the 3-week chart of the DJIA with the 7-period detrend oscillator. The placement of the horizontal lines on the oscillator formed part of our discussion of Figures 4.13 to 4.19.

Look where the oscillator has fallen to under price. The amplitude is equal to the amplitude circled in the first red oval. This market loves to produce "W" formations. Therefore, this is not a bottom.

A 2-week overlay chart of the S&P600 Small-caps and the Toronto TSX shows Canada is holding up very well. In fact, it is so strong it goes on my shopping list when a better bottom develops. That would mean a position in the Canadian ETF EWC.

**S&P SmallCap 600 Index - SML (WI) - 2 Week Bar Chart - USD - No Layout**

Chart by Optuma

TSX

SP600

1,277.61

# JANUARY 26 (WEDNESDAY), 2022 MARKETS CLOSED

Toronto's TSX is going to produce another swing up. That supports further gains in Crude Oil. However, there is an interesting problem.

It is well known that crowds not only develop well defined swing patterns, but they also develop proportional relationships between price swings. It is common for the first and fifth waves to develop swings that are equal in length. The March 2020 panic lows creates the problem now. It seems unlikely we should take the length of the swing from the low to the pivot high marked '1' in a circle, then add that length to project the target from the price low at '4'. A more rational approach is to measure from the bottom of wave '2' to the bottom of wave '4'. Then project up from wave '4' to estimate the length of wave '5'.

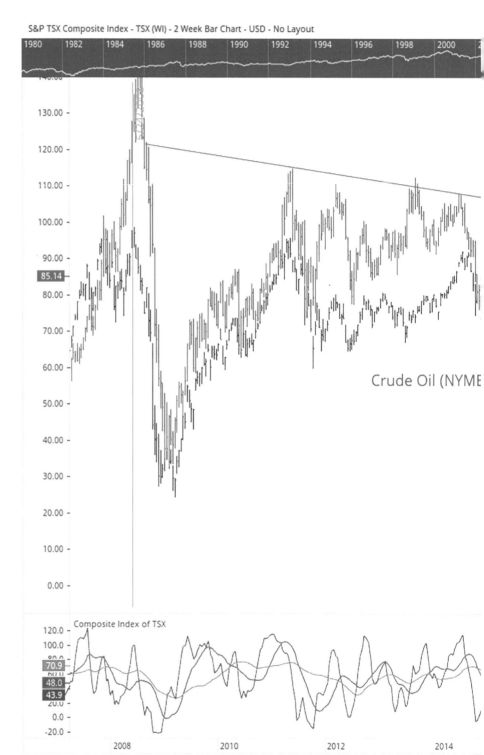

S&P TSX Composite Index - TSX (WI) - 2 Week Bar Chart - USD - No Layout

Crude Oil (NYME

Composite Index of TSX

Chart by Optuma

Toronto TSX (USD)

NYMEX)

# JANUARY 27 (THURSDAY)

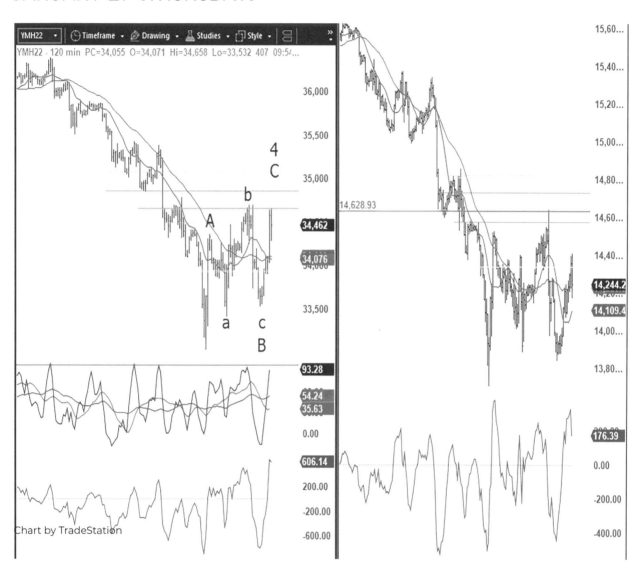

Chart by TradeStation

It is nearly 11:00 AM already on Thursday.
All that chop yesterday was the middle segment in a larger correction. I have seen this before. The equity markets are burning time to align with the cycle timing. Right now, no one has the winning hand.

The 120-minute DJIA futures and 60-minute NASDAQ futures show the detrend oscillator at highs in both. There could be a pullback. I am not very focused today. Taking the day off.

# JANUARY 27 (THURSDAY) (CLOSE)

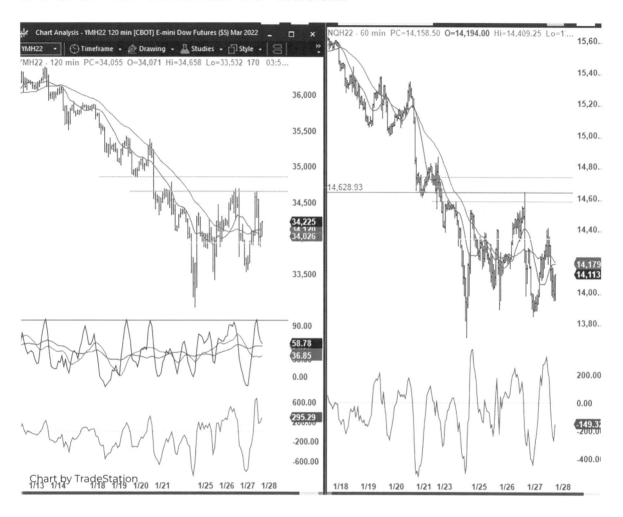

Chart by TradeStation

Knowing when to step aside and do nothing is just as important as knowing when to take up your battle stations. It is a battle that never ends. Experience teaches you to jump in when your survival looks good. Run away when it does not. At least that is true of short-horizon scalpers which is what I have been for my entire career in futures. Stocks I hold longer, but long for me is in terms of days or a few weeks. My specialty is short horizon, and a week feels like a life-time. Stay in the time horizon where you perform best.

I suspect a lot of people gave back their gains from Monday over the last few days. Notice the conflict. The 120-minute NASDAQ chart shows oscillators at the top. The 60-minute well below the zero line. The market can chop us to death when this alignment forms.

# JANUARY 27 (THURSDAY) (CLOSE)

Wow, look at Amazon and the Composite Index oscillator! This is a fourth wave consolidation, but it could rip bears apart with a sharp rally towards AMZN 3000. Then AMZN could fall to 2536. MSFT is holding up well. You could not pay me to sell this market here.

# JANUARY 28 (FRIDAY)

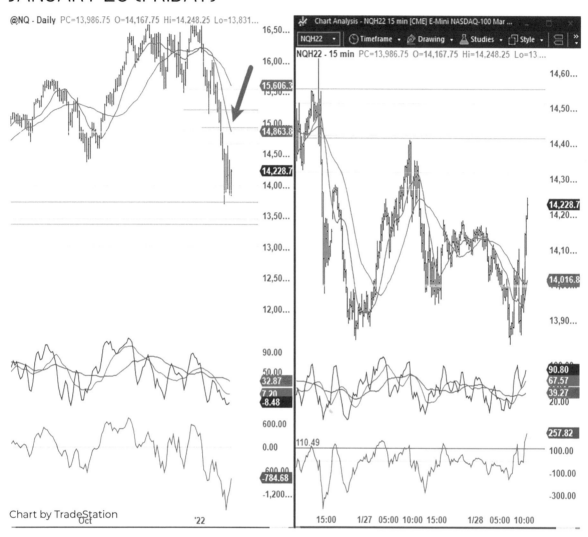

Chart by TradeStation

Amazon helped us call this move up nicely. NASDAQ could run up to the simple 33-period moving-average (red average on price) marked with an arrow. The bottom was Monday and chopped the rest of the week on low volume. People want out now.

We have several factors brewing that are not just technical. New York City and Boston will be hit tomorrow with a major snowstorm blizzard. Boston could see three feet of snow. That means traders who do commute will not be able to do so. People want to take profits, and this could build into a short-squeeze. I am not interested in buying. The weekend is here.

# JANUARY 29 (SATURDAY)

A blizzard is more than a snow event. It is a hurricane in winter with extreme high winds and total white-out conditions. The picture above is not of blizzard conditions outside the New York Stock Exchange. This is only the start of the storm. At the storm's height you would not be able to see your hand stretched out. Having worked in the NYC area for many years, I know that everyone is in serious trouble when the media panics. Airports are shutting down. This storm is going to be historic. Markets are people. The New York City traders want to head home by early afternoon to prepare. Many of us used to commute every day from other States into the City taking at least 1.5 hours one way or more.

The Boston forecast is for a paralyzing amount of snow. Traders begin covering their positions in the DJIA, S&P500, and NASDAQ futures. That in turn triggers others who have held a range-bound market for four days. It feeds on itself into a short-squeeze. We saw yesterday that Amazon was very oversold and warned us of this current rally. Knowing how people will react and influence others is a major benefit.

# JANUARY 29 (SATURDAY)

Check out this live footage of the blizzard in action. A reporter shows white-out conditions and video of 40-foot+ waves rolling up and right over battered homes on the coast near Boston!

https://weather.com/storms/winter/video/winter-storm-kenan-leaves-cars-buried-in-snow-hundreds-of-thousands-without

# BLIZZARD CONDITIONS

**Winter Storm Kenan: Feet of Snow, Dangerous Winds, Coastal Flooding**

If you ever saw the movie; *The Perfect Storm*, you will understand this current map. Conditions triggered a rogue wave of 100 feet tall in a true story. This is called a weather bomb. Boston is at the heart with conditions getting worse. Tremendous damage is taking place.

It is so severe that I am wondering if this will impact markets come Monday. Second-string traders will be on desks filling in for primary traders unable to travel. The second-string traders have less experience and usually trigger volatility in American markets. The risk will be on the sell-side as their job is to protect, not strategically trade. This is going to be challenging to analyze. I'll wait until Sunday.

Very early Sunday morning the news reports the area will recover by Tuesday. That means the storm will have little impact on the New York Stock Exchange. The diary log for a full month is coming to an end. The book opened with reference to a major earthquake; somehow it seems fitting that we conclude with another major event of nature, a blizzard.

# JANUARY 30 (SUNDAY)

There will be further gains on Monday. The signals in Amazon were very strong and several other stocks have similar patterns. But this will be corrective as the bottom is not in place.

When you become too focused on your own market, as I am currently, the thing to do is step back. Start the process from the beginning. Review all the global markets. I review all the DJIA 30 stocks, the key technology stocks for NASDAQ, then Russell 2000. Does the German ETF EWGS for their small-cap stocks agree? Do they give a similar message, or do they message a conflict? The message currently is that the decline is incomplete. However, the bigger picture tells us that the decline is a correction in an incomplete larger trending rally. Knowing this gives a sense of balance when trading in a very short horizon.

# JANUARY 31 (MONDAY)

Last day of the month. The NYSE was not impacted by the blizzard, and all is open. The American equity indexes rallied. The daily chart of Amazon shows the strong move up that developed today into resistance. The oscillators were right. However, this is not a topping pattern yet in the oscillators.

The market rhythms will go on whether we are there or not. But it is indeed a fascinating puzzle that is ever-changing. The markets I favor to lean on against equity indexes change. Is MSFT still my bellwether? Or will I lean on a new group or symbol for guidance? What international market will be my leading guide?

I have shared with you the transition from analyst to trader's mindset and back again. The thinking is very different. You cannot be both at the same time, at least I cannot, because the trader mindset is focused on the details of execution and risk. The analyst is the planner and strategist. I had promised you to log all the steps and execution for a full month. It was a very good month, but keep one thing in mind, I am a bear market specialist. I picked the month to track as a diary. That means I have a long history of seriously outperforming the market in declines, and then under-performing in rallies. Why?

It took me years to fully understand why. I am most comfortable trading a market that *is retracing a prior trend*. Only then do I have a sniper attitude and focus. But once markets move into new highs, I trade stocks with small under-leveraged positions and hold positions for a week or two. It is just not in my DNA to sit and watch anything. It sends me crazy! Everyone is different and traders need to understand what makes them tick. Charts in December warned me I absolutely had to write this final chapter in January 2022. Global equity markets showed us the same red flags for a major trend reversal. When a group of markets paint the same picture, count on a significant move to develop. I skipped Chapter Six. Now I'll go back to write about the price projections you have watched me use in all time horizons. They are a critical part of the process for me. I will find a way to record what followed our experience in this diary log. Laughing, inserting or hiding charts behind a chapter is a very W.D. Gann thing to do. I have just crossed over to the dark side.

Speaking of time, I need to move on to focus on tomorrow's open and the start of a new month. That means I will now scan charts for Asia, Europe, Forex, Oil, Rates, Bitcoin, Metals, and then the underlying stock sectors to rebuild and re-balance my outlook. If I see conflicts, I will then need to look at individual stocks within the sectors, as though I need to take the temperature under the surface of a sector or index. Look at stocks in like sectors on different exchanges across other continents. I'll check all my cycle work, price projections, and overlays. It is all here in this book with examples how I apply these methods over and over again. Technical Analysis has supported me for three decades with the freedom to act independently and go where my heart leads me. And, it is a blast and tremendous fun to stalk the world's markets like a hawk. I sincerely hope that you will enjoy similar longevity and have tremendous fun along the way.

## Do not think you have to do all this alone! Join one of the societies referenced throughout this book. We all speak the same language as you do.

# CFTe Certification

**A well planned Syllabus and Study Guide is online now ready to provide you with the game plan you need to succeed.**

The IFTA Certified Financial Technician (CFTe) consists of CFTe I and II, which together constitute a complete professional program.

The two examinations culminate in the award of this internationally recognized professional qualification in Technical Analysis.

Examinations

The exams test not only technical skills but also ethics and international market knowledge.

CFTe I: This multiple-choice exam covers a wide range of technical knowledge and understanding of the principles of Technical Analysis, usually not involving
actual experience. This exam is currently offered in English, German, Arabic, Spanish, French, and Chinese. CFTe I practice (mock) examination (Chinese).

CFTe II: This exam incorporates a number of questions requiring an essay-based analysis and answers. For this, the candidate should demonstrate a depth of knowledge and experience in applying various methods of technical analysis. The exam provides a number of current charts covering one specific market (often an equity), to be analyzed as though for a Fund Manager. This exam is offered in English, German, Arabic, Spanish, French, Italian, and Chinese. actual experience. This exam is currently offered in English, German, Arabic, Spanish, French, and Chinese.

CFTe II: This exam incorporates a number of questions requiring an essay-based analysis and answers. For this, the candidate should demonstrate a depth of knowledge and experience in applying various methods of technical analysis.

# IFTA.org

**Download the free Syllabus and Study Guide**

**Visit**

**https://IFTA.org**

# AUTHOR'S CLOSING THOUGHTS ...

CHARTS WERE CAPTURED IN A REAL-TIME SEQUENCE THROUGHOUT THIS BOOK FROM OCTOBER 2021 THROUGH JANUARY 2022.

THERE IS AN EXCEPTION, A CLUSTER OF MAJOR TIME CYCLE BEATS TARGETED THE MONTH OF JANUARY. THE SIXTH CHAPTER HAD TO BE SKIPPED IN THE WRITING PROCESS TO STAY IN SYNC WITH THE MARKET CYCLES. THE SEVENTH AND LAST CHAPTER RECORDS A DAILY INTRADAY TRADE-LOG FROM JANUARY 1 to JANUARY 31, 2022.

SEVERAL GLOBAL EQUITY INDEXES WARNED THAT JANUARY WOULD BE A HIGH RISK TOP. YOU WILL FIND THAT CYCLES TRUMP ALL OTHER TECHNICAL METHODS THAT THEN OFFER CONFIRMATION.

THE WAR WAS NOT A FACTOR IN THE ANALYSIS AS IT DID NOT BEGIN UNTIL AFTER THE BOOK WAS COMPLETED AND IN THE PRODUCTION PHASE THAT LOCKS ALL CONTENT AND LAYOUTS.

This book shares with you the practical methods used by one trader. You will find other methods that speak to you, but this book may help you see how different techniques are combined and why others are excluded in changing market conditions. Technical analysis is incredibly powerful.

Best Wishes,
Connie Brown

Aerodynamic Investments Inc.- March 4, 2022

support@aeroinvest.com

# INDEX

confluence, 262

consolidation, 183

continuation, 180

corrective, 178, 281, 292

cyclical, 94

distribution, 133

double bottom, 160, 246–47

engulfing, 180

fractal, 156, 175

head-and-shoulders, 213, 345

key reversal directional, 162

topping, 383

triangle, 182

weakest, 247

wedge, 20, 203

peaks, 52, 79, 84, 96, 119, 129, 205, 211, 232, 243, 250

highest, 103

narrow, 131

Pearson correlation coefficient, 148–50

period cycle, 113–14, 119

fixed, 78

periodicity, 77, 79, 100–101, 106–7, 109

period rhythm, 118

periods, moving-average, 118

phase, 79, 101–2, 105, 114

pivot, 156, 160, 173, 211, 213, 218, 227, 233, 257–58, 292, 299

plotting, distribution bell-curve, 144

point-and-figure, 9, 236, 332

position size, 11, 179, 255, 275

positive correlation, 134–35, 140, 142, 145, 149

Presidential Cycle, 91

price

closing, 15, 17, 19, 115, 117, 138, 145, **149**, 153, 191, 198, 205

contracting, 52

declining, 52

price bottoms, 62, 207, 213, 280

price gap, 20, 129

open, 362

price projection method, simple, 179

price projection methods, 62, 178–79, 223, 234, 385

price reversals, 118, 206, 218

significant, 207

price swings, 16, 25, 114, 175, 233, 278, 353

Price targets, 44, 180, 217, 233–34, 256, 316

price trends, 83, 218

price volatility, 192

Principles of Market Cycle Analysis, 107

PROPORTIONALITY- Cycle amplitude, 107

# R

rates

10-Yr Treasury Constant Maturity, 313

benchmark, 34, 41, 96

ratios

harmonic, 107

mathematical, 78

recession, 29–30, 33, 42, 90, 96, 101

rectangles, 233, 266, 285, 299, 316, 325, 358

regression line, 141

resistance, 157, 159, 167, 169, 199–200, 207, 210–11, 213, 223, 258, 260–61, 344–45, 363

calculating, 261–62, 311

exceeded, 159

resistance confluence zone, 269

resistance targets, 306

resistance zone, 264, 267, 335

retracement, 261, 263, 280, 358

retracement level, 261

retracement ratio, 316

retracing a prior trend, 385

Rhea, Robert, 99

rhythm, 77–80, 85, 114–18, 122, 126, 175

rhythmic fluctuation, 113

ripples, market shock waves, 15

rising inflation, 96

rising inventories, 96

rising slope, 85, 89

risk management, 11, 14, 26, 30, 34, 159, 165, 273–75, 291, 294, 382, 385

Robert Prechter Jr, 175

RSI, 202–3, 205–14, 217–18, 221, 223, 225, 227, 229, 232–33, 313, 337

RSI divergence failures, 218

RSI formula, 211

R-squared, 141, 148
Russian Nikolai Kondratiev, 100

scatter plot, 134–35, 138, 140, 142, 144
Schumpeter, Joseph, 100–101
seasonal chart study, 82–83, 131
sector weightings, 59–61
Secured Overnight Financing Rate (SOFR), 39
sellers, short, 24
selling pressure, 18–19, 156, 159–60, 203, 223
sentiment, 21, 24, 33, 36, 44, 52, 60, 156, 176, 232, 306
Simple equality swing, 345
simple moving-average (SMA), 145, 159, 162, 190, 192, 198, 213–14, 221, 223, 227, 230, 232
Skewness, 90, 130, 144
slope, 29–30, 33, 85, 134–35, 140
Slow Stochastics, 157, 161, 245, 249
Solar-flares, 125
Solar Sunspots Cycle, 100, 125
spectrogram study, 119
spectrograph, 102–3, 106
spikes, 129, 137, 160, 362
square root, 191
Statistical Adequacy, 94
statistics, 13, 126, 129, 137, 144–45
Steidylmayer, Peter, 133
Sterling Overnight Index Average (SONIA), 39
St. Louis FRED Economic Data, 27–28, 86, 88
Stochastic formula, 249
Stochastics, 163, 197, 213, 239–40, 243, 246, 248, 250–51, 253, 313, 329
    stochastics period, 313
StockCharts.com, 9, 131–32, 221, 236, 332, 341
Stoller Bands, 191, 193, 195, 223
Stoller Bands on RSI, 223
stops
    physical, 46
    trailing, 193
strong bars, 162, 169, 257, 262, 273, 316
strong bars and gaps, 162, 257
Strongest bars, 258, 346
Summation Principle, 105, 107
supply-chain disruptions, growing, 93

swing amplitude, 7
swing projection, 285, 299
swings, 20, 160, 162, 173, 176–78, 255–56, 258, 261, 264, 280–81, 297, 299, 314
SYNCHRONICITY- Cycle troughs, 107
synthetic cross-rates, Forex, 43–44

termination wedge, 20, 203
test on lower volume, confirmation, 18–19
theory, long wave, 101
third wave rally, 316
Thirty-Second Jewel, 125, 165, 239, 319
thrust, 180
    fast, 338
    strongest middle, 256
time cluster, 319
time horizons, 173, 175, 202, 207, 209, 211, 217, 227, 232, 234, 249, 325, 330
    lesser, 175
    longer, 137, 175, 195
    multiple, 232
time period, 15, 17
time ratio, 305, 342
time signal, 59
timing, 7, 21, 81, 93, 95–97, 366
timing offset, 91
trading, tri-screen, 207
Treasury Yield Curve Rates, 27
trend, 10, 15, 18, 90–91, 134, 139, 203, 205, 209, 211, 213, 225, 229
trend analysis, 43, 52, 63, 65, 118, 200, 203, 205, 209, 211, 218
trend line, 19, 160, 162, 180, 215, 227, 246, 291
trend lines on oscillators, 227
trend reversal, major, 63, 217, 225
trend reversal signals, strongest, 247
triangles, 10, 180, 183, 211, 280, 326
    corrective, 280
    expanding, 180
troughs, 79, 84, 95–97, 105, 160, 197, 203, 205, 227, 232
trough-to-trough, 98
Tulip Bulb Mania, 165, 167, 182

# U

Unbound oscillator, 198, 200, 218, 221, 253
unconscious crowd, 167
uptrend, 17–18, 20, 203, 209, 217, 232, 324

# V

value R-squared, 140
variance measures, 148–49, 191
velocity, 198
visual examination, 113, 116, 142
volatility, 34, 94, 97, 382
volatility bands, 191–93, 195, 223
volume, 17–20, 133–34, 137, 177, 241–45, 341–42, 344, 349, 358

# W

Wave, Sine, 84
wave structure, 79, 175, 177–79, 217, 227, 229, 233, 281, 285, 289, 292, 332, 338
wavelength, 79, 84, 107
wave swings, five, 177, 234, 289
weighted indexes, 60
weightings, 60, 126, 244

# Y

yield, 27, 29–30, 33–34, 225
yield curve, 26–30, 33–34, 60
Yield Curve, inverted, 30-31, 33
yield curve graph, 33

# Z

zigzag (corrective price pattern) , 292, 365
zones, hot (cycles), 83, 357

CPSIA information can be obtained
at www.ICGtesting.com
Printed in the USA
BVHW011750080523
663791BV00002B/8